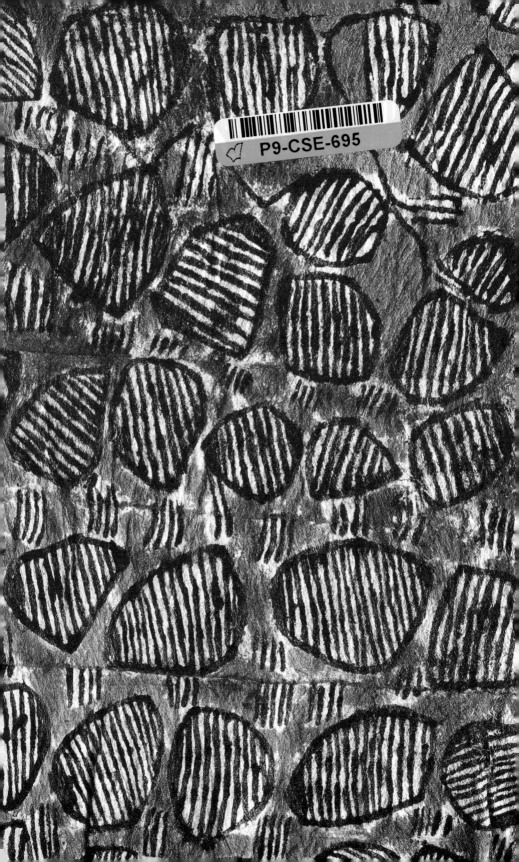

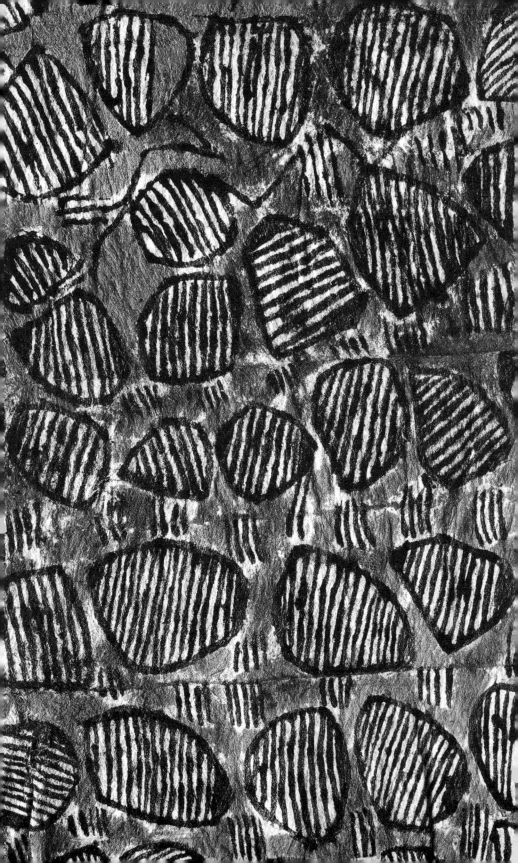

ALIVE
IN AFRICA

ALSO BY WILLIAM F. WHEELER

Efe Pygmies Archers of the African Rain Forest

ALIVE
IN AFRICA

My Journeys on Foot in the Sahara,
Rift Valley, and Rain Forest

WILLIAM F. WHEELER

THE LYONS PRESS
Guilford, Connecticut
An imprint of The Globe Pequot Press

For Linda, my loving wife.

The Lyons Press is an imprint of The Globe Pequot Press.

Cover design by Diana Nuhn
Photos by William Wheeler
Text design by Sheryl P. Kober
Africa Illustrations by Lee Mitchelson/Mountain Tribe Studio

Library of Congress Cataloging-in-Publication Data is available on file.
ISBN 978-1-59921-402-3

Printed in China
10 9 8 7 6 5 4 3 2 1

❖ CONTENTS ❖

CONTENTS

❖ ACKNOWLEDGMENTS ❖

I am forever thankful to my friend Dallas Clites, who not only encouraged me to take up photography, but critiqued every one of my thousands of images of Africa. To my wife, Linda, who so patiently taught me how to use the computer while putting up with my impatience. To Peggy and Lester Green, missionaries in the Congo whose encouragement, friendship, and hospitality can never be repaid. To my editor at The Lyons Press, Holly Rubino. To Ivan Gaylor who loves my photographs. To Ileana Pelaez who gave me many good ideas. Nancy Nenow, Gwyn Enright, Neal Matthews, Kitty and Owen Morse, Char and Larry Glacey, Bob Vinton, Bill McGill. And to all my friends who gave me encouragement. And to the Africans, whose laughter made it all fun. ◉

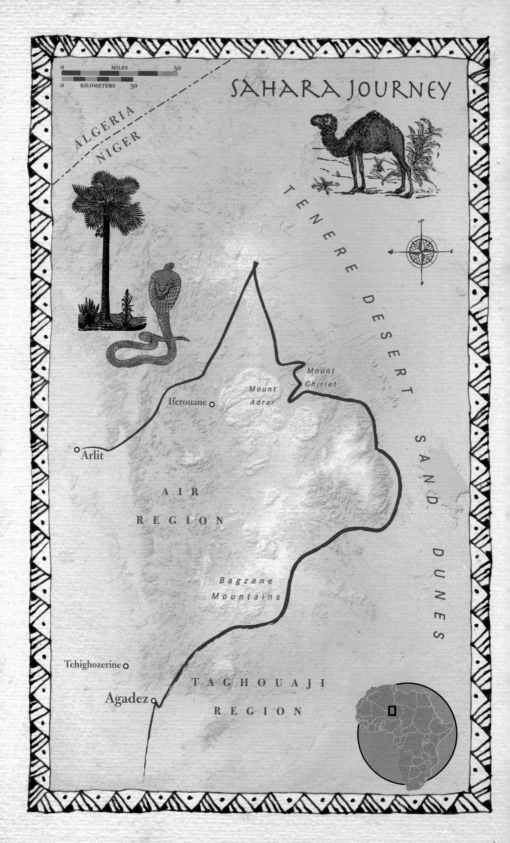

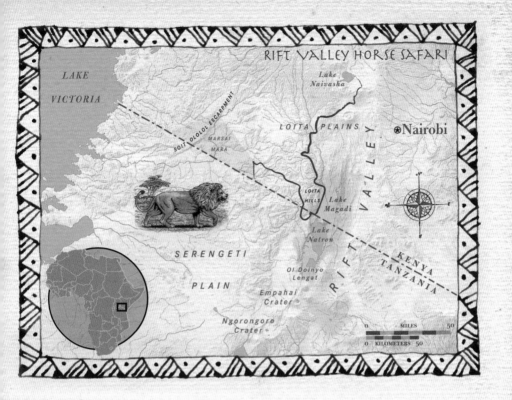

RIFT VALLEY HORSE SAFARI

LAKE VICTORIA

Lake Naivasha

LOITA PLAINS

SOIT OLOLOL ESCARPMENT

MARSAI MARA

⊛Nairobi

LOITA HILLS

Lake Magadi

RIFT VALLEY

SERENGETI

Lake Natron

PLAIN

Ol Doinyo Lengat

KENYA
TANZANIA

Empahai Crater

Ngorongoro Crater

0   MILES   50
0   KILOMETERS   50

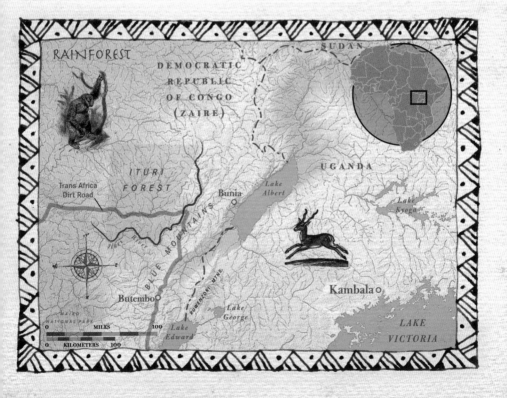

RAINFOREST

SUDAN

DEMOCRATIC REPUBLIC OF CONGO (ZAIRE)

ITURI FOREST

Trans Africa Dirt Road

Bunia

Lake Albert

UGANDA

Lake Kyoga

Ituri River

BLUE MOUNTAINS

RUWENZORI MTNS.

Butembo

Kambala

MAIKO NATIONAL PARK

Lake George

Lake Edward

0   MILES   100
0   KILOMETERS   100

LAKE VICTORIA

❖ PROLOGUE ❖

"Why do you travel like that?" the elderly purple-haired lady asked as the final image of sand dunes and camels faded from the screen. Lights came on in the Rancho Santa Fe Garden Club, and I faced a group of highly educated, successful, and well-traveled men and women from Southern California's most affluent community.

Her question took me by surprise. Dumbfounded, I replied, "Because I always wanted to." But my answer was embarrassingly inadequate and left me frustrated.

I had never wondered why I traveled, or thought anything unusual on the way I went about it. Everyone, I assumed, would want to abandon normal everyday life to explore a remote wilderness on foot, leaving behind the creature comforts we have come to depend upon.

There had never been a stated purpose in my travels—no endangered species to study, no vanishing cultures to document, no goals to strive for, or mountains to climb. I had no desire to test myself in any way, to pit myself against the forces of nature, to conquer, win, or lose. There was no survival contest, and no death wish. I was not a professional adventurer, anthropologist, photographer, writer, or even physically qualified for extreme wilderness travel. My body was riddled with weaknesses and idiosyncrasies. Without regular sleep or three meals a day I failed to function. Worst of all was my delicate stomach—the organ most essential for rough adventure.

An unexplainable instinct seemed to be guiding me. Although I didn't know the purpose, the plan was clear from the very beginning. I would travel on foot through the remotest and most untouched wildernesses of Africa, alone except for a nomad guide whose native language I would not be able to speak. Each of the journeys would last forty days, time for the excitement and newness to wear off and to reach a state of equilibrium, both physical and psychological, with the foreign environment and culture.

Reminders of my own civilization—radio, Walkman, books to read—
would be left behind. Like nineteenth-century explorers, I would rely on
camels, donkeys, or porters to carry all the necessary food and supplies.
Without global positioning systems or experience with map and compass,
nomads would show me the way. There would be no support team, no
following Land Rovers, no food drops, no satellite telephones, and no
emergency contact devices. Without a watch, only daily entries in a journal
would keep me from becoming completely lost in time.

It was years later, after my travels were concluded, even after I had
finished this manuscript, before I seriously came to grips with the purple-
haired lady's question that had continued to nag me. I rewrote my book's
introduction eleven times. All were inadequate and thrown away. I began
searching deep inside, peeling back layer after layer of my past until one day
the significance of a silent but unforgotten event unfolded.

Severe asthma had kept me confined to the house during childhood.
Nine hospitalizations and long miserable nights sweating in a hot steam tent,
a crib draped with plastic, had beaten me down. Worst of all, I had not been
able to go outside and play with my friends. One night as Mother tucked
me into bed, I began to wheeze. The copper kettle on the night table started
belching clouds of white steam. Tenderly wiping the droplets of hot water
from my face, she tried to comfort me. "I will leave the light on. Just call out
if you need me." Then she left.

Almost immediately my breathing became labored, as if strong metal
bands were clamping around my chest. It took all my strength to barely
move any air in and out. I rolled closer to the kettle, and the hot steam seared
my face until I could no longer bear it. Exhausted and dripping sweat, I tried
to call out, but it was too late—not enough breath was left to make a sound.
Panicked, my lungs closed off completely, and I stopped breathing. I quit
struggling and gave up.

I knew I was dying. Anger suddenly raged through my body, anger that I
would never go out to play again, never run in the yellow fields of straw grass
behind the house, never smell the flowers that grew in our garden, or marvel
at the secret world of ants and butterflies. These were great mysteries of

nature that I loved, and I felt cheated, angry with God for taking me away. As the room turned gray, a humanlike image materialized above my bed. Arms reached out and picked me up, the touch filling my body with overwhelming warmth, an indescribable feeling of love and compassion. The anger immediately vanished, and as I was taken away toward the ceiling of the room, I knew I was going to a better place.

I looked back at my body, lifeless and still on the bed. Detached physically and spiritually, I was on my way to a new world just as real as the one I was leaving. Then, a voice filled the room, saying, "Put him back!" Instantly I was back in bed, my face in hot steam, breathing.

As a child I regarded this as just a normal experience. I never even thought to tell anyone about it until recently. But the memory has always remained just as clear as the night it happened. And I can still hear that voice saying, "Put him back!" Whether it was real or the delusion of a dying child I do not question, for that experience has been a guiding force in my life, as real as anything that happened to me.

Ever since that night, I have considered life a precious gift, to be lived fully and never taken for granted.

However, I quickly learned that living fully was not the same as living dangerously. By my sixteenth birthday I had used up thirteen of my nine lives. I survived being tied up and thrown into a river and three automobile accidents that totally destroyed the car I was in. I drowned twice, resuscitation was stopped, and I was left for dead. My pelvis was broken in a horse accident, my clavicle in a motorcycle accident, my jaw in a car accident. Although those years were long ago, friends back home still call me "Wild Bill."

To experience as much of life as possible, I rushed the milestones, quitting high school for college, receiving my MD degree at twenty-three and retiring at forty-three, long before I had enough savings. The world of awe and wonder that as a child lay just outside my house had grown beyond the forests and streams of the rural farming community I loved. I began to dream of faraway places and cultures.

One day working at my desk, I suddenly looked up and asked: If anything was possible, what would I do, regardless of risk? I picked up a yellow sticky pad and without thinking wrote: cross the Sahara desert by camel, travel on horseback among the wild animals of east Africa, and live in the rain forest with pygmies.

I pasted the sticky on the wall and leaned back—shocked! The idea scared me to death. My spine tingled up and down from fear. Any one of these endeavors seemed impossible; all three, the dreams of an idiot.

As the months went by, and the yellow note remained on the wall, I began to toy with the logistics of traveling in the Sahara by camel, a mental challenge that became fascinating, but only a game. Then, three years later I found myself planning a real journey—I had gone too far! I lay awake at night, unable to sleep.

Africa was a natural choice for me. A continent of great extremes, it contained the world's largest desert, vast untouched rain forests, hunter-gatherers who lived nearly uninfluenced by the outside world, and exotic wild animals left over from the Pleistocene found nowhere else on earth. Human life began in Africa, and only in Africa was it possible to sense what life was like for the first people, living on foot among lions, elephants, and other dangerous creatures.

In the Sahara I was beaten into submission by the wind and sun. Nights brought an end to the suffering, and in the crystalline depths of the dark universe it almost seemed possible to reach out and touch God. It was the hidden evil in my guide's agenda that tested me to the limit, in an escalating battle of two indomitable wills.

The tropical rain forest was an immense sea of sweltering vegetation, a riotous explosion in which life was constantly being created, mutated, and destroyed. In the deep silence of the forest, giant trees and tannic streams seemed alive with spirits, as if time had been rolled back ten thousand years.

Walking with only a spear across the grasslands of east Africa's Great Rift Valley quickened my wits and refined my adrenaline; life became an intense game of Russian roulette in the bush.

These journeys left me with a deep sense of humility and an enlightened awe for the beauty of the world all around. The tribes and cultures I encountered imparted upon me a greater compassion for our common human condition, and an understanding that in our hearts we are all the same.

Finally, alone in the vast wildernesses of desert, forest, and grassland, I came closer to God. And that, I discovered—that was what I was searching for all along. ◉

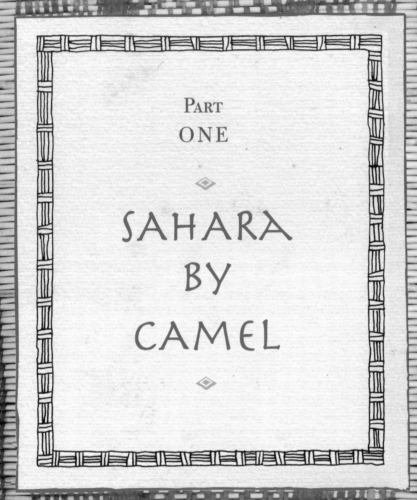

Part
ONE

❖

SAHARA
BY
CAMEL

❖

CHAPTER ONE

The Messenger

The diaries of my African safaris fill one bookshelf on my library wall. Some of these old-fashioned explorer-type foot journals are enclosed in black boxes with gold lettering, but most have plain board book cloth with simple titles, such as "Horse Safari," "Donkey Safari," or "Pygmy Safari," written on the spines.

Of these twenty-one handwritten records, there is one I treasure most. Often I am drawn to that diary just to pick it up and run my aging palms over its worn covers. A tattered black cord binds the journal, and I remove it not to read illegible words scrawled late at night by dirty fingers under the flame of a dripping candle or to recall the hardship of camping exhausted in some faraway *oued,* or dry streambed, but to reunite myself with a particular scent that lingers still after all these years.

It is a peculiar odor, unlike any I have ever encountered. I first discovered it on an ancient Ethiopian manuscript, its goatskin parchment stiffened and worn rough by centuries of blowing wind and sand. This, I now know, is the scent of the Sahara, and once you have lived there for a time among nomads or traveled its desolation on foot with camels, it becomes part of you, thoroughly permeating every living cell. The desert is then with you forever, and you are no longer who you once were.

Of all things meaningful to me about that diary—wear marks from forty days chafing against the camel's back, peculiar stains, crudely drawn maps, sketches of landscapes and camps—it is the black cord, knotted and worn thin, that stirs my emotions. It is the memory of the delicate thread that bound our tiny caravan together in the desert.

O. Henry and I in the Sahara

It was a mistake to remove the black cord from O. Henry's neck, the act of a confused and desperate person. Forty days on foot in the Sahara had erased the past and left me disoriented. Permanently knotted there by a nomad, the black cord held a leather pouch containing a Koranic verse, a talisman blessed by a marabout (teacher of Islam). Bilal, my nomad companion, called it "gris-gris," a good luck charm so to speak; but I removed it at the camel market in Arlit, the oasis where I sold O. Henry.

For forty days O. Henry had carried me faithfully across the desert—empty plains of desolation, mountains of volcanic rock, endless seas of golden sand. More than any humble beast of burden, he had become my guru, a trusted friend in an alien land. During those long and tedious hours together I came to appreciate simple things: the taste of water, sleep, and the harsh beauty that was all around. In a world of sand, wind, and sky, my thoughts grew uncluttered and I came to know my inner fears and recognize far-off longings in tired eyes. In the emptiness of the desert my innermost self was exposed, and for a time tranquility and peace reigned. Then, in a fit of confusion, I removed the gris-gris in Arlit.

I last saw O. Henry at the camel market, a haughty Tuareg buyer leading him away. He was hauling O. Henry unmercifully by the nose ring without regard for a camel's exquisite sensitivity. O. Henry's head was high above the crowd, his brown eyes filled with fear. I seized the rope and he lowered his face to mine, eyelashes flickering, lids closed in relief. I rubbed my bearded cheeks over the soft flesh of his nose, the way he liked, lingering over the familiar scent of camel hair and skin. My eyes clouded over, and for a brief moment my emotions trembled. Then, my head dropped, and I submitted to the code of the desert. I handed O. Henry back to the impatient Tuareg and turned away.

O. Henry was taken outside the walls of the market and brutally forced down on the ground, legs bound tightly together. There was a flash of steel, silver white under a midday sun, then pools of blood ran red on yellow sand. Rendered asunder by the knives, O. Henry's body was sold for meat.

This, then, was Sahara: stained pages in a diary, a tattered black cord, and a delicate scent stamped indelibly into memory.

I first encountered the Sahara incidentally, seven years before. I had taken a four-month leave from my medical practice and purchased a second-hand Land Rover in London. My intention was to drive it to Zaire, the old Belgian Congo, to satisfy my childhood fantasies of Tarzan and the primeval rain forest. All I knew about the African rain forest at that time was what I had seen in movies of the 1950s.

My only previous experience with Africa had been a brief vacation to Egypt and Kenya. People there told me Zaire was the most corrupt country in Africa, that there was no infrastructure, and I would need my own Land Rover to travel about. They said I would be crazy to go there.

Then, consulting a map to plan an overland route to Zaire, I discovered the Sahara. It stretched completely across the continent of Africa, three thousand miles from the Atlantic coast of Morocco and Mauritania to the Red Sea of Ethiopia and Somalia. It was immense, the entire continental United States easily fitting inside its boundaries. There was no way around it. To me, the Sahara, the world's largest desert, the grandest and most romanticized desert of all, was nothing more than a nasty unknown separating me from the rain forest of my dreams.

I knew nothing about the Sahara, or any other desert for that matter. I had met no one who had ever been there, read no books on the subject, and knew nothing of mechanics or what to do should the Land Rover break down and I became stranded. Driving across the Sahara seemed too formidable, too grand, too frightening, so I just ignored it. I even laughed about it at cocktail parties in San Diego. Now I was sorry.

My first view of the desert, after crossing the Atlas Mountains of Morocco, was from the cocoonlike interior of the Land Rover out into an immense expanse of empty space—silent, barren, ugly.

I had a French map, Michelin 153. Large areas were colored egg-yolk yellow—sand dunes. There were only two routes across the egg yolk, each red line indicated as *piste*. They were not paved roads, but a wide band of tire tracks in sand that I measured fifteen hundred miles across the egg yolk to the black circle of Gao, a village near Tombouctou on the Niger River in Mali. Once into the empty desert, Gao would be the next source of fuel for the Land Rover. That's all I knew about the great desert.

I had four-wheel drive and a compass, my first experience with either. Stashed inside the Land Rover were twenty gallons of water, one thousand liters of diesel fuel, camping equipment, and enough Top Ramen dried noodles to last four months. Sand tires were mounted on the front wheels and road tires were on the back, an arrangement I was told that would break the half axles, whatever they were. I had metric wrenches to work on an English-system vehicle. No matter; I didn't know how to repair it anyhow.

Three days later, and two hundred miles into the Sahara, I awoke to an orange fireball burning its way slowly out of the black horizon. The flat, ugly desert of the previous days was transformed into a golden sea of sand. I had camped in a palm oasis on the edge of the Great Western Erg, thirty thousand square miles of orange sand blown into star-shaped dunes one thousand feet high. For the next week and a half I drank tea with passing nomads and lay at night with oasis dwellers on the soft dunes beneath an ink-black heaven to watch stars and planets glide by silently overhead. As that first month in the desert passed, I witnessed for the first time the sickle moon change phases and discovered why celestial secrets long ago revealed themselves to desert mystics. Having forgotten my quest for the "real" Africa, I had fallen in love with the Sahara.

Halfway across the desert I stopped the Land Rover on an empty plain of sand and pebbles. Around me unfolded an absolutely flat and endlessly barren landscape, 450 miles of utter desolation. It was completely devoid of life, even bacteria. Rain had not fallen in centuries, recorded temperatures were the highest in the world, and humidity had fallen to 2 percent. It was the Tanezrouft, a desert within a desert, a place of extremes. Nomads called it the "Desert of Thirst." The word itself means "emptiness." Most Land Rover travelers chose the more frequently traveled Hoggar route. I was afraid to cut off the engine for fear it might not start again.

At the horizon, where sand and sky imperceptibly merged, was a dark band of trees. As I continued, the trees grew taller; then, like kaleidoscopic images, they were transformed into a modern city of glass skyscrapers. The tall buildings melted down into amorphous lumps, and a caravan of camels emerged floating on shimmering waves of heat across the sand. I left the Land Rover emitting toxic fumes and ran across the sand toward five veiled nomads in desert robes. They were Tuaregs, grand masters of the desert. Leading sixty camels, they had walked ten days across the waterless desert, and six more days remained to reach the other side. They shook their empty water bags and laughed, unyielding in their faith that Allah would provide. I gave them all the water I could spare, and then watched spellbound as they hurried on into the blue void.

As they rode off, the oldest nomad turned his camel and unexpectedly charged at full speed straight toward me. At the last second the immense white bull veered, his shoulder knocking me aside. For a moment I was enveloped by exotic perfumes—oils of camel's skin, goat-hair woolen blankets, dried leather, and human sweat. The old man dismounted, and we touched fingertips, laughing. We were of different worlds, the nomad and I, and although we could not speak a common language, we recognized a similarity of heart.

As the caravan disappeared across the horizon, I felt an urge to abandon the Land Rover and join them. The idea seemed far-fetched, and although I tingled with excitement, the thought frightened me. But from that moment on I was determined that someday I would cross the Sahara by camel.

Ten days later, near Gao, I met a nomad named El Bechir, "The Messenger," an allusion to Muhammad, the Messenger of God. He could speak some English and was a Tuareg, a desert tribe often called "Blue Men" because the dye from their indigo-stained veil rubbed off on their skin. They were a fiercely proud and independent people who carried swords and resisted any government interference with their lifestyle.

For a week we traveled together in the Land Rover, off road through the countryside while he taught me the life of a desert nomad, a life of complete freedom living close to nature. I learned how to find a well by following animal tracks; how far sheep, goats, and cattle can be pastured from the well and still safely return to water; how to survive a sandstorm; and how Islam was ingrained in the life of desert dwellers. I also learned that a woman breast-feeding a child and accompanied by a lactating female camel can cross the entire Sahara without any water at all as long as the camel has fresh grass to eat.

A Tuareg indigo veil.

Each year El Bechir traveled with his camels in a great circular arc across northern Mali for a thousand miles searching for pasturage made by the fickle rains of summer. That year the rains had failed, and both camels and nomads were beginning to starve. The caravan I had witnessed in the Tanezrouft was, he said, a desperate attempt of nomads to reach the markets of Algeria before their camels died of starvation. If they survived the desert crossing, they would be sold for meat, although much of their body weight had already been lost. El Bechir predicted that if the rains failed that year there would be a famine worse than ever before.

The rains did fail, and the famine that summer of 1984 resulted in horrifying images of starving African children shown nightly on CNN.

That last night together around the campfire, I promised El Bechir that I would return to travel with him and his camels. However, planning this was difficult, as the only way he could be contacted was by mail, which he picked up once a year when he passed near Gao herding his camels.

Three years later I flew to Niamey, rented a Land Rover, and drove up the Niger River road to Gao. After two weeks searching the Sahel bush country for El Bechir, I gave up and went back to California.

Over the years I made several more unsuccessful attempts to contact El Bechir. Unable to forget the desert or its long-suffering people, I finally decided to execute a camel journey during the winter of 1991, regardless of problems.

Although I was nervous about the journey, once my mind was made up nothing seemed to stop me. On my Land Rover trip I had been shot at by bandits while climbing the Ruwenzori Mountains in Zaire, but I just kept climbing. When problems became too big to handle, I had the habit of just ignoring them. At times I had even risked my life because of some seemingly purposeless idea.

I obtained visas, purchased airline tickets, and then couldn't sleep from the shock of undertaking a difficult but incredible journey. My wife, patient and understanding, and I didn't talk much about my plans. When I was gone, she just went on with her life, and when I came back, it was just as if I had never left. However, before we were married, each time I left on an

African trip there was a breakup, seventeen in all, each more painful than the last. Finally, after we were married in a Maasai ceremony in Tanzania the pain ended, and there were no more problems with my going away. However, my two daughters always felt abandoned when I left.

Several months before my departure, the Tuareg of Niger attacked and robbed a government armory. Military troops retaliated by killing men, women, children, and livestock.

In Mali the Tuareg also revolted, and Gao was under martial law. Officials at the U.S. Embassy informed me that the Tuareg were fighting a guerilla-style war for independence. The desert north of Gao had been declared a war zone and travel was forbidden by the government. Tuareg working in the oil fields of Libya had returned with money and guns. Lawless bandits had stolen all Land Rovers from the relief organization World Vision, leaving one driver on foot in the desert. A doctor working for Doctors without Borders had been killed along with his wife and child. A French couple crossing northern Mali in a Land Rover had been murdered. Government troops were reported to be massacring entire villages of innocent Tuareg women and children.

Although this turn of events was disturbing, my camel trip plans had been foiled too many times before, and I was determined not to delay any further.

Then, two weeks prior to departure I received a postcard from a friend traveling in Algeria. A disheveled Tuareg had approached him asking for money. The Tuareg told my friend that he was from Mali where he had informed French journalists about the government massacre of Tuareg women and children. The soldiers had come after him, but he fled Mali on his camel, traveling nearly 300 miles to the border, then riding 250 miles across the Tanezrouft in seven days. His camel died on the last day, and he finished on foot. His wife and children were in prison in Gao, and he was trying to get to France for help. He said that he knew an American named Bill Wheeler.

The last sentence on the postcard read: "There stood El Bechir."

Mali was now out of the picture. I would not travel there without El Bechir and miss the rich cultural experience that only he could provide.

That would have to wait once again. I decided to go to Agadez, an oasis on the southern edge of the Sahara in Niger where I could buy camels and hire a Tuareg nomad as a guide. My plan was to travel north across the central volcanic Aïr mountain region and into the Ténéré sea of sand, then cross the eastern section of the Tanezrouft to end the journey at the oasis town of Tamanrasset in Algeria, where the camels could be sold. It would be a distance of over seven hundred miles, nearly forty days in the desert. Like Moses wandering in the Sinai, I half expected some religious experience.

I learned of a student, Flagg Miller, at Dartmouth College, who was writing his senior thesis on the Victorian desert travelers T. E. Lawrence, Sir Richard Burton, and Charles Doughty. Interested in his bibliography, I telephoned him. When I described my plans, he was amazed that such a nineteenth-century-style camel journey was possible today.

Although we were strangers, I had immediately liked Flagg. Only twenty-two years old, he was less than half my age, but we shared a common interest in the desert, camels, and the Muslim world, as well as in music. He played the fiddle, and I had played classical and flamenco guitar since college. Although I had planned to travel alone, I thought his youthful insight and unspoiled innocence would give a unique view of desert life. I planned to treat Flagg as an equal in every decision. To me the age difference made no difference.

Flagg had experience backpacking in America and, more important, had spent a year in Tunisia learning Arabic. Dartmouth College recognized the value of such an unusual journey near the end of the twentieth century and awarded him a grant and a two-month leave of absence from school.

We met for the first time two weeks later at Orly Airport in Paris on our way to Niger. He walked off the airplane with a curious but detached regard for his surroundings. Tall, lean, blue-eyed, and with a wild crop of yellow hair, Flagg bore an uncanny resemblance to Peter O'Toole in the film *Lawrence of Arabia.*

"Bill," he said, holding out his hand to the older man wearing a tan safari hat, blue jeans, and leather hiking boots, waiting at the bottom of the passenger exit ramp. Although I was six feet, he stood several inches taller.

"And you are Flagg," I responded smiling. "Did you bring the two plastic five-gallon water containers?" I asked anxiously.

There was little time between flights, so while having a quick cup of coffee we went over our checklists of necessary gear. Although Flagg was quite relaxed, I knew how difficult it would be to find replacements in Africa. I was relieved to find everything in order.

We boarded an Air France flight for the final leg of our journey. My attention was focused out the window, and the excitement mounted as the azure Mediterranean passed quickly below, then the dark cliffs that mark the north coast of Africa. The snow-covered peaks of the jagged Rif Mountains in Morocco rose sharply, and suddenly we were over the Sahara with its cloudless, clear blue sky. Orange sand stretched to the horizon, which from an altitude of thirty-five thousand feet was slightly curved. Beyond that was the deep blue of endless space.

The clarity of the air and the altitude provided a view of the desert like that seen from a satellite orbiting Earth. Astronauts said what impressed them most about Earth was the orange desert with its beautiful patterns of giant sand dunes. But more than anything, it was the complete absence of human encroachment.

Flagg was deeply immersed in Richard Burton's *Pilgrimage to Al-Medinah and Meccah,* one of the nineteenth-century desert classics he brought along for the trip. There was little conversation. I was spellbound, fixing my eyes down below watching immense fields of transverse dunes

being swept across the desert floor by constant winds, like parallel waves rolling over an ocean. Vast regions of star-shaped dunes were whipped up by chaotic winds to heights of one thousand feet. Long, monotonous, empty sections, barren and gray, were etched with spiderlike drainage patterns of ancient riverbeds. Through my small window I measured off twenty miles on the ground below—one day's travel by camel, 120 seconds in our Boeing 747.

On the southern side of the Sahara a brown haze hid the desert below. The pilot announced that because of a sandstorm, the earlier morning flight had been unable to land.

We descended through the brownout to land at Niamey, Niger, two thousand miles into Africa. On the floor of a dingy room at the Ténéré Hotel we sorted out our three hundred pounds of baggage, food, and camping equipment, then began trudging, exhausted, from one government ministry to another, all in unmarked buildings that were mostly empty. We needed permits to travel by camel in the Aïr region, which is the Tuareg nomad region north of Agadez, as well as visas with authorization to enter Algeria through an unmarked border in the desert. Each time we located the proper office, a uniformed official told us to come back tomorrow; or just waived us away with "pas de problème"—no problem. But I knew there would be a problem if we came across police or government officials looking for a bribe. They would demand permits whether required or not. After three days we gave up, hired a taxi, and left without any permits at all. ◎

CHAPTER TWO

The Last Oasis

It was moonless and dark when we reached Agadez, sometime after midnight. A sandstorm had slowed our progress to barely twenty miles per hour. Sand was blowing in sheets across the road, white layers that fluttered like shimmering veils suspended in the headlights. Soft dunes were forming over the narrow tarmac highway, making driving dangerous. Our taxi passed through an opening in the village wall, and we entered a sand-swept maze of mud-walled buildings, dark and unlit.

Down a lane of soft sand we found a one-story adobe structure, the Tiden Hotel. The guardian, an elderly Tuareg with a medieval crusader-style sword slung beneath his robe, helped us drag our baggage into the sand courtyard. Our room was a mud-walled hut with bare concrete floors and one small, wood-shuttered window with iron bars. There was no electricity and no bathroom. The beds were hard mats over sagging iron with no sheets. We collapsed, exhausted, in our sleeping bags.

"Allahu Akbahr. . . Allahu Akbahr . . ." Piercing screams shot us awake from deep sleep. It was still night, but the unearthly voice continued, working itself higher into a fanatical frenzy. I quickly dressed and went outside. It was bone cold as the first gray light of dawn etched the outline of a conical structure towering over the village, the minaret from which the muezzin of Agadez had called the faithful to prayer for four centuries. It was said to be the tallest adobe minaret in Africa. Then the sun rose, burning instantly through my cotton long-sleeve shirt.

Agadez was a small desert village of sandy lanes and one-story adobe houses plastered with mud. Everything was the color of sand. The streets were sand, walls of houses were sand, and anything not constructed of sand had been wind blasted until it had taken on sand's tan color. Sand made its way into the daily wash, staining people's clothes an off yellow. Even food did not escape the omnipresent tiny grains, which gave a gritty consistency to everything desert dwellers ate.

Yet the village was free of dirt, all filth blown away by a strong northern wind that swept the Sahara clean each winter. The harmattan, which means "evil thing" in Arabic and is called "Hot Breath of the Desert" by the Tuareg, churned dust into great clouds that hung suspended for months in a thick, dirty-gray blanket overhead. Often the sun was blocked out down to the Atlantic coast of west Africa.

Violent Sahara windstorms whipped up dust and sand into trade winds that carried them across the Atlantic, dropping millions of tons each year into the rain forests of Brazil. Particulate clouds often reached the east coast of Florida carrying bacteria and fungus that killed coral and caused toxic red tides that poison shellfish and manatees.

El Bechir had told me how a sandstorm could appear unexpectedly on a clear day as a thousand-foot-high ominous wall of orange sand, several miles wide and moving rapidly across the desert. He had survived one lying beneath his camel in total darkness for five days. Such storms could sandblast the paint off a Land Rover. A train was blown off the track once in Algeria.

As the village stirred, I began to explore the sandy streets. Agadez was a tribal crossroad, a trading center located where the Sahel grasslands met the real desert. A mixture of tribal people from the agricultural south—Hausa and Djerma—and the more northern desert nomad tribes—Arab, Tuareg, and Wodaabe—were already moving along the main avenue toward the market.

I turned into the narrow deep-sand passages between mud-structured houses. Veiled Tuareg men in flowing robes stood in shadowed doorways, while black Peul women with blue-pigmented facial tattoos and numerous saucer-sized earrings plied the otherwise empty passageways, balancing calabashes of goat milk and water on their head. Donkeys trudged toward the central market heavily laden with crates and wares, while untethered sheep and ragged street urchins wandered about just trying to stay alive.

The mosque of Agadez.

A Bella girl.

An imposing mosque surrounded by a high courtyard wall dominated the center of the village, the Grand Mosque of Agadez. Originally built in the sixteenth century, its adobe surface was plastered smooth with mud while twisted tree trunks projecting from its cone-shaped minaret served as scaffolding for annual repair work.

Next to the mosque was a two-story mud structure, the palace of the sultan of the Aïr Tuareg. The sultanate, created five hundred years ago by the spiritual leader of Islam, was still respected by the Tuareg but had been reduced by the government to solving intertribal disputes and disagreements.

Outside the village walls I discovered a foreboding landscape of shifting sand and desiccated bush. Lacking grass or grazing of any type, hungry goats had eaten the few acacia bushes down to brittle stumps. Donkeys and sheep stood listless in the shade of the thick mud walls, heads down, ribs protruding. The sky was a sickly gray, filled with sand and dust from the harmattan. Often this "evil thing" had a strange way of making the locals weak, and they stayed indoors.

Our journey would begin in the desert north of Agadez, where Tuareg nomads survived with their camels by constantly searching for pasturage in remote areas. Our plan was to continue north to the border of Algeria where the desert was waterless, lacking even the deep hand-dug wells that allowed nomads to survive. Agadez was the last oasis, the end of the line.

I returned to the Tiden Hotel where Flagg was still asleep. As I rummaged noisily in our duffel bags for breakfast, he awoke.

"Is it morning?" he asked wearily, head still tucked deep inside his sleeping bag.

"Did you hear that call to prayer?" I asked, grinning, wishing that Muslims had not adopted modern-day amplification.

"Yeah, he needs to turn that down!" Flagg replied.

We lit our petrol stove in the courtyard and began heating water for coffee. Two thin, unkempt German men in their early twenties were bending over a plastic bucket washing clothes under a water spigot. Neither was wearing a shirt, and their pants were wrinkled and dirty.

"How long have you guys been here?" I asked.

One of them straightened up stiffly, face haggard.

"You better be careful!" he said, ignoring my question. "Everyone here is a thief," he frowned.

His companion, with tangled hair and hands heavily grease stained from mechanical work, stopped washing to explain.

"We drove a Peugeot 405 overland from France to sell in west Africa." He wiped his hands on his jeans and continued. "Crossed the Algerian border four days ago and stopped here to rest for a few days. Parked the Peugeot inside the courtyard, there," he pointed to the locked gate, "where it would be safe."

"Right after we arrived, two Africans from Ghana came to the hotel and said they wanted to buy our car. They took it for a test drive and never came back. We went to the police, but they don't do anything. Africa!" he muttered in disgust as he stooped back over the bucket.

"Is there any place to eat here?" I asked.

"There's a restaurant by the main street, on your left." He looked up from scrubbing a sock. "A hut made out of straw. The food makes you sick."

"Did you eat there?"

"Yes, it's the only place."

"Did you get sick?"

He laughed. "We've had the runs since we arrived."

Flagg and I finished our coffee and oatmeal, stuffed passports and several thousand dollars' cash into secret money belts, and then mentally braced ourselves to search Agadez for permits and finalize the remaining details.

Outside the hotel door a ragged street hustler spotted us and attached himself.

"Que Voulez-vous? Allemands? Américains?" he yelled excitedly as he raced in front of us, trying to block our way. "What do you want? Do you have Peugeot? I give you good price. I show you the camel market." He continued in French. The young west African was insistent and too much in our faces.

"*Balek* [Out of the way]!" I shouted in north African Arabic while Flagg threw unrecognizable Arabic phrases at him.

The hustler kept up an incessant tirade, "Americans are good . . . I am your friend . . . bad people in Agadez. I show you everything."

We darted into a quiet lane leading away from the market area.

Myriad tasks lay ahead, heavy burdens that felt like anchors dragging in the sand. We needed to buy camels, saddles, ropes, cooking pots, flour—everything necessary to survive forty days in the desert. Each item was critical, as there would be no place to buy things along the way. Most important, however, was to find a guide who could be trusted. ◎

CHAPTER THREE

A Simple Nomad

The history of Sahara exploration had not been encouraging. By the beginning of the twentieth century, only three Europeans had successfully crossed the desert. Many had tried. Of the first 200 would-be explorers, 165 died in the desert, many at the hands of their Tuareg guides. Major Gordon Laing was the first to reach the fabled city of Tombouctou in 1826, only to be murdered by his Tuareg guide who also stole his camels. Alexandrine Tinne was killed at a lonely well by her guides who divided her property between them. Canidem Douls was strangled by his Tuareg guide in his sleep. French Colonel Paul Flatters and the famous monk Charles de Foucauld were murdered by Tuareg. In 1881 two priests were warned, "Beware of your Tuareg guides; they will betray you!" A few days later, their guides fulfilled the prediction.

The Tuareg were a fiercely independent people, proud of their reputation for treachery and deceit. Of North African Berber extraction, they were driven into the desert by Arab invaders who conquered much of Africa during the eleventh century. But the invaders never subdued the Tuareg, who became onerous trolls of the desert, raiding caravans and extracting protection payment in order to cross their land. During the colonial period, the French also had difficulty controlling the Tuareg.

That was all long ago, I thought, and with tourism and television spreading Western culture around the world, things were different now. Despite the lack of restaurants, there were two tour agencies in Agadez and an airstrip. There was even an ice cream shop.

We searched out Rhissa Boula, an educated Tuareg whom we hoped might help us find a nomad for a guide. Everyone seemed to know him so we found his office right away. "Bonjour, bonjour," a jovial, round-figured Tuareg greeted us from behind a well-organized desk. Dressed in a pressed blue cotton boubou, a pullover gown typical of desert village dwellers, he rose and held out his hand. "I am Mano Dayak," he said in English, then pointed to an adjoining office without windows. "Rhissa is in that room."

Hunched over a stack of accounting papers, Rhissa Boula was a Tuareg of small stature with an attractive olive complexion and wearing Western clothes. It was clear that he was well educated. Humble, polite, and concise, he appeared extremely busy, so when he agreed to help us find a guide, I was relieved and immediately grateful. Instinctively, I felt I could trust Rhissa. He said to come back the next day. We left excited, but somehow I just could not believe it would be that easy.

We found the commercial market in the center of the village, next to the mosque. Everything Agadez had to offer was sold under a maze of tin-roofed stalls. Laid out on canvas sheets were ingredients for magic spells, witchcraft, and traditional medicine: old bones, bird feathers, lizard and snake skins, animal teeth, even a shriveled, dried-up crocodile and an old, moth-eaten lion's head. We were swept along in a jostling crowd of colorful tribal people jamming the narrow passageways, bargaining loudly and haggling over prices.

After four stressful hours, we had purchased a heavy cast-iron pot for cooking bread, ten kilograms of flour, handwoven hemp ropes, an iron sacking needle, and grain sacks to be stuffed with straw and used for saddle pads. As we departed loaded down, street hustlers taunted us calling, "Où est le chameau? (Where is the camel?)"

In the privacy of our room, Flagg and I tried on desert *chèches*, the fifteen-foot-long head scarves that Saharan nomads wear. The Tuareg called them *tagulmust,* wrapping them in many thick folds with a veil to hide their faces from the eyes of strangers. It also protected them from the evil jinn, spirits of the desert, which could enter through the nose and mouth. For me, however, it was the ideal protection from the sun and wind, as well as a way to retain precious breath moisture. Seeing our images reflected in the mirror, faces behind veils of blue cotton, I felt we were leaving the world of computers, faxes, and ringing telephones and stepping into some midnight script of camels, desert, and cloaked intrigue.

The restaurant the Germans told us about was an open-sided structure of woven straw mats with a gravel floor. The menu had only one choice: couscous with chunks of tough goat meat swarmed by flies. By sundown we both had cramps and diarrhea. We took antibiotics and returned for supper, where the two Germans were finishing a stomach-churning plate. They informed us that the police still had no news of the missing Peugeot. We tried not to laugh. They had no idea that the police might be in on the deal.

The following day Rhissa introduced us to an elder Tuareg immaculately dressed in a clean, pressed white boubou. An unusually long white tagulmust was wound in intricate folds around his head, but unlike other Tuareg, the veil was loosely draped below his chin, leaving his face exposed. His skin was olive, lips thin, and when we shook hands, I noticed his palms were smooth and soft. He had worked many years as a guide leading tourists, and he spoke English. When Flagg began describing our plans, the gentleman abruptly stopped us—his price was US$60 per day.

We were shocked! The annual wage in Niger was less than $300. His soft palms and high price told me he had quit the life of a nomad many years ago. I was depressed by the thought of being pampered by a trained guide. I explained to Rhissa that we were buying our own camels and planned to take care of them ourselves. We needed someone only to guide us to the water holes, and in the beginning teach us how to care for the camels.

"Perhaps my cousin will do it," Rhissa replied, nodding his head. "He is a simple nomad and has never worked with tourists. He lives with his camels in the desert north of here, in the Aïr."

"Perfect!" I said, relieved at the possibility of a real nomad untainted by tourism and Western culture.

"I'll send someone with a Land Cruiser to look for him," Rhissa said, standing up from his desk. "I'm not sure I can find him. He lives the nomad life. Check with me tomorrow."

When we returned the following afternoon, a veiled figure was sitting cautiously in the courtyard outside Rhissa's office, back pressed stiffly against the adobe wall. He wore a faded forest-green robe, more voluminous than the boubou of villagers, and a once-white tagulmust now yellowed with sand and dust. Unlike the Tuareg we had seen around town, he carried a sword in a heavily worn red leather scabbard slung by a sash from his shoulder. The veil of his tagulmust completely hid his face, and his body was covered down to the sand by the loose-fitting gown. Only his hands were exposed, and dark featureless eyes that furtively avoided all contact.

> The veil of his tagulmust completely hid his face, and his body was covered down to the sand by the loose-fitting gown. Only his hands were exposed, and dark featureless eyes that furtively avoided all contact.

The only clues to his age, which I guessed to be thirty, were his smooth, wrinkle-free eyelids and the flawless brown skin of his hands, clasped tightly together in his lap. He was clearly restless and uneasy in the village setting.

Rhissa introduced him as Bilal, his cousin. Like a lot of Muslims named for religious figures, Bilal's name was taken from a black slave freed by Muhammad. He had climbed the Kabbah wall when Muhammad overran Mecca in AD 630 and became the first to call the faithful to prayer.

The veiled figure did not rise or acknowledge our presence in any way. I held out my hand, but he ignored the gesture, eyes shifting away.

"As-salaamu alaykum [Peace be upon you]," Flagg said to the nomad in a north African dialect of Arabic.

"W-alaykum as-salaam [And upon you be peace]," Bilal said, returning the traditional Islamic greeting, but then he clammed up and refused to speak further in Arabic. Flagg tried French, but after a few uncomfortable exchanges Bilal shifted about restlessly, refusing to acknowledge us in either language.

Rhissa argued with Bilal for a moment in Tamasheq, the Tuareg language, which neither of us understood. Then, with Rhissa as our interpreter, we briefly outlined our plans and tried to settle the guide price. Bilal flatly rejected our offer of $12 per day, a reasonable price, we thought, considering the economy. After a tense discussion we agreed on $20, but Bilal still did not seem happy.

A curly-haired villager in a freshly ironed blue boubou rushed into the courtyard. He greeted Bilal in Tamasheq, then sat down close to him, holding hands affectionately. He introduced himself as Elias. From then on, Flagg spoke to Elias in French, who then relayed our questions to Bilal in Tamasheq. I thought Elias was an unnecessary intrusion and asked Flagg why he didn't just speak to Bilal himself, since they were both fluent in Arabic and French.

"There could be cultural differences." Flagg replied, wrinkling his brow with uncertainty. "We need to give him time to adjust to being around Western people."

With Elias interpreting, we went over our plans in detail. On a topographical map nailed to the wall in Rhissa's office, I traced our intended route, pointing out geographical place-names—Agamgam, Chirlet, Gréboun. Bilal had been to many of them by camel, and he pointed out the location of water holes, calling them by their Tuareg names, while I calculated the number of days of travel between them. Bilal explained that we could not depend on the wells, they might be dry; we would ask nomads along the way about sources of water.

As our journey unfolded on the map, I discovered that Bilal had never been to the desolate northern area near the border of Algeria. However, whenever we talked of desert travel, Bilal seemed confident, and I felt we could depend upon his knowledge. It was his eyes that bothered me, featureless muddy orbits that always avoided mine. Throughout our meeting his face had remained completely concealed behind the veil. Cultural differences left me hanging.

I explained to Bilal that Flagg and I would do all the work of taking care of the camels—saddling, packing, and ankle-hobbling them with a short rope at night to prevent them from running away. We would also draw the many gallons of water they needed from the deep wells, a hard labor in hot sun. We wanted to learn how to ride camels and how to do everything necessary to survive in the desert, like nomads, but we needed him to teach us.

With an abrupt turn Bilal left the map and sat down. His body stiffened, and he shifted about uneasily, whispering in an angry tone to Elias.

"Who will guard the camels during the night?" Elias asked, wrinkling his brow.

"We will," I replied, suddenly anxious.

Elias crossed his arms and leaned back passively against the wall. "The camels must be let go to graze during the night. They can go far, and there are many bandits in the desert. Someone needs to guard them or they will be stolen."

Despite our objection, Bilal and Elias insisted that he bring along a Tuareg friend to guard the camels at night. Perhaps his story was true, or maybe he just wanted more money, but I did not like the idea. Another person meant another camel, more food, more expenses, and more delays. But worst of all Bilal would prefer the friendship of another Tuareg to us, and there would be little chance of developing the close bond we hoped for. Also, we were infidels, and to Bilal, a Muslim, that was an unbreachable barrier. In Mali some marabouts had been inciting locals to kill Americans.

"How can a person stay up all night guarding camels," I asked Elias, looking straight at his face, "then travel all day with us? What do you Tuareg do?"

Bilal's eyes darted about the room. There was no answer.

I leaned back in my chair, hands folded. "We will just have to do the best we can, doing it ourselves."

Bilal leaned over and hissed to Elias in an angry tone.

"The camels will be stolen!" Elias insisted, straightening up.

Irritated with his persistence, I cut back "So? We're buying them, we'll take responsibility. If they get stolen, I'll take that chance."

The discussion ended. Bilal had washed his hands of the camels. Although I hoped things would work out, I knew that this potentially serious problem had been left unresolved. And worse, Bilal had lost face to a Westerner, a cultural affront for a Muslim Tuareg. I felt a fire ignite between us. I ignored it.

Rhissa had taken time from his busy day to graciously do us as favor, and I could not ask him to find us a third guide. So to head off another situation that might derail the journey, I explained to Bilal that he must bring all of his own food, enough for forty days.

"I want to stick to our planned route," I explained, calmly. "There will be no villages where we can buy food along the way."

Bilal shrugged with indifference.

"A nomad needs only flour, tea, and sugar." Elias explained with a smug look.

That, I knew, was true. Nomads lived on a monotonous diet of bread made from unleavened flour cooked in the sand, and millet boiled to porridge, like southern grits. Essential to their happiness, however, was a three-times-daily ritual of tea, a syrupy sweet mixture of Chinese tea known as "gunpowder," with handfuls of rock sugar. Also, I suspected that because of strict Islamic halal practices, Bilal preferred to bring his own food and would not even touch ours. The meeting ended, and I was relieved to find that food was not another big problem. For the time being, Bilal seemed satisfied. ◉

CHAPTER FOUR

The Camel Market

When we left Rhissa's office Bilal and Elias started straightaway for the camel market. When we tried to go with them, Elias stopped us.

"We must not be seen together," he explained. "If the Tuareg see you, the price will be high."

I knew it was essential to obtain certificates of ownership that showed the hand-drawn brand mark burned into each camel's neck. Without legal proof of possession, properly signed by the chief of the market, any stranger riding across the country on a camel would be regarded as a thief. I wrote out our names and instructed Elias to put two camels in my name and two in Flagg's. He slipped the paper into his boubou, and they left.

The camel market was a sprawling area of livestock and mixed tribal people outside the west wall of the village. Clouds of dust enveloped bellowing herds of long-horned cattle being driven about by Wodaabe nomads wearing conical hats of straw and red leather. The hoarse braying of lost donkeys floated over the bleating of sheep and the constant din of human voices. Camels were couched on the ground, resting on their chest calluses with legs tucked beneath them. Others stood tied to poles or hopped about awkwardly on one front leg, the other flexed and hobbled by a rope at the knee.

Flagg and I went to the goat and sheep market, an acre of dark urine-stained earth thickly matted with pea-sized droppings. Young goats galloped about playfully while large rams with spiral horns were tethered to stakes. On the far side of the market we could see Bilal and Elias engaged in casual conversation with Tuareg camel owners—not physically examining any of the camels.

We disappeared into the commerce area, crowded alleyways lined with stalls covered with canvas and straw mats and packed with miscellaneous wares. A multitude of tribal people milled about shopping for goods.

"Bonjour, monsieur," a cheerful voice called out. A black man of the Hausa tribe, identifiable by three catlike slash scars across both cheeks, was making a rope from fibers stripped from a plastic grain bag. It bore the inscription, "Donated by the People of the United States of America, Not to be sold."

His fingers and toes were heavily callused and split open from years of work, and his broad smile revealed a mouthful of cracked and broken brown-stained teeth. Three abrasive cords of tough plastic looped around his big toe were being twisted and braided into a half-inch-thick, hard cable. It was impossible to tie a knot in the stiff rope, useless for any purpose I could imagine.

He explained in French, of which I had minor proficiency, that the rope was used by nomads to draw water from deep wells in the desert. A 150-foot section required twenty days of work, netting him, after paying for the bags, less than 65 cents (US) per day for his labor. I had brought a long nylon rope from the United States for the purpose.

Cone-shaped blocks of gray salt were being carefully stacked by an elderly Tuareg. The coarse, gritty-looking material appeared to be more like concrete than something to eat. The old Tuareg told me that nomads and camels preferred the natural mineral-rich Sahara salt, found only in remote locations far out in the desert.

The salt trade was a remaining piece of Sahara history, the only trade still conducted by camel caravan. Each year the *azali* (salt caravan) leaves Agadez on a four-hundred-mile journey across the Ténéré sea of sand to the remote oasis of Bilma, where salt is extracted in evaporation pits. The caravan returns to Agadez a month later, each camel carrying nearly five hundred pounds of salt.

During the fifteenth century, salt was so valued in west Africa it was traded on an equal weight basis for gold. Agadez, at the center of east-west and north-south caravan routes, became rich from the gold and salt trade, reaching its zenith during the sixteenth century.

"*Allahu Akbahr* . . . ." The call to prayer settled the market confusion like a gentle wind bending a field of wheat. The sun was setting and dust clouds scattered the failing light to create a soft orange glow over Agadez and its lonely minaret. Like a medieval village in a faded tapestry, it seemed to say, "Day has ended and all is well."

The next morning, still hopeful for the return of their car, the Germans told us they had discovered an Algerian consulate in Agadez. Excited by the renewed possibility of obtaining the visa that had eluded us in Niamey, we searched for an hour through unmarked passages. Finally, I spotted the green and black flag of Algeria waving on a pole behind a ten-foot-high mud wall.

We forced the unpainted iron gate open and were confronted by the consul general, a Berber from North Africa, hurrying across the courtyard on his way out. He stopped to say it would take five days to get a visa, and Algiers must be radioed for approval. We dutifully filled out the necessary forms but decided not to leave our passports.

While checking in at the gendarmerie, necessary to avoid problems in Agadez, the chief of police, a Djerma tribesman, informed me that permits to travel in the Aïr were not necessary. He insisted that it would be impossible for us to find a guide; then with a condescending smile he offered to supply us with one. I decided to avoid him.

Outside the office, a middle-aged Tuareg who had seen me at the camel market asked if I needed a camel guide. He showed me his ID card and said he would be happy to get $15 per day. When I hesitated, he dropped his price. He seemed desperate. He was so pleasant that I was tempted, but I felt committed to Rhissa.

Bilal and Elias were waiting for us at the hotel. They had purchased a seven-year-old riding camel for $400. That was $100 more than the going price, but Flagg and I were too excited to care. We went immediately to see our first camel, held in a corral near the market.

Relying on previous experience with horses, I attempted to inspect the strange beast that towered over me looking down with indifference. His front shoulder was level with my neck, and it was impossible to reach his head to tie the lead rope through the nose ring unless he lowered it. He could kick backward, forward, and sideways, so, unlike a horse, there was no way to protect myself when around him. If he didn't like me, he could pick me up in his mouth and break my forearm, an injury so common it was known as the "camel fracture." However, he seemed to be a quite docile animal, just bigger than I was used to.

Most important was to make sure he had been castrated. Tuareg men took pride in riding big male camels, but a mature bull could be extremely dangerous, especially if in rut, when they are highly excited and in an insane state like elephants in musk. Then everyone stays away.

As I tried cautiously to inspect the private area between his back legs, Bilal told Flagg in Arabic how his grandfather had been tragically killed by a bull camel at the Agadez market some years ago.

"Tch!" Bilal made a glottal clicking sound often used by Tuareg men for emphasis. My grandfather had taken many caravans across the desert," Bilal explained with pride, standing more erect than usual. "He knew camels better than any Tuareg of Aïr!"

He shifted his sword around his waist and continued. "He was walking through the market to see a friend. When he passed near a big male camel, it grabbed his arm in his mouth and lifted him into the air. My father could do nothing. The camel flung him between his front legs and dropped on him, crushing him with the hard chest-bone callus. He died without saying anything."

Having satisfied myself that the camel had no testicles, I tried to open his mouth and check his teeth. He growled menacingly at me and raised his head high up out of reach. I asked Bilal for help, but he just looked at me with a blank expression as if none of this was important.

I disagreed. Sand eventually wore down a camel's teeth to useless stumps. When no longer able to chew the coarse Sahara browsing materials, they died of starvation, usually at about twenty-five years of age. Like a horse, a camel's age could be estimated by the number and length of teeth. Although I had no experience at this with a camel, I felt compelled to try. At least I could tell if his teeth were badly broken or missing.

A tug on the sensitive nose ring lowered the camel's head to within reach. Despite loud growling protests, I grabbed his lower jaw and prized open his mouth. A blast of rotten hot air hit my face, belched up from his ruminating stomach over a slobbering tongue and nasty evil-looking fanglike teeth. I quickly let go.

Finally, I tried to check the bottoms of his feet, broad spongy footpads that allowed him to walk over soft desert sand without bogging down. If they were torn or infected, our journey could be jeopardized. When I tried to pick up his front foot, he kicked sideways at me, narrowly missing. Bilal took over and made him lie down, a position in which the front pads were folded up and visible, but the rear feet were tucked forward under his body, pads to the ground. Neither Bilal nor the owner was willing to pick up the camel's back feet. They said it just wasn't done. His long, powerful legs and clawlike toenails looked dangerous. I decided not to try.

Bilal had not test-ridden the camel, but he assured me it was good and that the owner spoke only the truth. This was the way camels were bought, he said, simply on testimony of the owner. As a teenager I had worked for a country horse trader and seen him swear that the spooky killer an inexperienced father was buying for his child was safe for a baby; however, I had no choice but to trust Bilal.

Marabout amulets to protect against Jinns.

Next morning, Flagg and I were on our way to the village market to purchase the remaining supplies when Bilal and Elias spotted us and tagged along. It irritated me that they were not at the camel market.

"What are you looking for?" Elias asked, prying.

Thinking they might be helpful, I replied, "Where can we buy camel saddles?"

Elias stopped us. "The Tuareg don't sell them here. Bilal can get you one from a friend."

We pushed on to the market despite his protests. Once there, Elias and Bilal took over and became our guides. With them bargaining for us, we purchased hemp cord, iron rings, and canvas material to make girths for the saddles. Whenever Elias and Bilal were not around, I noticed that prices fell significantly. When I confronted Elias about this, they quickly departed for the camel market.

I discovered a wonderful treasure of new Tuareg camel saddles stashed in the back room of a shop. They were covered in burnished red and green leather and fitted with shiny brass and tin decorations. The haggled price was $35 each. Excited, I purchased one with a comfortable seat for myself and another for Bilal. Flagg decided to wait and see what Bilal had for sale.

The camel saddles had a two-foot-tall pommel horn that fits between the legs when seated. Three brass-covered, ornamental, tapered prongs branched from the end of the horn, which I thought were dangerous and might impale my body if the saddle came loose and I fell off. The group of curious Tuareg who were following me groaned in horror when I borrowed a saw from a workman and hacked off the decorative prongs from my new saddle.

Back at the hotel I found Flagg admiring a saddle that Bilal had just sold him—at twice the price I had paid. When I showed him mine, he seemed perplexed about the price difference; however, he dismissed it. "Bilal's saddle was a real nomad saddle," he said, "and of better quality." I could see no difference.

When Bilal and Elias arrived, they scoffed at my saddle, saying it was no good, but when they left, Bilal picked up his new saddle and carried it away over his shoulder as if there were no problem.

The second camel was an old, gray gelding purchased for $460. Once famous as a racing camel, the twenty-year-old had been retired. He was unusually big and Bilal assured us that he had enough stamina left for one more journey. We had paid 50 percent more than the going price and knew they were skimming commissions for themselves. We consoled ourselves, however, with the thought that they would have cost even more if we had tried to buy them, and we would have been shown only the sick, deformed, or disabled.

Over the next two days, Flagg and I stuffed and sewed saddle pads, prepared the ropes, and scoured the marketplace for remaining items. We worked away excited and happy that we were almost on our way.

One essential item continued to elude us, a packsaddle. Bilal said that the Tuareg do not use packsaddles and insisted that we would not find one. A day later I discovered an elderly Tuareg nomad at the camel market with a well-used packsaddle made from two tree forks bound together with rawhide. When Bilal saw it in our pile of stuff, he was angry and left.

Each time we returned to the Algerian consulate there was a lock on the gate. We finally ran into the consul general in the town market and were told that visas were impossible. Radio contact with Algiers had been terminated, and the border was officially closed. He hurried away. All hope of Tamanrasset as our final destination was lost.

Late that afternoon, Bilal and Elias came to our room. Elias announced, with a sense of finality, that they had purchased the last two camels, a twelve-year-old brown riding camel and a pinto baggage camel. At $460 each, I thought this a healthy profit for them, but it was a huge relief to finally have the necessary camels. Flagg and I jumped about the supply- and baggage-filled room tingling with the prospect of leaving.

Bilal shared none of our excitement, he seemed nervous and in a hurry. He wanted to leave immediately for his camp in the Aïr to say good-bye to his family, and he asked us to give him $100 to supply them with food during his absence. I counted out the money but before turning it over decided to ask for the camel certificates. Elias faltered, then tried to evade the subject. When I persisted, he said the certificates were at the market being prepared.

Flagg and I insisted that we go immediately to the market and get them, but Elias and Bilal refused. We demanded to have the certificates before Bilal left Agadez. Bilal and Elias argued viciously in Tamasheq; then Elias hesitatingly pulled two folded pieces of paper from inside his boubou. The certificates had Bilal's name on one, Elias's on the other.

Flagg and I were shocked! Desperate to get going on the journey before something worse happened, I reluctantly gave Bilal the money, insisting that he return within two days with no further delays. Then we took Elias with us to the camel market where for $5 the *chef de marché* issued new certificates in our names.

The following day we inspected our four camels corralled at the camel market. The only fodder available, a tough natural grass, was expensive, since all pasturage around Agadez had been grazed down to the roots. Water had to be hauled from far away by donkey, and it seemed we were paying steep premiums. Although Flagg had never ridden a camel before, he saddled the gray gelding and rode him around the market while onlooking Tuareg men laughed and jested. At least we no longer heard the irritating yell, "Où est le chameau?"

In the corral next to ours, a uniformed official was lovingly admiring two recently purchased long-horned cows. Feeling proud of my new camels, I introduced myself. He was Sammy, chief of the local militia and a Hausa. The sun was setting, a time when Muslims let their hair down and are traditionally hospitable to all. I risked everything and openly told him about our intended camel journey. He was envious, thought it was a wonderful adventure, and sincerely wished us good luck.

The day ended in an orange glow, nomads and camels silhouetted against the setting sun. *"Allahu Akbahr . . . "* the muezzin's voice floated over Agadez like a soothing blanket, calling for prayer, supplication, and submission to the will of God. Our laborious chores were completed, supplies packed and ready, difficulties seemingly over. ◎

The camel market at sunset.

CHAPTER FIVE

Into the Desert

Three more days passed and Bilal had still not returned. Expenses at the camel corral were mounting, as was our impatience. Finally I gave in and asked Rhissa to find us another guide. He introduced Sidi, a jolly, middle-aged Tuareg who did not bother to veil his face. Sidi was happy about the guide fee, easy to get along with, and said he would be ready to depart early the next morning. After nine days in Agadez, we were bursting to leave. I was happy to be rid of Bilal.

Back at the Tiden we met an exhausted, unshaven, and disheveled American man in his thirties. He had just escaped from Algeria where Muslims were rioting against American policy in the Middle East. They sided with Saddam Hussein, who had just invaded Kuwait.

He had crossed the border at I-n-Guezzâm in a Peugeot driven by two Frenchmen, and they were confronted by a crowd of angry Algerians stoning cars and yelling anti-American slurs. He lay in the back seat pretending to be sick, speaking only French, and denying his U.S. citizenship. He was still shaken by the experience.

That night a crowd of scruffy-looking locals wearing headgear and robes gathered at the Tiden in front of a battered black-and-white television set brought to the lobby. No one was talking and everyone was staring intensely at the TV. What appeared to be fireworks were bursting over a dark city skyline, but the excited newscaster's voice was garbled and unintelligible and left me wondering what kind of celebration was occurring. We sat down among them to watch.

Flagg whispered to the man next to him in Arabic, asking what was happening. He said the United States was bombing Baghdad. Flagg and I were taken by surprise, having been out of touch for two weeks. The Gulf War had started. We tried to show no reaction, but when not staring at the exploding bombs, the rough-shaven Muslim men stared at us. We went to our room. Eighty percent of the country was Muslim, and that was just another reason to get out of town as soon as possible.

Before sunrise Sidi knocked on our door. In the gray of dawn we loaded our quarter ton of equipment into the back of a rented pickup and drove to the camel corral. While Sidi returned to Agadez for his personal gear, Flagg and I threw ropes over the camel's necks and pulled their heads down. With them crying "waaaaaaa," like babies, we threaded lead ropes through the metal rings piercing their sensitive nostrils.

My only previous contact with camels had been a five-day camel trip two years earlier in the dunes north of Djanet in Algeria. However, I thought my experience with horses would be easily transferred to camels. One by one we led them out of the corral and made them lie down by hissing, "shuss . . . shuss," and tugging downward on the nose rope. Then we knee-hobbled each camel by tightly binding the left foreleg to the upper leg with a short piece of rope. That prevented the camel from suddenly standing while we worked.

Flagg and I saddled the three riding camels, then began packing the baggage on the pinto, but each time we attempted to put the packsaddle over his hump he growled and lunged at us with an open mouth full of vicious teeth. Sidi arrived and quickly finished the job.

Just when we were ready to depart, Sidi came forward holding the hand of a friend who had been in the crowd of Tuareg watching us. He insisted that we take him along to guard the camels. Despite my absolute refusal, Sidi persisted, and our imminent departure was put on hold. While we argued, the crowd of curious onlookers pressed closer around our loaded camels.

It was now midmorning, and the sun was hot on our faces. The argument was leading nowhere. I removed the knee hobbles, and the camels immediately began to rise, roaring in protest amid deep-throated groans.

Awkward heaps of flesh lurched skyward, then faltered before surging upward again. Saddles tilted dangerously as rear haunches unfolded and straightened stiffly beneath them. Forelegs shot forward, slamming footpads into the ground and heaving forequarters skyward, whiplashing everything in reverse. The pinto baggage camel lurched from the ground with four hundred pounds lashed tenuously to the creaking frame pack.

Gathering the nose ropes, I started leading the four camels north, into the desert. Flagg, still in discussion with Sidi, threw a curious glance in my direction, then cast off to join me. Sidi said good-bye to his friend and ran to catch up. We were off!

By noon the sun was searing our backs beneath our cotton shirts. A hot wind blew in our faces at gale strength, and the sky had taken on a brown hue, the color of sand. Sweat flowed in hot trickles down my face and chest, only to evaporate into the dry air leaving salt on my skin. In spite of the heat, I wore my chèche, leaving only dark glasses exposed.

> *A hot wind blew in our faces at gale strength, and the sky had taken on a brown hue, the color of sand.*

Two hours out of Agadez, we gave up walking, couched our camels by tugging on the lead rope and mounted. Sidi was riding bent forward holding his throbbing head between his hands. The aspirin was buried deep inside the baggage.

The packsaddle was leaning to one side, twisting and digging with each step into the pinto's back. Twice I dismounted to adjust the load, but the heat and wind quickly exhausted me. We continued with the baggage listing precariously.

Nine miles out of Agadez, we halted in the shade of a threadbare acacia tree. Sidi dismounted, staggering as he unwound his chèche and dropped it on the ground. He poured water from a *guerba*, a goatskin water bag, over his head and collapsed, sprawled on the sand. He refused to move into the shade, as sparse as it was, and would not let us help him. Sidi just lay there roasting in the sun while Flagg and I drank the hot water in our canteen, ate peanut butter sandwiches, and wondered what to do.

We had to keep going, but Sidi was unable to stand. Yellow stomach fluid was drooling from his mouth onto the sand, and the sun was baking him alive. With no previous experience on our own with camels, we decided to search for a protected place to camp, then return for Sidi.

Two miles to the west was a dark band of vegetation—palm trees. It was the ancient riverbed of Teloua where water seeped to the surface in shallow pools and small gardens were cultivated in the shade of date palms. With our four camels in tow, we found our way through the thick bush to the edge of the *palmeraie* where we were stopped by a thorn limb barrier, constructed to keep livestock out. Inside, an elderly Tuareg was mending his irrigation ditches.

"*As-salaamu alaykum!*" I shouted, startling the old man. He was surprised to see two Westerners in khaki pants and blue jeans leading camels.

"W-alaykum as-salaam," he replied, running to open the thornbush gate.

I turned to Flagg and said, "Hamdullah, praise be to God."

Flagg went through the formal salutations in Arabic, then asked permission to camp inside the man's palm grove. He led us to a carpet of green grass in the deep shade of the date palms, heavy with clusters of golden-yellow nuggets. Water gurgled nearby in the irrigation ditches, reminding me of King Faisal's words to Lawrence of Arabia in the movie: "Arabs do not like the desert; they like the oasis, the sound of cool water. Only mad dogs and English like the desert."

Flagg unloaded the camels while I hurried back for Sidi. Twice I lost track of our footsteps in the acacia bush and wandered about in circles. Finally, I found him lying where we had left him, roasting in the merciless sun. I shook him until his eyes opened, but he was unable to speak. When I pulled him to his feet, he fell down again. With one of his arms over my shoulder, I began dragging him back to camp. After some yards he revived and wobbled along unassisted, but near camp he collapsed again. Each time I moved him into the shade, he crawled back into the sun, so I gave up and left him there, retching.

We hobbled the camels and released them outside the palmeraie to browse on the brittle acacia and stubble of coarse grass. I drew a bucket of cool water from the well and poured it over my sweat-drenched body.

Late that afternoon, Sidi stopped vomiting, and I gave him some antibiotics. However, when our Tuareg host returned and discovered Sidi sick, he became alarmed, rounded up a little donkey, and trotted off toward Agadez for help. Explaining that I was a doctor and that I had given him medicine made no difference.

Near sunset it began to cool down. Sidi revived and came into camp, wrapped himself in a blanket, and began to sleep peacefully. Beyond the palmeraie the horizon glowed red, the entire sky taking on a brilliant orange hue. I noticed a dust trail approaching rapidly from the south, then the high-pitched whining of a motor running at a high rpm. A Toyota Land Cruiser pulled up to the edge of the palmeraie and, to my utter dismay, out stepped Elias and Bilal.

Despite my insistence that Sidi was recovering and that the antibiotics would cure him by morning, they quickly loaded him into the Land Cruiser and started back toward Agadez. Bilal said he would return later that night with his sword and blanket. I shook my head. I no longer cared if the devil himself was our guide, as long as we kept going. ◉

CHAPTER SIX

A Land without Mercy

I n the crisp dawn air, spirals of white vapor formed over our hot oatmeal. Bilal had left camp an hour before sunrise with a flashlight to track down the camels. By the time he returned, daylight was breaking, and the heat had returned with a vengeance. Eager to get started, Flagg and I saddled the riding camels while Bilal prepared tea over a small fire of twigs. He loaded the baggage camel effortlessly, clearly more experienced than Sidi. My confidence was restored, Agadez forgiven, and we were happy to be on our way.

Once free of the sheltered palmeraie, the hot desert wind bore down on us again. We struggled against it for an hour on foot, then mounted. The sun rose higher, torching the barren earth and jagged rocks until they radiated heat like an open furnace. I was protected from the hot blast by a long-sleeved shirt, chèche, and ski goggles over my eyes, but despite leather gloves, my hands shriveled like prunes.

We rode into a oued, a dry riverbed of soft sand churned up by the hooves of goats, sheep, and donkeys on their way to a well. Dom palms with branching trunks and leafless, thorny acacias covered in dust lined the banks. Bilal pointed to a half-eaten, red applelike dom palm fruit, saying that baboons lived there. We couched our camels at the well, an unprotected four-foot-diameter hole hand-dug some thirty feet into the sand.

A forked tree trunk buried upright next to the well was tilted so a rope could be thrown over it to draw water. We lowered our plastic bucket into the dark hole and brought it back half full with murky liquid the color of sand. While Flagg and I filled two of our jerricans, a painstaking job of pulling the heavy water-filled bucket to the surface, Bilal rode ahead, hopeful to find a Tuareg garden with red peppers and tomatoes to spare.

Inside one of the jerricans I noticed something brown bobbing around on the surface—a camel turd. I could not fish it out and decided not to mention it to Flagg. I never saw it again.

We were riding over rock-strewn ground when my saddle suddenly tilted and began to slide forward down the camel's sloping withers. I braced my feet against the back of his neck, but then the saddle leaned precariously to the side. The girth had come loose and was dangling between the camel's front legs.

I pulled on the nose rope to stop my camel, but he growled and twisted around in a circle, trying to keep up with the others and making things worse. The pommel stake between my legs prevented me from leaping free, so I was trapped in the saddle, fighting an unruly camel and sliding uncontrollably off toward the rocks.

At the last second, Bilal saw me and leaped from his camel. He caught the edge of my saddle, and with the weight of my body on his shoulder wrestled the uncooperative camel to his knees. I toppled gently off onto the ground.

My camel had been a problem since Agadez, growling and refusing to obey commands. A single leather rein draped along the left side of his neck extending to a metal ring in his nostril was used to guide him. To turn right I drew the rein tight against his neck; to turn left I pulled it away. The problem was that his nose, like that of all camels, was exquisitely sensitive to the ring, and he hated any pressure on it. Although a camel could be trained with the nose ring to fall on his chest at a full gallop and slide to a stop, most camels howl with anguish and pain whenever pressure is applied. When my camel did not want to cooperate, he lashed his head around like a snake, pivoting 180 degrees to stare straight into my eyes and growl menacingly. He could spit in my face or grab me with his teeth and throw me off, and there was nothing I could do.

He also refused to couch or lie down when I wanted to dismount. The signal was a "shhh . . . shhh . . . shhh" sound while pressing the sole of my foot into the back of his neck. Unfortunately, this particular foot action was also the signal to go faster. When he did couch, I was pitched violently forward as he dropped to his front knees, then whiplashed backward when his rear legs collapsed. A safe landing was verified by a heavy "thud" as the resting callous of his chest bone hit the ground.

Bilal's camel was more cooperative, so I asked him to trade since it might avoid problems during what was going to be a long trip. He refused and then became angry when I insisted. I remained firm, knowing that an injury on my part would end the trip. After the switch, Bilal started riding ahead of us, silent and brooding.

We paused for a moment at the top of a hill. The sheltering palms of Teloua were still visible ten miles behind us, a dark belt of luxurious green curving toward the horizon. As we rode farther into the hill country, it faded out of sight.

The western sky was blistering orange when we stopped to camp in a dry streambed. Strands of yellow grass stood nearby, brittle broom straw for our camels' hungry mouths. Desiccated leafless bushes survived tenaciously along the edges of the streambed, but otherwise it was a landscape of rock and earth. An overhanging bank protected us from the wind, but the hot, arid air had sucked my skin dry, like the scorched countryside around us. Long after sunset, the rocks were still hot to the touch, and when I crawled into my tent to sleep, the ground beneath was uncomfortably warm. Dirty and exhausted I fell immediately asleep.

At sunrise I was relieved to find the hobbled camels nearby, grazing peacefully. Horses would have run home during the night. Bilal's recalcitrant camel and the pinto had become friends, rubbing noses whenever they met and howling anguished moans when separated. Flagg's camel, the old gray, was a loner and stayed away from the others. My tan gelding hated the gray, growling and baring his teeth whenever he came close.

While finishing breakfast, we named our camels based on their personalities.

"I think I will call my camel McGoo," Flagg said pensively while sipping tea from his Sierra Club tin cup. "The title fits his lofty nature. I think he is a wise old camel."

Flagg saddles up Igor.

McGoo walked with his nose tilted toward the sky, and when Flagg tried to catch him he just held his head higher, glaring at him with disregard.

"The Tuareg say that camels know the hundredth name of Allah." I said, shaking a packet of instant oatmeal into a bowl. "Man knows only ninety-nine names. That's why a camel holds its head high and looks down at humans like they are stupid!"

Bilal's brown gelding became Lion Mane for his deep-throated roar and the thick black hair that grew on the back of his neck.

My tan camel was gentle and well-behaved, a delightful travel companion. At times he seemed philosophical, and during the long day's ride he appeared to dream of faraway places, perhaps greener pastures. I decided to call him O. Henry for the surprise twists to William Sydney Porter's stories my mother loved so much, and for his pen name, the source of which remains a mystery.

We named the pinto baggage camel Igor the Terrible for his awful disposition, broken teeth, and fetid breath. Whenever Flagg or I approached him, he growled horribly, lunging at us with an open mouth. His huge, transparent blue eyes burned like those of an evil mythological beast, and I sensed a bitter confrontation somewhere in our future. Flagg had developed a symbiotic relationship with the pinto, so for the time being I stayed away and let him handle the camel. Under Bilal's supervision Flagg and I loaded the camels, then moved off on foot. We walked for two hours, then couched our camels and mounted. In one smooth motion, Bilal vaulted effortlessly into the saddle with his camel still standing. Impressed, I asked him to show me how.

Stepping with his right foot on the side of his camel's knee, Bilal placed his left foot in the U-shaped curve of the neck and stood up, then swung his right leg over the saddle and sat down—a seamless procedure. On my second attempt I succeeded clumsily, after a struggle. I was determined to learn the nomad way of doing things.

O. Henry was a slow walker, and I began to fall farther and farther behind. Continuously jabbing my foot into the back of his neck was exhausting and seemed futile. By midmorning I was a mile behind Flagg and Bilal. Frustrated, I slapped O. Henry hard on the rump with the lead rope and forcefully jabbed my foot into his neck. He woke up and shifted into an effortless seven miles per hour "pace," a comfortable side-to-side rocking gait that T. E. Lawrence and his Bedu companions employed to ride eighty miles per day, covering vast distances in the Arabian desert. Bilal groaned when I moved effortlessly ahead of his Lion Mane.

We camped on the bank of a dry riverbed, among dust-covered bushes and scattered dom palms. Some of the palms were dead, pencil-like trunks with ragged, broken-off tops. Our camels strained their necks to reach the few shriveled leaves left high up in the acacia trees. With their long legs and globular bodies, they resembled giraffes, which the first European explorers thought they were related to.

An elderly Tuareg camping in the nearby oued came to greet Bilal. After proper salutations, he approached me with his few personal possessions to sell. His clothes were tattered and he looked in serious need, so I purchased two ragged saddle pads. Then he offered me an old heavily worn silver Agadez cross, a revered silver pendant symbolic of earth and sky. Bilal said that it had been his grandfather's, so I tried to give it back, but the old man insisted on selling it.

The sun set in a yellow haze, a platterlike disk balanced delicately on the horizon. An indigo-veiled Tuareg riding a big, white male camel trotted urgently along the opposite bank of the oued, black robes swirling behind him in a trailing cloud of dust. A sword in a red leather scabbard was slung loosely around his saddle, and tasseled wool trappings hung down below the camel's belly, swaying rhythmically with the jostling pace. The glowing sun burned into the far side of the oued, capturing for a moment the mysterious black rider in its brilliance; then in a fiery explosion, both vanished into the empty desert.

Bilal was praying some distance away, as he had done each day before sunrise, at noon, and after sunset. He stood facing Mecca with his sandals removed. After washing his hands with sand he held them over his face and began reciting the "Fatiha," six verses that compose the opening chapter of the Koran. Then he kneeled and pressed his forehead into the sand twice, leaving a white patch on his brow. After repeating the ritual three times, he sat peacefully, offering private prayers.

I respected his belief and admired the rigorous daily devotions of the faithful. Islam, Judaism, and Christianity were all born of pastoral desert people and traced their lineage to a common source, Abraham. Islam, however, as practiced by nomads, seemed closer to its roots.

That night tribal music drifted from the Tuareg camp. Goatskin drums and high-pitched singing were accompanied by an infectious melody played on a single-string primitive, guitarlike instrument. The air was hot and still, and I lay in my tent listening, too weary to join them. Despite wearing the chèche to retain breath moisture, the arid wind had parched our throats, and Flagg and I had hacking coughs and bloody noses. Each night I covered my body with mineral oil, but my fingertips had split open, leaving painful cracks that kept me awake.

I thought about how desperate the old man had seemed, selling his precious few heirlooms. The music from the camps was happy and did not sound like that of a suffering people. However, while crossing the Sahara by Land Rover during the 1984 drought, I had found that desert people submitted easily to the will of God and during starvation could smile and share their last morsel with a stranger. On that trip I had passed right by starving people without recognizing them. I decided to visit the old man in the morning to investigate.

I found their camp set in the soft sand of the riverbed. Their tents, four highly mobile structures, were made of woven straw mats lain over an oval framework of bent poles. Inside, the elderly Tuareg of the night before was carving a bed from an acacia tree trunk. He smiled and motioned me to sit on the sand inside his tent and watch. Chips flew from his primitive adze as he skillfully sculpted the brittle wood into a barbell-shaped wooden post, two of which would support a platform of poles. Over that would be placed a straw sleeping mat with a geometric pattern in red leather woven into it by his wife. Although the bed and tent appeared heavy and cumbersome, everything could be taken down quickly and loaded onto a camel's back.

In a nearby tent another nomad was carving a wooden pulley for drawing water.

He stopped to welcome me. A young boy whose bare head sported a Mohawk-style haircut sat next to him scraping smooth the surface of a paddle-shaped, twelve-inch-long wooden writing palette. For a small fee, a verse from the Koran would be written on it by the marabout. It would be hung in the entry of the tent to protect them from the jinn.

In front of the other tents women were laboring over smoking cooking fires, stirring blackened pots that bubbled with a thick paste of millet flour. In spite of the intense sun, they were completely covered by heat-absorbing dark indigo scarves draped over their heads and voluminous black dresses that hung in long folds to the ground. In the shade of tent walls, young mothers sat in the soft sand suckling babies, while unmarried adolescent girls clad in light cotton print dresses trudged back and forth hauling loads of firewood and water.

None of the women wore a veil or tried to conceal their faces in any way. In a unique reversal of Muslim custom, only Tuareg men wore veils. Nomad women were free of the constricting Islamic codes forced on villagers. Also, I noticed, they were not shy or afraid of my presence.

As I surveyed the contents of their open tents and stared into cooking pots, they relentlessly peppered me with questions in Tamasheq, laughing with broad smiles whenever I responded in limited French tainted with a deep southern accent. The young girls, busy keeping a close eye on toddlers,

A Tuareg camp at the sandy oued.

A Tuareg girl.

had pretty olive skin, thin Berber noses, bright round eyes, and shy smiles. They turned away giggling whenever I caught them looking curiously at me. Long braids of crow-black hair hung down their backs, and the idyllic pastoral scene, with smoking fires and primitive mat tents, was reminiscent of an Edward Curtis photograph of a nineteenth-century Native American camp.

All married women wore the silver cross of Agadez, a dowry gift from their husbands, along with numerous strands of red and yellow glass beads and shiny triangular metal pendants. Small purses of red leather also hung around their necks containing precious needles, coins, and bits of string.

The women began aggressively trying to sell their jewelry and other personal items, so I returned to camp. As we rode away, Bilal pointed to a tree that had been stripped of branches and hacked down to a jagged stump.

"There was no rain this year, and the Tuareg here have nothing to eat." He slowed his camel as we surveyed the area. "When the grass was eaten, they took long sticks and knocked leaves off the trees for their goats to eat. After that, they cut off the branches. Now even the trees are dying. It is finished, there is nothing left. They are selling their jewelry to buy salt and cereals."

We rode on through a desolate land of bare stumps, fallen dom palms, and dying acacias stripped of their limbs. It looked like Armageddon.

Bilal continued. "When the rains come in summer, there is much grass and the camels grow fat. Then a camel can sell for more than two thousand U.S. dollars.

"Tch! In 1970 there was drought and camels sold for as little as $50. Many Tuareg died that year, in Niger and Mali. But the Americans sent food, and many were saved."

Then his voice turned bitter. "Tch! In 1984 the drought came again, but the Americans sent nothing. And this year, there was no rain, no water even in the largest oued. Tch! The nomad life is only hardship."

Bilal abruptly urged his camel forward, ending the conversation. I recalled that the word *Tuareg,* given to them by the early Arab invaders when they refused to accept Islam, meant "abandoned of God." The Tuareg, however, in their own language of Tamasheq call themselves "free people," or "people of the veil."

At midday we passed six mat tents in a dry streambed. Two women were pounding millet in a wooden mortar carved from a tree trunk and winnowing the grains in shallow, rimmed baskets. The few precious cereals they had extracted by this laborious and inefficient work were kept in pear-shaped gourds with narrow necks. The women's black dresses were tattered and soiled, their faces stained with dirt, and there was no laughter. We did not stop.

As we rode, the landscape became even more barren, with suffering and hardship all around. For the first time we passed camps of starving people who stared silently at us with blank faces. The energy and excitement of the camel trip was drained out of me, replaced by a sadness that invaded every pore. It was a land without mercy.

Our only luxury was a three-kilogram bag of dried dates that Flagg had purchased in Agadez. The taste of crystallized raw sugar had become addicting, and we were feasting uncontrollably on the crunchy fruit at every meal. When we stopped for lunch, Flagg discovered tiny black bugs crawling in the sticky mass, as well as white larvae wiggling out of little holes. He heaved the disgusting bag over a hill, but I quickly retrieved it and hid it in my duffel.

That afternoon we rode onto a flat plain strewn with volcanic rock. Bilal found a narrow trail leading through the black lava, jagged rock whose sharp edges could easily lacerate the soft footpads of our camels. Only twelve to eighteen inches wide, it was an ancient caravan route used since Roman times, centuries of shuffling camels' feet wearing the rock smooth. Known as the Garamantian Road, it was once the main trade route connecting black Africa to the Mediterranean.

Until camels were introduced in the seventh century AD, trans-Sahara trade was carried out on the backs of humans and horses. Red garnet had been the first product out of Africa, then elephants and other exotic beasts were driven across the desert after their depletion from north Africa by the Romans for their Coliseum games. In the Middle Ages, ivory and ostrich feathers were considered fashionable by Europeans; then slaves and gold became the dominant trade.

In 1849 Dr. Heinrich Barth, a German explorer, crossed the Sahara to Agadez along the same caravan route we were traveling. He continued on to the fabled city of Tombouctou, the second European to do so and return alive.

Bilal and Flagg on the Garamantian Road, which was once the main

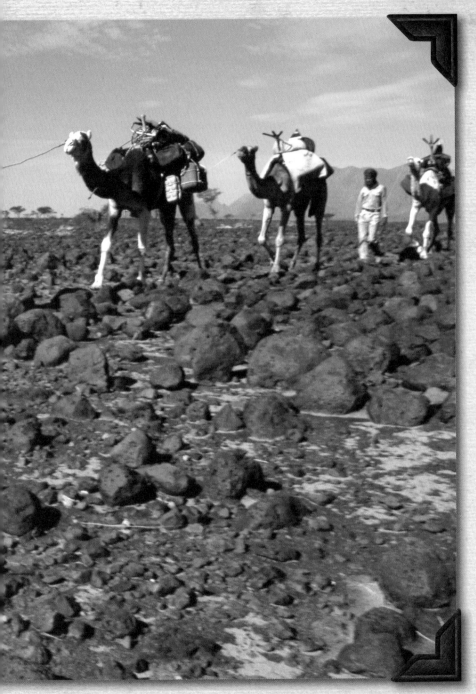

...orth-south trading route between black Africa and the Mediterranean..

At sunset we stopped in a rock canyon to camp, shielded from the wind by twenty-foot walls with red and yellow quartz. As the light faded the air turned bitter cold, and wind bit through our down jackets. While Flagg and I huddled around a small fire of broken twigs, Bilal knelt in prayer some distance up the canyon. ◉

Making camp in the rock canyon.

CHAPTER SEVEN

Unforgiving Way of the Nomad

Travel by camel had quickly forced upon us a demanding routine, the unforgiving way of the nomad. It was a lonely life but without boredom. There was no time for personal needs, and they were soon forgotten. We rode late into the sun each day, not stopping until grass was found for the camels. Their needs were always a higher priority than our own, and it was only after unloading, hobbling, and leading them to pasture that we turned to ourselves.

Tents were set up and food prepared in darkness, then, exhausted and dirty, we fell immediately and deeply asleep. Morning always came too quickly, and with bodies still stiff and aching from the previous day's march, we groped about in darkness and freezing air to take down our camp and start all over again. Bilal had cut his prayer to three times a day, instead of the five required by the Pillars of Islam.

Before dawn could etch the horizon with its blue-gray light—a squinting luminescence that shadows the muezzin's thread and calls the faithful to prayer—Flagg would set out across the empty desert following our camels' tracks. If they were not found before the first warming rays of sunlight stirred them from the night's cold, they shuffled off rapidly in search of grass, often for miles, driven by hunger. Flagg often returned to a pot of cold macaroni, and if the camels had not been found, Bilal was sent out after them.

By day we rode or walked without mercy. If one of us fell behind, or stopped to empty his bladder, the run to catch up was exhausting; so we learned to drink in a miserly way and to disregard our bodily functions. Only at the scorching midday zenith did we stop to unload the camels, rest, and let them graze. Then we pushed on in the relentless sun.

We rode all day over rolling hills, the ground littered with broken quartz of yellow, red, amber, white, and transparent orange. Late in the afternoon the wind picked up, and the air thickened with a foglike suspension of dust, the harmattan that had plagued us for the last five days since leaving Agadez.

A dome-shaped mountain known as Bagzane could be seen far away, a monolith of black rock shrouded in a gray haze. We were approaching the Aïr massif, the rugged six-thousand-foot volcanic highlands where Tuareg tribes retreated to hide during wars, including the current insurrection.

We stopped in a mile-wide river of sand where there was some brittle grass for our camels. The wind grew stronger, kicking up fine particles of sand that swirled around us.

As we unloaded the camels, a Tuareg came running barefooted from his tent, hidden among some low bush nearby.

"*Be careful!*" he shouted, pointing toward Mount Bagzane. "It's dangerous here."

The gusting wind whipped his ragged gown around his body while the excited nomad explained that a bandit named "El Khuf" lived on the plateau above Bagzane and came down at night to steal camels. With the moonlight obscured by sand and dust clouds, he was sure there would be a raid tonight. Bilal had heard of El Khuf, his raids were famous among the Aïr Tuareg. He insisted that we not let our camels graze during the night, but keep them in camp, closely guarded.

I thought El Khuf possibly a bit of folklore used to scare us for some unknown reason, perhaps so the nomad next door could steal our camels. However, what concerned me most was that this was the best grass we had seen in days and if we followed his warning our camels would not be allowed to graze. After dark, Bilal knee-hobbled the camels and made them lie down next to our tents. Although they had eaten almost nothing over the last five days, I hid my sympathetic agony and deferred to Bilal. I would have taken the chance and let them eat.

By morning the wind had stopped, and for the first time since arriving in Niger, the sky was clear and blue. Bilal had set the camels free at first light and they were grazing peacefully nearby. The harmattan, the oppressive, dust-filled air that had physically weakened my body, was gone. The dome of Bagzane was clearly visible, and El Khuf, the bandit, seemed like a cruel joke.

We rode toward Bagzane invigorated by the clean air and warm yellow sunshine. At the base of the mountain Tuareg women were drawing water for their goats at the well at Abardokh. We borrowed their goatskin guerba and rawhide rope and filled our jerricans. Then Flagg and I doused ourselves with cool water, thoroughly refreshed and energized by the openness of the landscape and clarity of the sky.

At midday we found pasturage for our camels and decided to camp. They had eaten little since leaving Agadez, and I was amazed at their ability to survive on the meager browse we had encountered. We made a fire from scavenged pieces of dead bush limbs and baked bread in the cast-iron pot by piling coals around the sides and on top of the lid. That night the wind returned with a vengeance, vibrating the tent walls so violently that sleep was impossible.

To our surprise, the air was clear again the following morning. We had been traveling north for six days toward the central Sahara where centuries of wind had sifted and cleansed the desert of dust particles. Days were growing hotter, nights colder, and we would be encountering diurnal temperature swings of up to one hundred degrees Fahrenheit, enough to split boulders. Such temperature extremes had caused the Colossus of Memnon in Egypt to sing, emitting a high-pitched sound at sunset when the granite statue contracted.

We entered a lava field of molten basalt that had gushed from the center of the earth to cover the sandy desert floor with a thick layer of sharp, black rock. All around us rose sharp-rimmed volcanic cones born of rifts in the earth's crust.

Long ago tectonic plates collided in the center of the Sahara, uplifting domes of crystalline granite. Violent volcanic eruptions covered them with a mantle of basaltic lava to create the central Sahara massifs: Aïr in Niger, Hoggar in Algeria, and Tibesti in Chad. Wind and erosion sculpted them into jagged peaks, and the sun burned the exposed bedrock to a shiny black patina— the "geography of hell."

For thousands of years rainwater flowed off the central mountains to create ancient riverbeds and shallow lakes. The water never reached the sea, but sank beneath the sand leaving immense flat gravel plains known as *tanezroufts*. The sand was winnowed by the wind and blown into dune fields, while the water became trapped beneath the desert against subterranean bedrock. This nonrenewable "fossil" water was being tapped in Libya, the largest engineering project in the world.

The Sahara massifs even affect life in America. When hot desert air collides with cooler mountain air, a low pressure system is created over the Aïr, which gives birth to tropical waves that become hurricanes that cross the Atlantic and devastate Florida.

Bilal pointed to a large three-toed footprint, saying that ostriches live in the remote valleys of the Aïr. I tried to imagine what it was like in the Sahara seven thousand years ago when herds of giraffes, elephants, and buffalo grazed on plains of waving grass, stalked by primitive hunters with stone-tipped spears.

Giraffes survived in the Aïr until the middle of the twentieth century; the last one was seen roaming the sandy lanes of Agadez. Crocodiles could still be found in the Guelta d'Archei, a narrow canyon water hole in Chad's Ennedi Mountains. And in the Algerian Tassili N' Ajjer, a few ancient nonreproducing cypress trees remained as living witnesses of that more moist and fertile era. Already twenty-five hundred years old when Christ was born, they were literally as old as the pyramids.

Bilal was out of food. We offered to share ours, but he reluctantly smelled it and refused, saying it might not be halal, clean for Muslims. So we detoured to Tabelot, a small isolated village where the government had forced a few Tuareg to give up their nomadic ways and settle down.

Twenty or so mud-walled houses were scattered along the bank of a sandy oued, shaded by dom palms. There was no electricity, and the only running water was flowing in the irrigation ditches of the gardens.

Bilal searched the irrigated gardens for a few vegetables to buy but found none. At the village store, a small one-room building with a few basics, he purchased a handful of dry tea leaves, half a kilogram of Bilma rock salt, one kilogram of sugar, and seven kilograms of wheat flour—simple fare. However, this was typical for Tuareg nomads whose normal diet consisted of one pound of millet or wheat flour per day made into gruel or bread. Many suffered from night blindness because of a lack of vitamins.

Fourteen miles north of Tabelot, we stopped at the Afassas oued to water our camels at the well, an open hole in the sand. I connected several nylon ropes before our bucket reached the bottom, nearly one hundred feet down. Although our camels had gone seven days without drinking, when we poured the first bucketful into the hollow dom palm trough they seemed uninterested. Flagg and I waited, perplexed, while their heads pivoted in all directions, large brown eyes surveying the area as if expecting something to happen. Then, in an unhurried manner, they began slurping up bucketsful of water as fast as we could draw them.

The camels drank far more than I had imagined, and we sweated profusely laboring in the sun to draw the thirty plus gallons necessary to satisfy their thirst. Between buckets they waited patiently. While Flagg and I labored in the heat, Bilal rested in the shade of a tree, watching us. I dumped the last bucket over my head, and we rode on.

The next day we reached the Tamanet oued and discovered a newborn infant wrapped tightly in a red blanket lying alone on the sand in the middle of the riverbed. Snuggled next to it was a baby goat, too young to accompany its mother grazing. Farther down the oued I found the child's mother cutting acacia branches for her goats. I was surprised that the baby had been left unguarded with the possibility of baboons or hyenas coming around. Bilal said there were none in the area.

Ahead of us was desert wilderness devoid of Tuareg camps, so Flagg and I decided to fill all of our four five-gallon jerricans. The well was deeper than the one at Afassas, and all our ropes tied together barely reached the bottom. During the hour it took to draw the twenty gallons, Bilal searched the oued for a nomad who could give directions. An old Tuareg man told him there was no more water until the Ajioua well, six days away on the edge of the Ténéré sea of sand. He had not been there in several years and said that the well was sometimes dry. We let the camels drink for a last time, then topped off our metal canteens.

We mounted and turned our camels east, toward the Ténéré. Soon we were in another lava field riding over a heavily worn trail, which Bilal said was the trail to Djado in northern Niger and to Libya. For thirteen hundred years it had been the main east-west route for pilgrims traveling to Mecca on the hajj, one of the five Pillars of Islam required of all Muslims. In AD 1324 Mansa Musa, king of the Mali empire, had traveled this way on a holy hajj. Preceded by five hundred slaves with golden staffs and one hundred camels, each carrying three hundred pounds of gold, Mansa Musa distributed his gold along the way, and it is said that he gave away so much that it depressed the price of gold in Egypt for twelve years.

The following day we dropped into a series of remote canyons that led us to a sandy plain bounded on two sides by mountains. The broad valley was sprinkled with patches of tall, ungrazed grass, evidence of its remote isolation. There were numerous tracks of gazelles, and from a hilltop we saw four female ostriches fleeing, plumes of gray with stubby, useless wings propelled by pistonlike legs. Staccato patches of dust thrown up by their claw-toed feet looked like machine gunfire following them. They were wild, and although we rode down the valley after them, we could not get closer than a fourth of a mile.

As we followed the sandy wash eastward, I noticed soft orange sand collecting against boulders and forming small rippled dunes beneath ledges. We were nearing the Ténéré sea of sand, nearly one hundred thousand square miles of immense sand dunes stained orange from iron oxides. At sunset they turn blood red and cast deep black shadows with razor-sharp edges.

We camped in the Indakat oued, near the ruins of a tomb of a marabout. Our arrival frightened three white gazelles, which ran off leaping in long strides across the sand. Flagg and I sat cross-legged by our cooking fire, backs to the wind. Tired and wind-whipped, we said little. After evening prayers the wind died, and Bilal joined us, raking glowing embers out of the fire with a stick. As he balanced his tiny blue enamel teapot on the coals, crammed full with mint leaves and sugar, I asked him about the Tuareg rebellion that had caused me to change my travel plans from Mali to Niger.

"Tch! I was near Tchin-Tabaradène when it happened," Bilal said, glancing sideways in my direction. "I had to go quickly to Agadez, or I would have been killed."

I was surprised that Bilal had been at the scene, and that he admitted it freely. Tchin-Tabaradène was far from Agadez, even farther from his camp in the Aïr, and his being there implied that he was involved.

> *The air turned brown with sand, and the sky took on an angry gray color as if a heavy blanket were hanging overhead. As before, my body grew listless and weak.*

He deftly flipped open the hot teapot lid with one finger, checked to see if it was boiling, then resettled the pot on the coals and leaned back, resting his elbow on the sand.

"Tch! It was not Tuareg that attacked the armory, but other people, I don't know, from the north." He sat up again, facing us, and his voice became angry. "The government sent military in trucks who shot Tuareg women and children, even their goats and camels. Hundreds, maybe thousands of Tuareg were killed; tch! no one knows. The government does not talk about these things." Abruptly, Bilal stopped talking and moved back from the fire.

I had expressed my sympathy for the Tuareg cause with every opportunity, hoping it would draw us closer together, but once again he turned cold and refused to continue the conversation He finished the tea and went back to his camp in darkness, away from us and the warm fire.

The next day we saw six more ostriches, three males with black feathers and hairless, pink-skinned necks. Each time we reached a hilltop, tan and white gazelles fled down the valleys, streaking over white dunes. There were increasing numbers of wild animal tracks: mountain sheep, addaxes, and a larger antelope that Bilal could not name in French. I collected an ostrich plume and pieces of petrified wood, and Bilal found an inch-long quartz arrowhead.

Since Bagzane, we had been free of the wind. Our days were warm with clear skies and occasional puffy white clouds overhead, while the nights were filled with stars. But as we neared the Ténéré, a cold wind began to blow in from the open desert at a constant twenty miles per hour. The air turned brown with sand and the sky took on an angry gray color as if a heavy blanket were hanging overhead. As before, my body grew listless and weak.

The countryside became increasingly bleak, flat, and empty. For four days we rode at a relentless four-and-a-half mile per hour pace, too fast to dismount and walk, too tired to talk. So we lay to in our saddles, shifting positions as the hours passed. By day we bundled ourselves against the blowing sand, and at night we huddled in darkness around a fire of twigs until exhausted sleep wiped the desert from our dreams.

We reached the eastern edge of the mountains and turned north, the Aïr massif a towering wall on our left, and the open Ténéré desert on our right. What the old man at Tamanet said would take us six days we had done in four. The wind was blowing nonstop now, off the desert at thirty miles per hour. The air was filling with sand, and the landscape was more desolate than ever. We could find no grazing of any kind, not even a brittle bush, and our camels began to starve.

The sun was settling behind the mountains, black volcanic rubble that cast a cold shadow over our tiny caravan. We had ridden for more than eight hours, thirty miles against a stiff headwind. In addition to the chèche, I wore swimming goggles to protect my eyes from the blowing sand. As the sky darkened we urgently pushed our camels forward, hoping to find Ajioua well before nightfall.

In the failing light, Bilal couched his camel and I dismounted to join him at a five-foot-diameter unmarked open hole in the sand. The absence of camel dung told me that no one had visited the well in months. I threw a stone down the dark shaft, but as I leaned over the open hole to listen, the wind blew my chèche off and I almost fell in. Lying in the sand on my stomach next to the well, I dropped in a larger stone, but only the echo of a sickening thud returned.

"There is another well, two days to the north," Bilal shouted over the raging wind noise as he turned to pick up Lion Mane's lead rope. He shrugged indifferently, "It may not have water. It is not used very much. I'm not sure I can find it."

We had only enough water left for three more days.

"What about farther on?" I yelled.

"After that, there is a good well," Bilal replied with a spark of enthusiasm. "It always has water."

"How far?" I asked.

"Six days." There was no emotion in his voice.

We would run out of water three days before reaching the second well. Bilal quickly shrugged it off and began unloading the camels.

I knew Bilal, like all Muslim nomads, accepted this to be the will of Allah. The very meaning of the word *Islam* was submission. My Christian faith was as strong as his Islam, but submission was not part of Western culture where fighting to win was the rule. I could not quiet the gnawing anxiety; however, there was no time to think further of it. The wind was getting worse and nightfall was upon us.

The long ride had exhausted me, and the cold wind was cutting sharply through the down jacket and two shirts I was wearing. In near darkness, I found an overhanging ledge of spotted leopard rock, a conglomerate that offered protection. A small dune of orange sand had formed beneath it and I set up my tent on its soft, rippled surface and crawled inside, thankful to be out of the wind and blowing sand. Flagg did the same nearby. Bilal found a smaller rock ledge, wrapped up in a blanket, and wedged himself into a narrow cleft barely large enough for his body. We were all too tired and cold to attempt supper.

It was still dark when I awoke and set off on foot across the desert searching for the camels with a flashlight. The wind had stopped, but fine particles of sand still hung in the air like a mist, and it was bitterly cold. Not far from camp I located their tracks, and after having followed them for half an hour I found them lying down, waiting for the cold of night to pass. Without a compass and in total darkness, I had no idea how far I had wandered or what direction our camp was in. Although I was completely lost, I had no fear or feelings of panic. After two weeks of desert travel my emotions were numb. I paused to take in my surroundings, marveling at the barren emptiness and silence.

I threaded the lead ropes through the metal rings in the camels' noses and unhobbled them one by one. Then, leading the four camels, I circled the area, and with the flashlight located my boot tracks leading away. I followed them back to camp, arriving in the first gray light of dawn to find Flagg heating water for coffee on our small kerosene stove we used to heat meals ready to eat (MREs).

At daybreak the wind returned, blowing even harder. The sand haze thickened, reducing visibility to less than a quarter mile. We moved off wearing down jackets, leather gloves, and goggles. The cold wind was stinging my face right through the chèche, so I tied a nylon stuff bag over it.

Mounted high up on my camel with only a slit for a view, I felt detached from the world around me, a disorienting sensation in which I floated dreamlike over a surreal landscape. Rose and green-tinted boulders drifted past scattered on the sand, and all around stood columns of polished basalt and wind-sculpted statues of brown sandstone, fading in and out among ghostlike sheets of blowing sand.

Outside my thick armor the howling wind played "Ave Maria," black-noted arpeggios of polished stones rippling in the sand below. "Ave Maria," I was once told, was written on a napkin by a barroom drunk and given to a stranger for a wedding present. Emptiness created beauty; suffering, the mother of joy.

As I drifted, lost on a magical carpet, the music reached a crescendo, and my mind slipped into the ether, reveling in the insanity. The wind surged in blasts, rising and falling as I struggled to push O. Henry ahead. I hadn't bathed in five days, my chèche smelled of camel urine, the land was bleak desolation, yet I saw only beauty around me. It was an illusion, born of the untoward monotony of eating, sleeping, and moving forward——the vision of a nomad. ◎

CHAPTER EIGHT

World of Sand, Wind, and Sky

"*We who have gone out to discover the meaning of the desert have found
only emptiness; nothing but sand, wind, soil, and empty space. The desert
seems to produce only one idea, the universality of God.... The Bedouin
had air and winds, sun and light, open spaces and a great emptiness ...
the heaven above and the unspotted earth beneath. There unconsciously
he came near God.*" —T. E. Lawrence, *The Seven Pillars of Wisdom*

In the desert Lawrence pushed his body and mind to extremes. At
times he rode fifty miles a day for a month, a total of fifteen hundred
miles, sustained like the Bedu by only a pound and a quarter of wheat flour
per day. Often he refused food, even water, and denied himself sleep. His
companions once showed him the walls of a Roman ruin, perfumed with
jasmine, violet, and rose; then they led him to an open window where the
wind of the desert swept past. He wrote, "This, they told me is the best; it
has no taste."

Of his epic desert experience, Lawrence wrote, "The effort for these
years . . . quitted me of my English self, and let me look at the West and its
conventions with new eyes: they destroyed it all for me."

The severe emptiness of the desert was what first attracted me, the
stripping down of life to the most austere and simplest terms—eat, sleep,
move forward. With each day's travel deeper into the desert I was casting
off all that was familiar, and life was taking on a new form, one that seemed
to have intense meaning but in reality had no purpose at all.

That was the beauty of it, the acceptance of emptiness and complete submission to the forces around me. Senses were heightened; slight variations in sound or a change in the direction of the wind became meaningful, even mystical. I was seeing the world with a new vision, one more sensitive and sympathetic than ever before.

At night the desert contracted, leaving us with our tiny fire and the heavens open above. Confronted by the vast emptiness of deep space with its stars, planets, black holes, and clouds of ice, I was shrunken into insignificance. Since the beginning of time humans have asked three questions: Is there life after death, Is there a God, How did it all begin (before the Big Bang)? The door to the universe seemed to be opening, and God seemed closer than ever. Stephen Hawking, the astrophysicist, once said, "Even if man explains the origins of the universe, we will not know why, and it is human to ask why."

A white addax hesitated at the top of a sand dune, eyeing us as we rode past, then disappeared with a few giant leaps. Late in the afternoon we found the Tigayin oued, flush with tall green grass. Nomads had not grazed the area since the last rainfall, and our camels surged forward, tugging heavily at their nose ropes to grab mouthfuls of the fresh pasturage.

At sunset the wind stopped, and the air cleared once again. After our pasta and meat MRE, we joined Bilal on his blanket as he prepared tea. Flagg asked if he knew the stars or the names of constellations.

"All nomads know the stars," Bilal said as he poured a shot glass full of tea, "but only the Tuareg names."

He dumped the steaming glass back into the pot and replaced it on the coals. Pointing to Orion, he said, "That one is Amanar, a legendary Tuareg warrior. The stars above his arm are his sword."

Bilal poured another glass, lifting the pot higher and higher as hot liquid splattered in the tiny glass, creating a frothy head. He turned and pointed to the Pleiades.

Petroglyphs at the Tigayin oued.

"Those stars," he said, "are Amanar's harem, and over there, pointing to an unfamiliar group, "is the guardian of the harem."

Satisfied the tea was ready, Bilal handed the steaming glass to Flagg. As we shared the customary three-round ritual, noisily slurping the steaming tea, Bilal explained how nomads navigate at night using the North Star, Southern Cross, and other stars and constellations. By day they recognized the shape of dunes, pattern of ripples in the surfaces, or even the texture of the sand. Blind guides were even said to have led caravans by feeling stones, the direction of the wind on their face, or smelling the earth.

Although Bilal had not traveled this area before, he recognized the hills and mountains from a description given to him by the nomad at Tamanet.

Relying solely on verbal information from a stranger, he was able to find the Ajioua well, a hole in the sand, five feet in diameter, invisible from fifty yards.

The next morning we left the camels grazing to explore a narrow canyon leading into the Aïr massif. The air was still, the sky clear, and as we struggled upward in soft sand, we began to sweat profusely. Sheer walls of black volcanic rock radiated heat, offering no shelter from the sun. Near the end of the canyon Bilal discovered petroglyphs, images of elephants, giraffes, rhinoceroses, and hippopotamuses, etched over seven thousand years ago into the black desert-varnished boulders.

At the end of the last ice age, twelve thousand years ago, the Sahara was a dry desert. Around 8000 BC monsoon rains quickly turned it into a lush savanna with trees, swamps, and lakes containing hippopotamuses and crocodiles. Neolithic spear and bow-and-arrow hunters left petroglyphs and rock paintings that testified to the herds of elephants, buffalo, and antelopes along with giraffes and rhinos that roamed the grasslands. Around 3500 BC the rains began to fail, and by the time the pyramids of Egypt were built in 2500 BC, the Sahara was a desert again. By the first century AD it was as arid and formidable a desert as it is today.

We climbed to a plateau on top of the canyon wall. Low dunes of white sand flowed to the east, brushed lightly with wisps of yellow-green grass. Near the horizon rose massive orange formations, dunes of the sand sea.

A solitary, windswept boulder stood at the edge of the plateau. The figure of an ancient hunter had been deeply etched into its polished black surface, arms outstretched toward the open desert. He appeared frozen in time, searching for vanished prey. I visualized what he must have seen—immense herds of buffalo and endless fields of grass, much like the Serengeti today.

Sixty miles out into the sea of sand was a dinosaur graveyard, well preserved skeletons whose giant bones could sometimes be seen protruding from the top of dunes. I wondered what the ancient hunters had thought when they encountered such immense skeletons.

Bilal picked up a quartz bird point, a small stone arrowhead lost by a Neolithic hunter. Nearby was a broken scraper and pieces of pottery with geometric designs, similar to Indian pottery I found as a child along the Edisto River in South Carolina. Farther on I discovered a prehistoric ax head lying on the sand as if it had just been dropped. It was perfectly heart shaped and made of white stone. Not far away protruding out of the desert sand was a four-foot-high block of white marble surrounded by chips and broken pieces—a primitive weapon-making area. A second ax head lay next to it. Flagg and Bilal had already started back toward camp, so I picked up one of the three-pound ax heads and ran to catch up.

Bilal frowned at the heart-shaped stone, saying he had never seen anything like it. He sneered at its authenticity. To pacify his displeasure, I threw it away, and we rode on.

We followed a steep trail into the mountains, then dropped into the Anakom oued late in the afternoon. On the far side of the oued was a wall of orange sand over five hundred feet high, the first large dunes we had encountered. Eager to get our first clear view of the Ténéré sand sea, Flagg and I started up the firm, windward edge of the tallest dune. Halfway up O. Henry's feet broke through the surface and he began to struggle in the soft sand. I couched him and continued on foot.

It was near sunset when we finally reached the top, high up over the oued. The sand was beginning to glow deep orange, and the shadows were darkening. I was transfixed by the view to the east over the seemingly endless Ténéré sand sea. It was a sea of liquid gold, a desert of dreams, orange dunes undulating to the far horizon like rolling waves in the ocean. Trackless and sterile, the sand sea shifted with the tides of the wind, continuously renewing itself and erasing any traces of human disturbance. It would be all too easy to lose our way there, in a world of sand, wind, and sky.

As we descended I studied the big wind-sculpted dunes. Razor-sharp crests flowed in graceful S-shaped formations that dropped precipitously to the desert floor. As the sun faded, the dune faces took on a deep crimson hue, and the shadows darkened to form abstract patterns in red and black. The soft, sheer faces made of tiny, noncohesive silica grains were so perfectly balanced that they avalanched in sheets at the slightest touch, like a fragile house of cards. The firmer windward surfaces rippled in artistic patterns formed by smoothly worn silica particles resonating with the pitch of the wind.

In the morning a Tuareg boy visited us from his camp nearby. He sold me a cloth bundle of arrow points he found while shepherding his goats. They were finely sculpted works of art, quartzes of red, amber, white, rust, orange, and yellow—evidence of the fine craftsmanship of Neolithic hunters.

We entered the big Ténéré dunes for the first time, winding our way higher and higher, following a wind-packed edge of sand that gave away with each footstep, cascading in avalanches down the steep slip faces. Near the top we halted between two enormous peaks. We were confronted by the stillness of the Ténéré sand sea, flowing endless beneath a pale blue sky. The sun was overhead, burning like fire in the sand. We plunged ahead, panting like dogs as we marched up and down the slopes, feet sinking with each step into the soft sand.

The Agamgam guelta.

Near sunset we reached Agamgam, a narrow, rock-walled canyon that would shelter us from the wind. Three days had passed since Ajioua and only two gallons of water remained, but for some unexplainable reason neither Flagg nor I had given it a second thought. Bilal had been told there was a *guelta, a* natural rock cistern, near the source of the canyon. We followed the canyon into the mountains until fallen boulders blocked our passage. While I set up camp, Flagg and Bilal proceeded farther on foot carrying the almost empty jerrican.

It was nearly dark when they returned. They had located the guelta a half mile away—a dark pool of stagnant water grown over with green slime. Dark watermarks on the canyon wall indicated it was only a fraction of its former size. Bilal set the jerrican down, depressed. "The guelta is going dry. There was no rain; that water is from twenty years ago. Nomads depend on Agamgam to pasture their goats; if it doesn't rain soon, Agamgam will be dry."

The sun had risen and the sand was already hot to the touch when Flagg returned the next morning without the camels. He had searched for two hours, unable to identify their tracks among the numerous prints of goats, antelopes, and other camels that had watered at the guelta. Bilal said there was nothing for camels to eat in the canyon, and since it was warm, they had probably traveled all night in search of food. He and Flagg left to try again.

The high-pitched tinkling of goat bells echoing off the canyon walls stirred me from a lazy sleep in the morning sun. Two Tuareg shepherd boys were driving a herd of fifty goats to water at the guelta. They stopped to show me a cloth full of arrow points, and several glass trading beads they had found nearby. I grabbed my empty jerricans and joined them.

A pungent odor of camel urine reeked at the edge of the pool. One of the boys waded out with a guerba, sweeping aside the thick layer of green algae. Water. We filled our containers, loaded them on their donkeys, and returned to camp.

It was noon when Flagg and Bilal returned with the mischievous camels. I had taken a bath, washed clothes, finished lunch, and was eager to get going. While Flagg and Bilal ate, I couched Igor and prepared to load him. But when I placed the packsaddle over his hump, he unexpectedly jumped to his feet, slamming me in the chest and ribs with his knee and knocking me backward onto the ground. As I struggled to regain my footing, he lunged at me with his mouth open, roaring loudly and trying to bite my arm with his sharp, broken-edged teeth.

Having previously been attacked by horses, I reflexively grabbed the lead rope and yanked as hard as I could, nearly ripping the metal ring out of his nose. He collapsed with a heavy thud on his chest bone resting plate; then, half rising on his back feet, he swung his head violently at me, mouth open and protruding fangs barely missing my body. I yanked him to the ground again, but he continued to roar and lash out, trying to grab me with his teeth. Attempting to control his head, I seized the metal nose ring and twisted his neck around sharply. Then, determined to subdue the fighting animal, I began kicking Igor in the chest. It was more a way to gain dominance than to inflict pain. His roars turned to high-pitched screams, and then finally a bitter, whimpering cry. When I let go of the rope, he remained couched and made no further attempt to bite.

I staggered about holding my sore ribs. Bilal had quit eating and was staring at me with wide-eyed disbelief. Both he and Flagg appeared shocked.

"What's wrong with Bilal?" I asked Flagg in a pained tone.

"He's kind of horrified!" Flagg replied. "He says Tuareg never hit their camels, even if they kick them."

Bilal was standing as straight and rigid as a stone. My roughshod method, reflexively ingrained by handling unruly and spoiled horses, had further distanced me from Bilal, perhaps even damaged my relationship with Flagg. At that point I didn't care, I was bent over with rib pain.

I returned to Igor to finish the packing. He cried "waaa . . . waaa . . ." like a baby when I cinched down the saddle, but he made no attempt to move until I finished and gave him the signal to rise.

O. Henry had quickly learned to respond to my voice commands, and I was convinced that camels were much smarter and more sensitive than horses. I suspected that Igor might seek revenge later in the journey when least expected. Perhaps that was the reason the Tuareg put up with their bad habits. Flagg agreed to handle Igor from then on.

The Aïr mountain Pass.

By midafternoon we had left Agamgam through a narrow slot in the canyon wall that opened out into the desert. We crossed several large dunes, then turned into the mountains again.

As we ascended over rocks, I noticed fresh red blood spattered on the trail. The mystery continued as we proceeded up the mountain until finally I noticed that Igor had a four-inch laceration in his rear footpad from the sharp volcanic rock. Bilal and I discussed what to do, knowing that as long as we kept traveling the cut would not heal. I suggested tying a grain bag around his foot, but Bilal insisted it was too dangerous to handle his rear feet, they were too powerful and a kick could be fatal. The Tuareg never bothered to train them for that procedure. We would have had to restrain him with ropes. There was nothing to do but go on. Neither of us expected Igor to survive the trip.

We pushed on over the pass, then as darkness came, we descended into Arakaou, the collapsed caldera of an ancient volcano. The eastern rim of the volcano had blown out, allowing orange Ténéré sand to be swept in by the wind. Over the years, a nine-hundred-foot-tall wall of sand dunes had formed down the middle, splitting the five-mile-wide crater in half.

A Tuareg was camped nearby on the sandy crater floor with seven camels. After unloading our camels, I joined Bilal and the nomad having tea at their fire, sitting among piles of baggage on sweat-stained blankets.

They were speaking in Tamasheq, but with limited French I learned that the nomad had just arrived from Algeria across the northern Ténéré desert, one of the most isolated and loneliest sections of the Sahara. It had taken him ten days to make the crossing by camel, a distance of four hundred miles, or forty miles per day.

Camels were in high demand at the Algerian oasis of Djanet, near the border of Libya, and he had traded four of them for flour and other staples that were expensive and difficult to obtain in Agadez. Camels were valued in Algeria for their meat, while wheat flour was cheaper by one-half to one-third than in Agadez. He had returned across the unmarked border without paying import duty, an onerous tax that created a thriving but illegal black market business for Tuareg camel drivers.

Bilal said he had been to Djanet as a boy with his grandfather. He poked the fire with a stick as he told the story.

"It was far across the sand. For many days there was little grass, and for six days we did not find water. Only the strongest camels survived." He paused to draw lines in the sand with the stick. "We traveled all day, and into the night after the stars were clear above us. Many Tuareg have died in that desert, but my grandfather safely led many caravans."

I had learned that recently the Tuareg had been taking their camels to Libya to trade them for guns to prepare for the rebellion. I wanted to learn more from Bilal, but he was just as distant as when we first met in Rhissa's office.

Our camp that morning was bathed in warm yellow sunlight. While taking down my tent, I noticed sickle-shaped marks in the sand. Bilal and I followed the tracks to a nearby bush.

"Arakaou is a place of vipers," he said as he dug around the bush with a stick.

The sand-colored snake proved difficult to find, burrowed beneath the surface with only a pair of slit-eyes exposed. In appearance it was similar to a small rattlesnake, and was just as poisonous although it was only one and a half feet long. Bilal flipped it out into the open where the squirming viper threw its body sideways in coils, like a North American desert sidewinder, trying to escape. Bilal quickly drew his sword and with one chop severed the snake's head from its body, which continued to curl and thrash about. As Bilal wiped his blood-stained sword in the sand, his eyes glared menacingly at me. "You must be careful!"

The sun heated up quickly as we left Arakaou. The floor of the crater was wind-swept, level right up to the edge of the sand wall. There seemed to be no point of entry into the steep dunes, no shadows to suggest an opening, only pale renderings of gray on tan. We veered aside, keeping the sand wall on our left. I could have dismounted and put one foot on the valley floor and the other knee deep in the soft side of a dune. Bilal turned his camel and disappeared into the wall of sand.

Suddenly we were engulfed by sand. Silently we pushed our camels upward, struggling over crests invisible in the shadowless noonday light. Occasionally our camels' broad footpads broke through the firm windward surfaces and they floundered; then we dismounted and led them higher on foot.

We were high up, nearly one thousand feet above the floor of the caldera. Ahead of us, orange dunes flowed in great mounds to a black mountainous ridge several miles away, the far rim of the caldera. We descended and rode into the dune field below, threading our way between steep, cresting waves and

over soft, rounded slopes that led to deep sand pits where our camels became bogged to the knees. After some hours the dunes flattened, and we found a narrow trail leading up the crater wall. Once again, Igor's foot began to bleed.

The next day found us deep inside the dunes. Early morning produced a dismal light, sand and sky without color. We rode without speaking, bounded by layer upon layer of gray on tan. At midday we were blinded by glaring images, a landscape void of any recognizable features. It was a world without shape or form; even the tiny ripples in the sand wiped clean beneath our feet. The sharp edges, which at sunset had formed sensuous patterns of red on black, had vanished, leaving only the hot knife of desert sand.

I rode half conscious, balanced in the soft padding of my saddle. The monotonous rocking and the gentle swish-swish of padded feet against sand were the tossing of a ship lost at sea, water lapping against an empty hull. There was no sense of forward motion, no shadows to measure things by, and at times I could not tell if we were moving ahead or standing still. One moment I would find myself near a large white dune, then another would appear magically as if dissolved inside the first. It seemed as if I were being transported through time and space. The sand held no dimensions, and even time seemed to have lost its way.

Overhead, the sky was cloudless and endlessly deep. It was a world of sand and sky, just a thin line separating the two. During those long hours, focusing on the line created an inner peace, like that of a monk meditating on the flame of a candle, or a lama listening to the ring of a cymbal high in the Himalayas until his mind became purified.

The sun reached its zenith and stopped. White light seared through my shirt. Prophets saw visions in the desert, and mystics sought refuge there from the chaotic world outside. Moses had seen God in a burning bush of Sinai, and Muhammad had wandered in the deserts of Arabia. In the Jordanian desert, Jesus had been tempted by the devil himself.

There were jinn in the desert; I had heard them myself a few days before Ajioua. The singing voices and drums were so insistent that I had started out alone across an empty plain to join them. Bilal had stopped me, saying I must ignore the voices or I would become lost and die. A nomad had told

Flagg and McGoo before the fall.

me of children's voices crying in the dunes, and of fire dancing in the sand around a bush that was never consumed.

O. Henry stopped suddenly, his eyes straining to see something far away. Was it tender tufts of grass, another camel, or the jinn? Perhaps it was simply to enjoy the view. He seemed almost human, or was it that, stripped to the essentials, I was becoming more like him. I seemed to be able to read his thoughts; the stiffening of his ears, changes in gait, vacant stares—all spoke of an inner world.

Near sunset, Flagg was leading McGoo along the crest of a steep dune when the edge suddenly caved in. The camel collapsed on his belly and started sliding helplessly down the nearly vertical face. Partway down he came to a precarious stop, bogged crossways on the slope. Each struggle tilted his ungainly body farther until he was dangerously near rolling down the face. Bilal had warned us about the steep side of dunes, where deep sand could easily break a camel's legs.

Although it seemed hopeless, Flagg climbed down the slope and tried to right the big camel by pushing from below, a risky position because if McGoo fell the camel could crush Flagg. McGoo's spindly legs flailed in the sand as he twisted about, finally turning to face uphill. Lurching violently, he succeeded in getting his front feet over the broken crest of the dune, and with Flagg pulling from above, he gave a final thrust, and his chest slid over the top.

It was our eighteenth day, and there was no grass in sight for the camels to eat. We decided to stop at a hill of white marble and let them rest.

At noon the following day we rode into an ancient lake bed, a broad plain of dust and shimmering heat waves that seemed to have no end. The sun beat down unmercifully upon us while silver sheets of water receded just ahead of us; this fata morgana both tortured and entertained us.

I was riding with a black umbrella to block the sun, but beneath my shirt and chèche I was dripping sweat. My mind retreated into its private world. A brass band accompanied O. Henry's monotonous pace, blaring John Philip Sousa's "Semper Fidelis." I had committed to memory every note of it during my college band days, especially the piccolo's shrill piece. It played

Flagg and McGoo watch the Anakom sunset.

brilliantly, better than a Walkman, and in the long hours of heat and dust O. Henry and I marched exalted across the empty plain.

At dusk we reached the Faris well, a staging area for camel caravans setting out across the Ténéré. It was simply a nondescript, flat place in the desert where an open well had been dug in the ground.

"The next well is ten days away," Bilal said in a discouraging tone, pointing north. "There was no rain this year. Perhaps it is dry." He lifted the saddle off Lion Mane, then hobbled and released him.

We had not encountered a nomad familiar with the desert to the north and Bilal had never been there, so we were unsure about finding water. Furthermore, I planned to first go east into the Ténéré sea of sand where there was no water at all. I had been looking forward to being completely immersed for a few days in the sand sea, where even footsteps make no sound. Also I planned to test the camels on the big dunes to see what they could do. Before leaving Agadez I had explained the importance of this to Bilal; however, he seemed reluctant to go farther.

O. Henry at the Issaoune oued.

I finished unsaddling O. Henry and went to where Bilal was sitting. "I must go into the sea of sand!" I exclaimed, frustrated. "My purpose coming here was to challenge ourselves and the camels against the big dunes, to see for myself what they can do." Bilal got up and walked away, sullen and quiet. He began gathering twigs for a fire.

While Flagg and I unloaded Igor and began setting up camp, a Tuareg camping nearby joined Bilal. They seemed to be discussing Flagg and me, periodically staring in our direction as they prepared tea. After consuming several rounds, they came to where Flagg and I were sitting on the ground, heating MREs in a pot of boiling water.

"This nomad says two tourists in a Land Rover were murdered by bandits north of here," Bilal reported. "They burned the Land Rover to make it look like an accident." They waited for a response, standing side by side.

We continued cooking without answering. Flagg fished an MRE out of the pot, cut it open, and poured the shredded chicken into a plastic bowl. We ignored Bilal and began to eat.

"The dunes east of here are dangerous!" the other Tuareg added in a concerned tone. "Too steep for camels; they will break their legs. There is a way around them, five miles south of here."

Flagg and I continued eating, unconcerned. The nomad turned to Bilal and began describing how to find the way around.

Finally I stopped them, insisting that we go straight into the sea of sand. If the dunes were too steep, we would make chest and tail harnesses, like those used on horses, to keep the baggage from falling. Bilal rejected my idea, saying that Tuareg do not do that.

I was getting nowhere with Bilal, and the stranger was interfering. Exasperated, I said that I would go alone with the camels if necessary. Flagg had remained indifferent to the whole thing but said he would go with me. The dunes didn't bother him; it was Bilal who bothered him. Before bedding down, I made harness straps and prepared a makeshift sun shelter to rest at midday in the dunes, where the sun would be fierce. Surface temperature in the dunes could reach 175 degrees Fahrenheit.

Flagg and I were up before sunrise, anxious to get going. Flagg tracked the camels for two hours but returned with a handful of empty lead ropes. Bilal was lounging on his blanket drinking tea with his Tuareg friend and refused to help. As we waited for him, the tension mounted. It was afternoon before Bilal finally left to track down the camels.

Flagg and I packed up the camp and prepared everything for loading. I borrowed a donkey from a Tuareg woman watering goats at the well, filled our jerricans, and hauled them back to camp. Four hours passed before Bilal returned. The hungry camels had traveled twelve miles while hobbled, and were still shuffling ahead in search of grass when he found them.

Bilal and Flagg crossing the ancient lakebed, and near Chirlet.

I was shocked when Bilal set the camels free again and began preparing tea with his nomad friend. Although less than two hours of daylight remained, Flagg and I insisted on getting away from Faris. I sensed that Bilal and his friend were plotting against us, perhaps trying to scare or delay us to get more money or to steal the camels during the night. And for some reason I did not believe the nomad's story about the dangerous dunes. After traveling twenty-one days by camel to get to the sea of sand, I was more determined than ever to go there.

Flagg and I saddled the camels and packed Igor. I saddled Bilal's camel and led it to where he sat, sipping tea. When I held out the lead rope, he said it was too late to leave. I demanded that we at least get to the edge of the dunes and be ready to start early the next morning. Reluctantly, Bilal slung his personal items across Lion Mane, and we departed just as the western sky ignited a brilliant orange.

One hour later we stopped in low dunes of white sand. Bilal threw his gear on the sand and took off immediately on his camel back to Faris, where he spent the evening with his friend.

We departed just after daybreak the next morning. Once again, Bilal tried to steer us south, away from the big dunes, but I ignored him. When we reached the edge of the sea of sand, Bilal dismounted and refused to lead us farther. He walked off, leaving Lion Mane standing with his nose rope trailing on the sand. Flagg picked up Lion Mane's lead rope, and we started up the first large dune, leading the camels.

We were sheltered beneath a clear Saharan sky that invigorated and restored my enthusiasm. As the sun warmed up, we took off our boots and walked barefoot in the soft sand, coarse orange grains that crunched, gently massaging the bottoms of our sore feet. We climbed higher, leading the camels along sinuous cresting edges that dropped into deep pits between huge dunes. The sand was sterile and clean, unspoiled by a single blade of grass. The edges of the dunes were firmly packed, and we followed their natural curves without danger at all. Flagg and I were thoroughly enjoying the beauty around us. Bilal followed at a distance, then after an hour took Lion Mane's rein and started leading us again.

From the top of a tall dune we saw the outline of Chirlet, an extinct volcano, fourteen miles to the east. The sheer walls of its eroded black plug, or inner core, was all that was left rising fifteen hundred feet out of the sand. The air was still, and intense sunrays were beginning to sear the sand. By midday the dunes became an open oven that cooked us with reflected light and radiating heat. Hot sand scorched our feet, but when we put on our boots it flowed over the tops, filling them. A thick saddle pad shielded my canteen from the sun, but the metal became too hot to touch. For the first time in the journey I removed the stifling chèche, but a swarm of flies that had followed us since Agadez attacked the salt on my face. I replaced the chèche and sweltered, rivers of hot sweat running down my cheeks.

Late that afternoon we reached Chirlet and followed its outer wall, searching for an opening. The volcanic mound was four miles in diameter and rose straight out of the sand several hundred feet tall, boulders balanced delicately on top as if a gentle push would topple them over. Several smaller, perfectly shaped volcanic cones of black lava protruded from the desert sand around the outer wall.

Bilal insisted on camping in the dunes outside Chirlet, saying there would be no grass inside for the camels. I could see no pasturage anywhere and the wind was kicking up, so Flagg and I decided against his advice and pushed on to camp protected inside the volcano.

We found a narrow canyon that led us inside Chirlet where Flagg and I were surprised to discover tall, untouched grass; but instead of sharing our relief, Bilal had once again lost face. He became hostile and camped far away, out of sight.

In the morning we headed northwest, crossing hard-packed dunes with unusual swirling patterns etched deeply into their surfaces. Milky plumes of sand blew off the crests, and by sunset we were facing a storm, visibility reduced to only a few hundred yards. As we unloaded the camels, clouds of sand enveloped us and whirling sheets pelted our clothing.

Into the Ténéré sea of sand.

Dunes near Chirlet.

Bilal knee-hobbled the camels so they could not move and left them couched on the leeward side of a dune. Flagg and I unloaded and set up our tents, then quickly crawled inside to keep them from blowing away. Despite our having put on the rain fly, blowing sand poured in.

Darkness rapidly descended, but the vibrating nylon and wind inside the tent made it impossible to light a candle. The air was stifling hot and filled with dust. Beads of sweat stood on my forehead. I lay in the darkness eating a cold MRE—sand grinding between my teeth—listening to the wind howling outside while sand slowly covered my body.

Once again I submitted to the forces of nature and discovered a strange beauty in what was going on around me. ◉

CHAPTER NINE

Ten Days in a Waterless Desert

By morning the storm had passed. It was freezing cold at dawn when I brushed the sand off my sleeping bag and went outside to release the knee hobbles so the camels could browse. Flagg was asleep, his tent partly buried in sand. Bilal was lying behind a dune, shivering beneath a single blanket. As the sun rose and warmed the earth, he just lay there, making no effort to get under way. We packed the camels and led Lion Mane to him.

We headed out of the Ténéré back toward the Aïr mountains. At noon the dunes flattened, and we came out of the sand sea and found the Tezirzek well. Bilal rode on past without stopping, saying it was dry. I dismounted and threw a rock down the hole but heard only the spatter of mud. A nomad family shepherding goats in the area said we would find water farther north at Adabda, a spring hidden in a mountain canyon. We could reach it by sundown if we rode fast.

Bilal was almost out of food, so we agreed to buy a goat from the nomad for him to eat. They haggled in Tamasheq over the price, but then Bilal suddenly turned away and rode off, saying there was none for sale. The nomad was as perplexed as we were about why Bilal had not taken the goat.

Bilal rode at a rapid trot without looking back, heading north along the edge of the mountains. Towing Igor the baggage camel we could not keep up, and soon Bilal was out of sight. We pushed as hard as we could, following his tracks.

At sunset we turned into the mountains and entered a rock canyon to set up camp. Bilal led the camels to an ordinary-looking granite boulder where underneath was a pool of clear, cold water, spring fed and waist-deep. It took nearly an hour of bucket work to satisfy our camels' thirst.

The night was windless. Flagg and I finished our MREs and lay on the sand next to a small fire, humbled by the crystalline depth of the heavens above. We welcomed darkness, which shrank the vast wilderness around us, limiting our space to a tiny fire of twigs and roots. The black void overhead was brilliantly illuminated with twinkling stars, constellations, and galaxies; and on clear nights we felt closer to heaven than earth.

Bilal had camped farther down the oued, out of sight. Unexpectedly he appeared just inside the orange glow of our fire.

"Tch! I am leaving tomorrow, going to Iferouâne!" he announced in a hostile tone.

We ignored him. Iferouâne, an administrative village in the center of the Aïr, was far off our intended route.

He moved closer, trying to get our attention. "Tch! This is a bad trip, no friendship. My food is finished, and you did not buy me the goat to eat." He paced around the edge of the fire, then added. "And the pay is too little."

Flagg and I were still wondering why he had not taken the goat at Tezirzek. Then Bilal said something that shocked me, although I had no idea what it meant.

"This is my country! I am Tuareg," he shouted in anger. "It is not your country." Flagg and I said nothing, hiding our surprise. Bilal stared straight into our eyes. His face was hidden by the veil of his tagulmust, but the wild venom in his eyes was unmistakable. Then he stormed down the dark oued to his camp.

We were stunned. He was threatening to abandon us in the desert if we didn't accompany him to Iferouâne. The journey would end there. Flagg and I recalled the problems we had had with Bilal: cheating us while buying camels in Agadez, mysterious behaviors that Flagg attributed to "cultural differences," and his growing withdrawal and silence. He had dragged his feet, refusing even to saddle his own camel. At Faris he had tried to sabotage our journey. I thought that we should let him go. We could return to the Tezirzek well and, we might hope, find another nomad to guide us.

Flagg was confident that we could finish the trip with no guide at all; however, he did not want to get rid of Bilal quite yet. He still had hope that

Bilal would change his attitude. Flagg devised a scheme to settle the issue. We went up the riverbed to his camp where Bilal was sitting in the dark without a fire.

"You can go to Iferouâne," Flagg said calmly. I added, "but you will have to walk. The camels are ours, and we are continuing north as planned."

"If you decide to continue with us," Flagg continued, "we will share our food with you. You can take what you want, we will reduce our rations." Flagg sympathized with Bilal, explaining that this was a hard journey for us also; forty days on camel would test anyone. Traveling together for such a long time, with cultural differences, had been difficult. Bilal just looked away, unresponsive. Flagg gave up and told him to give us his answer by morning.

By sunrise Bilal had changed his mind and decided to continue with us, but when we offered him our MREs, he opened and smelled one, then gave it back, saying it might not be halal. In succession he refused our wheat flour, coffee, tea, even the sugar, complaining that it was powder, not lumps. Then he started up again about his pay, and the situation rapidly began to fall apart. With no further discussion, Flagg and I saddled Bilal's camel and handed him the rein. We mounted and started north. Bilal followed.

The next water source was ten days away, and I knew this would push the camels and ourselves to the limit. If the weather was cool with plenty of fresh grass to eat, our camels could go indefinitely without water, but there had been little pasturage since Agadez, and any fat they once had was long gone. Their humps were shrunken, ribs and hips protruding, and skin beginning to hang loose over bony frames. Flagg and I had also lost weight.

Our jerricans were full, twenty gallons of water that would last the three of us exactly ten days. There was no room for error; however, any thought that the next well might be dry was quickly dismissed. For the camels, there would be no water at all.

We crossed rock hills, and I noticed blood again. Igor fell to his knees between two boulders, and during the struggle I saw that both rear footpads had four-inch bleeding tears. In addition, Bilal dug a two-inch thorn out of his front foot with a knife, creating another open wound. He shook his head, saying Igor would not survive.

That afternoon we rode onto a flat plain of gray sand and scattered charcoal rock. The wind howled in high-pitched screams, which made me think that must be what Sirens' voices sound like. Even the stones seemed to be shrieking from the yawning emptiness, which was sterile and lifeless. My mouth was parched, and the hot water in my canteen could not quench the nagging thirst. The voices drowned out all possible thought, and with the chèche bound tightly around my face, I felt as if I were trapped in an asylum for the terminally insane.

> *The voices drowned out all possible thought, and with the chèche bound tightly around my face, I felt as if I were trapped in an asylum for the terminally insane.*

I rode spineless, slumped forward in the saddle with my eyes closed, but each time sleep came near, I was jolted awake by the sensation of falling. I persevered in a numbed state, leaving O. Henry to follow the others. At times I awoke to find him wandering forty-five degrees off course. No one looked back. I was falling farther and farther behind.

Flagg stopped to tighten his saddle cinch, and I caught up. I couched O. Henry and fell off on the sand beside him, asleep in the shade of his body. Ghostly forms appeared in my dreams, shadows of Flagg and Bilal passing by on their camels. I forced myself back into the saddle and plodded forward again, too weak to steer O. Henry or keep my eyes open.

Near sunset Bilal found a little browse for our camels and stopped. I put up my tent and fell instantly asleep. Flagg shook me awake later that night to eat, but I only drank a half cup of hot tea. I sat upright until a wave of nausea passed, then slept again.

For two days we rode with the full impact of desolation. The landscape was unlike anything I had ever experienced, a wilderness where words, if spoken, were never heard; even the stones were silent. The air was still, the horizon ringed with a steel-gray pallor lacking even a streak of a cloud. There was no sign of life, not a bird, no telltale track of an animal, not even a single tuft of grass. We were surrounded by mounds of coal-black volcanic rock, heaps of russet-colored stones, and polished blue boulders scattered at random over the flat plain as if they were the giant playing pieces of an ancient god left on a gaming board. It looked more like the surface of a distant planet than any earthly environment.

On the third day we encountered tracks of antelopes and gazelles, then were confronted again by the Ténéré sea of sand. We made our way into the dunes, following a dry oued that had once flowed with water into the sand sea. Walls of sand towered hundreds of feet on either side of us, shrinking our tiny caravan into insignificance. Some dunes were the color of rust, coated with iron oxides, while others were lightly dusted with fine white gypsum powder.

Deep inside the dunes we found a flat wash with mature acacia trees, the largest we had seen, and a sprinkling of yellow grass, the best for our camels we had found since Bagzane. We set up camp at the base of a gnarled trunk whose spreading limbs and sand-stained leaves provided the luxury of shade. Everything that we saw—plants, leaves, grass, even the stones—was varnished yellow from blowing sand.

That afternoon I noticed a low-pitched humming that seemed to come from all directions. Strange, I thought, as there was no wind. It persisted for about thirty seconds, then faded off, only to recur again in cycles. The dunes were singing as layers of sand shifted deep inside the massive formations. The Tuareg believed it was Rul, an evil jinni that tortured travelers lost in the desert. As I lay beneath the tree watching our camels graze, the resonant tones came and went like deep-throated chants of Tibetan monks.

Near sunset I set off to climb one of the dunes but was so weak that I gave up halfway and fell asleep on the warm sand. I awoke when the air turned cold, and I returned, still exhausted, to camp. That night Flagg and I tried to make bread, but the wind created a blast furnace of our fire and we could not remove the pot. In the morning a solid chunk of charcoal was all that was left in the blackened pot.

I scrubbed the pot in coarse sand, but the torching flames had turned the stainless steel a golden brown.

Dawn bathed the dunes in delicate shades of pink. Wispy clouds hung over them, fleeting white streaks painted across a pastel sky. The early light stained our oued into a fragile palette—pale yellow sand spotted with mint-colored puffy bushes and rust-stained acacias whose twisted trunks brought tortured agony to an otherwise peaceful pastoral canvas. Bilal was wiping the blade of his sword, having hacked another viper to death.

Despite my exhausted state, I was determined to go farther north and pressed Bilal to continue on to the border of Algeria. He insisted there was no source of water there and we would not have enough to get back to the nearest well. Flagg said he was looking forward to getting back home, having a beer with his friends, and playing some fiddle music. He also did not want to go any farther. He reminded me that the nomad at Tezirzek had said bandits north of here had seized a second group of Land Rovers.

I tried to persuade Flagg to rest a few days at Temet and allow the camels to graze while we explored the area, but he pointed out that the heat had caused us to drink more water than expected and we had just enough left to make it to the next well, still five days away. Both he and Bilal were anxious to start.

I gathered the lead ropes and set off for the camels, grazing on nearby grass. The journey had exhausted them, and their coats were dull and heavily sweat stained where saddles and baggage had rubbed. Their fatty humps were shriveled, rib cages skeletal, and the hollows beneath their eyes had deepened into empty pits. Igor had several bald spots on his back, pressure sores from the weight of the baggage, that would soon fester and break open. As I threaded the ropes through their nose rings and started back to camp, I felt I was leading prisoners to the gallows. We had ridden them for twenty-seven days without a single day of rest. A cloud of fatigue settled over me as I realized my own pitiful state. ◎

CHAPTER TEN

Hidden Agenda

We mounted and rode southeast in the direction of the Tadek well. At dusk we found ourselves in a forlorn moonscape where we stopped to camp inside a rock amphitheater, encircled by jagged volcanic ridges. The waxing moon illuminated grotesque gargoyle-shaped boulders, sculpted by blowing sand. Polished slick by the wind, they glistened in the pale yellow light.

Bilal strode over to where Flagg and I were cooking. "Tch! You are in trouble!" he said confidently. "If the police from Iferouâne see us, they will arrest you."

"Why is that?" I feigned indifference while adding garlic pepper to a tasteless MRE.

"This is my country!" he stated emphatically in a loud voice. "You have no permit to travel by camel. It must be stamped in your passport at Agadez. The police in Iferouâne are bad people; they will take your camels and keep you in prison. Maybe, after a month they will send you to Agadez."

Bilal's body language was stiff and arrogant, and he was smirking. The danger was real enough, but I thought he was exaggerating. Police in remote villages sometimes threaten tourists to extract bribes or whatever else they might want, and any official had the power to stop us, check our passports, use any excuse to cause problems; however, I knew that Bilal didn't have an official guide permit required by the government and might find himself in bigger trouble than we would. I sensed that he was trying to control us, manipulate us for some hidden motive. But what?

"Bilal," I said in a condescending tone, mouth full of food, "let's just avoid Iferouâne, stay north of it."

"Tch! What will I do?" He shrugged hopelessly. "I have no more food."

"You go to Iferouâne alone," I said, leaning back on my elbow. "We will camp in the bush and wait for you, a day's ride away."

He was quiet for a moment, thinking.

"The police will take your cameras," he said, angry again. "You have no permission to take pictures here. It is a very serious problem in the Aïr!"

I shuddered. He had found our soft spot. All the things we had tried so hard to obtain without success—permits to travel in the Aïr, permits for photography—could come back to haunt us. I tried to hide my sudden anxiety.

Bilal sensed my weakness. "Tch!" he continued. "We cannot go to Arlit. The camels are in bad shape, they cannot make it. The baggage camel is very sick, he will die before Arlit. This is a bad camel trip, no good company," he snarled.

Then Bilal clenched his teeth and stared straight at us, demanding that we sell him Lion Mane. It seemed urgent. After thoroughly running down the camel's weight loss and bad health, he offered us CFAF12,000 ($50 in U.S. currency).

I hid the shock of his laughable offer. "When we reach Arlit, we will give you a cheap price," I assured him with a straight face, "for all the camels, if you want them."

He paced back and forth, tense and unsatisfied. Methodically, he berated the poor state of the camels, his pay, the bad trip, and on and on. We ignored him until finally he sulked back to his camp.

The night was clear, and Flagg and I lay on our camel blankets watching the stars move slowly overhead. A satellite passed among them, and I wondered if anyone back in the civilized world felt as close to the heavens as we did that night. Lacking a radio, or even a watch, we had been out of contact for nearly a month, isolated in one of the remotest wildernesses on earth. I felt unexpectedly safe and at peace, as if in direct contact with God. Bilal was the nagging thorn that pricked my flesh.

The mood was interrupted by what at first appeared to be a falling star. It descended to the horizon without burning out, then turned in a great arc and accelerated straight toward us, parallel to the earth. It passed overhead at supersonic speed, five pieces in V formation trailing rocketlike plumes of green and red while emitting multicolored sparks. Within seconds it reached the far horizon and disappeared.

Bilal said he had seen similar phenomena many times, although he did not know what it was. I wondered if the Gulf War had gotten out of control, and what we saw were intercontinental ballistic missiles, or perhaps Libya had fired rockets on Chad. It could have been space debris, a defunct satellite that had reentered Earth's atmosphere and broken into pieces, but we would not know for sure until we reached Arlit.

> *We tried one last time to make peace by promising to sell him the camels cheap, or even give them to him for his guide payment if he would just cooperate and be happy.*

The next day Bilal degraded the camels again, insisting that we sell him all of them. We ignored his offer, which was ridiculous; however, Flagg and I assured him that we would give him a good deal, half the market price, when we reached Arlit. He became angry, saying they were in such bad shape that we would not be able to sell them. Then he demanded that we give him $200 to buy a camel in Iferouâne. When we refused, he started in again about the police, the permits, and the poor state of our camels.

For the rest of the day Bilal rode far ahead of us, brooding. We caught up with him late in the afternoon when he stopped to camp. We tried one last time to make peace by promising to sell him the camels cheap, or even give them to him for his guide payment if he would just cooperate and be happy. He sulked away and camped out of view. The next morning he remained isolated, drinking tea alone on his blanket until I saddled his camel and brought it to him. Then he rode ahead of us, fast, and out of sight.

Flagg was giving up on Bilal. Although he no longer attributed his weird behavior to cultural differences, he had no other explanation. We recounted all the effort spent in Niamey, and again in Agadez, trying to obtain permits. Everyone had insisted that a permit was not necessary. We decided to call Bilal's bluff.

That night we went to Bilal's camp and told him we had decided to go straight to Iferouâne and give ourselves up. When Bilal readily agreed, fear came over me. The bluff, which I felt so sure would work, had backfired. I felt isolated and afraid. His defiant words, "This is my country!" rang in my ears. We were sure he was trying to control us. But what was his agenda?

Flagg stoically resigned himself to Iferouâne and the end of the trip, but I was afraid of what the police might do. The police and border guards had proved to be the most corrupt of all during my Land Rover trip. They were constantly looking for any excuse to demand money. I had been arrested in Zaire and my passport taken without being given any reason at all. I tried to convince Flagg of the danger.

"The police can just lock us up for no reason," I said anxiously, "and keep us in some hellhole of a jail until we give them whatever they want. By the time we get free, Bilal would be far away."

"And our camels probably with him!" Flagg added with a nervous laugh. ◉

CHAPTER ELEVEN

Desecration by an Infidel

I was still trying desperately to sway Flagg toward Arlit when we reached the Tadek oued the afternoon of the following day. We unloaded the camels beneath a shade tree in the riverbed, then led them to the well. They had not been watered in ten days, and we labored for an hour to draw the nearly two hundred gallons of water it took to fill their thirsty bellies. We released them to forage on the acacia trees that grew along the riverbank.

Flagg and I set up our tents in the oued and lay down on the soft sand, our bodies aching from exhaustion. We were awakened by the high-pitched whine of a motor running at its peak rpm. A white Toyota Land Cruiser was advancing up the streambed, all four wheels spinning in the deep sand. When it reached our camp, it sank to the frame and stopped. Two turbaned men jumped out and began hurriedly shoveling sand while a rather obese figure wearing dark glasses and a pressed blue boubou emerged from the backseat. He adjusted his sunglasses and stared straight at us. Bilal whispered, to my horror, that he was the chief of police from Iferouâne!

Smoothing his robe, the burly man strode purposefully across the sand to our camp. He paused briefly to intimidate Bilal, then proceeded straight to Flagg and me.

"Bonjour, messieurs," he addressed us in an educated French accent. "How are you enjoying my country, seeing it by camel?"

The chief knew right off we were Americans but didn't ask to see our passports, or anything else for that matter. He was curious about what sights we had seen and if our camels had been good to us. The Land Cruiser spun free, and his assistants signaled him. Before leaving, he mentioned that he was returning from the north after investigating the murder of tourists traveling by Land Rover, "a disgraceful thing for bandits to do," he added. Then with well wishes and a friendly handshake he returned to the Land Cruiser and sped away down the oued.

Flagg and I were both dumbfounded and ecstatic. Bilal's threats had proved untrue. While we were talking with the chief, I had noticed Bilal furtively slipping away down the oued, out of sight.

When Bilal returned, we offered to wait for him while he went to Iferouâne to resupply his food, but he said he had bought a bag of flour from a Tuareg camped nearby and was prepared to go on to Arlit.

We remained camped at Tadek the following day. Writing in my diary, I noticed that we had traveled thirty days without a day of rest. Except for my diary entries, I had no means of keeping track of time. Flagg and I bathed at the well, then spent the rest of the day sleeping on our mats beneath the tree. It was Sunday, and for a moment I thought of people back home, off work watching TV.

Late in the afternoon three Tuareg women came to the well and began drawing water for their goats. Their lips and fingers were stained purple from indigo used to dye men's ceremonial tagulmusts and the cotton head scarves and dresses of women. Two herdboys assisted them, heads shaved like Mohawk Indians with a strip of hair down the middle.

Near the well a male camel was bellowing loudly and threatening any Tuareg that came near. Saliva dripped from his mouth, and an inflated red balloonlike membrane the size of a basketball dangled from his lower jaw, a sign he was in rut and sexually excited. He appeared dangerously insane and everyone was staying away.

A young female camel was led to him, and the riverbank echoed with deep-throated roars as he mounted her. His eyes glazed over and his body shuddered periodically during his orgasm, which lasted for forty-five minutes. The Tuareg said the breeding would continue every few hours until late into the night.

Flagg woke me that evening to eat. I had tired of the constant diet of meat MREs and Rice-A-Roni, and the dates had run out weeks before. Before Bilal had gone sour on us we were drinking Tuareg tea three times

Women at Tadek well.

a day, but it had caused such severe stomach cramps that I thought I was developing an ulcer and had given up the only enjoyment I had left.

Bilal had disappeared again, but Flagg found him spending the evening at a Tuareg camp celebrating the circumcision of a young boy. I could hear the singing and goatskin drums but was too exhausted to join them. The shrill ululating of the women and periodic roar of the breeding camel kept me from a restful sleep.

We left Tadek the next morning, following the sandy oued as it wound its way beneath dom palms. We stopped briefly at a Tuareg tent where women were preparing pots of millet for the feast after the circumcision, which was to be performed at midday.

Flagg dismounted and began exploring the nearby ruins of the sanctuary of a marabout. The adobe roof had fallen in, but inside Flagg found a handwritten Koran bound in goatskin. When Bilal discovered Flagg reading the holy book he was shocked and began yelling at Flagg, angrier than ever before. The holy book, had been desecrated by an infidel, an unforgivable sin.

Flagg desperately tried to explain that he had studied the Koran and could recite parts of it. And that he was reading it in the original Arabic, something most Muslims could not do, although many had memorized the entire book word for word without knowing the meaning. Flagg pleaded with Bilal, almost in tears, but any bond that had remained between us had been irreversibly severed. ◉

Tuareg camp at the Tadek oued.

CHAPTER TWELVE

Sandstorm

Late that afternoon I was a mile behind when I noticed Bilal veer away from Flagg and dismount. After looking around suspiciously in all directions, he bent down and appeared to be drawing something in the sand. He quickly caught up with Flagg, and they disappeared into an area of granite boulders.

It was out of my way, but I decided to investigate. An arrow had been drawn in the sand pointing in the direction of our travel, and beside it a message written in the ancient dot-dash script of Tifinar, the alphabet of the Tuareg similar to cuneiform. I erased everything with my foot and hurried to catch up. For the next hour we rode over solid rock that would have made it difficult for anyone to track us.

Flagg and I concluded that Bilal had conspired with a Tuareg from Tadek to steal our camels during the night. We laughed at outwitting him again. That night we knee-hobbled the camels and kept them couched next to our tents; however, during the moonless hours something spooked them, and they jumped up, roaring and hopping about. I went outside but found nothing.

For two days we followed the Eroug oued, an uninteresting, dusty riverbed that broadened into a vast floodplain formed by runoff from mountains and hills as far north as Temet. We encountered Tuareg camps, but they seemed more desperate than before. Black-shrouded women ran toward our camels, begging to sell their possessions. Bilal explained that they had nothing to eat and no money to buy flour. Unlike the seasonal *soudure,* an annual period of starvation that occurred while people waited for the summer rains, the rain had failed, and their suffering continued without relief. The udders of the camels and goats no longer produced milk, and the lactating women's breasts had gone dry. Infants and children suffered the most.

The moon rose full that night, bathing our camp in a pale light. The dry lake bed turned a ghostly blue, and leafless bushes cast skeletal shadows across lacy patterns in the cracked mud. We had been in the desert for thirty-four days, more than a full lunar cycle.

The following night we camped at the Tessadrek well in an area of bush not far from several Tuareg tents. A group of well-dressed elders were sitting on a blanket, one of them preparing tea. Bilal did not go to greet them as he had always done but told us to keep away, that they were dangerous. He unloaded his baggage behind a bush and stayed out of sight.

After Flagg and I set up camp, I decided to investigate.

"As-salaamu alaykum," I greeted the six veiled men, holding out my hand to the eldest seated nearest the boiling teapot. We touched fingertips gently, then slid them apart in the manner of a Tuareg ritual handshake.

"Bismallah (Praise be to God)," I announced as I sat down cross-legged on the straw mat among them.

"Hamdullah," the old man replied, then rapid-fired questions to me in Arabic. When they realized that I could not speak Arabic, all conversation abruptly halted. It was awkward, sitting there in the circle with them all staring at me. They had no idea who I was. After some uneasy moments, the men began to whisper among themselves, then the old man offered me the first glass of steaming tea. They watched intensely as I sipped the hot liquid with a noisy slurping action, emitting visceral "ummm" sounds, trying to follow custom. After I had finished and returned the glass, the old man filled all three glasses and passed them to the others.

Flagg joined us, greeting them in Arabic with the proper tonal accent. The men were immediately taken aback, but after establishing that Flagg was fluent, they proceeded with all the formalities—"Peace be upon you. How is your health? Your family? Your camels?" and so on—with praises to Allah liberally sprinkled in between. Flagg discovered that the men were not Tuareg but rather a religious group of Arab scholars traveling about the countryside teaching and preaching Islam.

They were curious about our journey, asking about wells and place-names, amazed that we had traveled so far. When Flagg mentioned Bilal, they threw a disapproving glance in the direction of his camp. As educated Islamists they regarded him as inferior.

That night we heard a faint throbbing of drums. The moon had not yet risen, so Flagg and I set off in darkness with a flashlight. We fumbled through bushes and among palms for a mile, then followed the sound out into an open plain. The full moon began to peek over the horizon, an orange globe rising from a black void. A golden sheen spread over the sand, and we discovered ten young girls sitting together in a tight circle. Their singing and drumming stopped when they saw us approaching.

They were unmarried teenagers, clad in colorfully patterned cotton dresses. Long strands of braided hair fell over their shoulders and hung down their backs. Their younger brothers, standing outside the circle, came forward to welcome us, having learned earlier that two foreigners had arrived at the well. We sat on the sand some distance away, and the girls began to sing again, celebrating being together at the well. The moon rose higher, illuminating their faces in its yellow haze and outlining the slender palms of the oasis behind us. Their voices were filled with laughter and excitement. They could have been young people anywhere, on a moon-filled night.

The next morning we watered our camels at the well, a hand-dug shaft about one hundred feet deep. Tuareg of all ages were trying to control several hundred anxious camels and goats waiting their turn around the well. Wooden pulleys creaked as rawhide ropes, stretched tight as steel cables, were pulled by donkeys straining under the load of the heavy water-laden goatskin buckets. Boys sporting Mohawks rode steel-faced donkeys, pounding their bony skulls with clubs to control them, while girls in wind-blown shawls and uncombed tresses ran along behind, throwing stones and shouting. Young men, stripped to the waist with pant legs rolled up, hoisted the full water buckets into troughs carved from palm trunks.

Drawing water at Tessadrek well.

Herds of goats milled nervously around, waiting their turn, while old men flailed long sticks whenever a camel tried to bully its way in. Goats were bleating, camels roaring, donkeys braying, and voices shouting, but order was kept so each person's livestock was watered in time.

At midday we stopped on a nearly barren plain to let the camels browse on a few scattered islands of dry bush. We sat under a leafless tree, too hot to eat. Soon we were all asleep. When I awoke, the camels were gone. Except for the few clumps of bush, I could see for miles over the open plain. While Flagg and Bilal slept, I set out following their tracks, but when I finally caught up with them and tried to return, I lost my way. Thinking that I had passed our tree, I doubled back, but after wandering for a half hour I realized I was completely lost.

The desert around me was flat and open except for the isolated islands of bush, which all looked the same. I decided to stay where I was and wait for Flagg and Bilal to wake up and come look for me. A half hour later I saw Bilal coming toward me with a perplexed look on his brow. He had been watching me for some time, only a hundred yards away from our tree.

A wind started suddenly out of the north, and Bilal became anxious to get going. Flagg and I quickly loaded Igor as the wind increased rapidly, and by the time we began saddling our riding camels, it was a hard blow. Each time I threw the blanket over O. Henry's back, it blew back in my face. Sand began to swirl around us. A sudden gust blew the saddle off McGoo before Flagg could cinch it down.

During the struggle I noticed a solid wall of brown sand extending from ground level to sky, a mile away and approaching rapidly like a tidal wave—the front of a boiling sandstorm. Just before it hit, the wind stopped, and we were encapsulated by an eerie electrostatic stillness. Large drops of water spattered on the sand, and then the storm hit with full intensity. I fitted my sand goggles over my eyes just in time to witness Bilal disappear into the moving wall of sand. Unable to walk against the raging wind, we mounted our bellowing camels and turned them into the storm.

Walls of sand were forming and reforming all around us. Although we tried to stay close together, Flagg and Bilal were faint forms that periodically vanished behind curtains of sand.

Walls of sand were forming and reforming all around us. Although we tried to stay close together, Flagg and Bilal were faint forms that periodically vanished behind curtains of sand. The sun was completely blocked out, and we could not orient ourselves. It was impossible to maintain a direction of travel, and I quickly realized we were wandering in circles.

During a momentary distraction Flagg disappeared. I stopped O. Henry, afraid to move. A curtain of white sand collapsed in front of me, and I saw Flagg holding McGoo no more than thirty feet away. Bilal had dismounted and was struggling to adjust a pair of antique aviator goggles over his eyes. He had found them a few months ago near a wrecked motorcycle, both lenses badly shattered.

The storm surged around us, sand streaming in horizontal layers like snow in a winter blizzard. At times I was scarcely able to make out Flagg's camel, only fifteen feet ahead. My leather gloves looked as if they had been hit with a sandblaster.

After two hours the body of the sandstorm passed. We headed for the leeward side of a mountain and rode along its base until sunset, when the wind stopped completely and the sky began to clear. Far away I heard deep rumbling sounds, like artillery.

Bilal after the sandstorm.

"Beaucoup pluie (much rain)," Bilal said as he pointed to the west. Large drops of water began to spatter in the sand, turning it blood red. We urged our camels into a fast walk, searching for a sheltering cleft in the mountain to camp.

As I slung the last piece of baggage into my tent, the rainstorm hit full force. I piled everything against the inner walls to keep the tent from collapsing. Flagg joined me, but Bilal refused, insisting on staying outside with the camels.

The storm continued into the night, which was wet and miserably cold. We tried to cook outside the tent door, but the wind blew the stove away. Flagg and I sat with our backs to the wall, watching the tent vibrate and the aluminum poles bend and shudder. At times we had to use our bodies to prevent the tent from caving in. Finally the storm passed, leaving a constant drizzle of rain. Bilal, thoroughly soaked and cold, finally decided to join us.

As this was our last night together, I thought this was a gesture of friendship. I was wrong. Bilal refused to try any of the food we offered him and started complaining again about the camels, his fee, et cetera, et cetera. I told him that we really wanted to be friends, but if he couldn't stop complaining, he should just leave us alone. He slept outside on wet blankets.

By morning the storm had passed, and the air was clear again. Camel saddles, supplies, and everything left outside were spattered with red mud. Before heating water for coffee, I had to disassemble the stove and clean out fine particles of sand. I cinched down O. Henry's saddle girth for the final time, the cracks in my fingertips as painful as ever. To relieve Igor of his heavy burden, we dumped the water in our jerricans into the sand. ◉

CHAPTER THIRTEEN

Blood on the Sand

That final day it felt good to walk next to O. Henry, the morning sunshine warm on my back and a gentle breeze on my face, purified after traveling a thousand miles over empty desert. Although dirty and unkempt, my body and spirit had reached equilibrium with the environment. After thirty-seven days in the desert, I was at peace.

Bilal slowed his camel and dropped back beside me. I ignored his gripes and repeated insistence that we were dependent on him to sell the camels, since only he could attest to their previous owners. I steeled myself to ignore Bilal and enjoy what was left of the desert before Arlit.

We were traveling over an open plain of sand and gravel, a *reg*, undisturbed by plants, animals, humans, or living material of any kind. The land was flat and clear to the horizon; there were no distant hills or mountains, not even a rock or stubble of grass to mar the emptiness. It was the beginning of the Tanezrouft, the sterile void that had fascinated me since first crossing it in the Land Rover. To Western minds the Tanezrouft was a bore, but it fascinated me with its mirages, illusions, and shimmering waves of heat and light. It was the absolute emptiness that drew me to it, where the outside world could be tossed away and all perception could instead travel inward to the deepest recesses of one's mind. There, I had hoped to discover something of my inner self.

As we moved on, fata morgana took shape around us. What appeared as a distant mountain was slowly transformed into a full-scale battleship marooned on desert sand, as if a receding tide had beached it there. As we came closer I saw a central control bridge and artillery turrets mounted on the foredeck, then it crumbled into sand. A cloaked nomad appeared at the horizon, leading a camel, but it too dissolved, and I found only a small stone resting innocently on the surface of the sand. We had no explanation, nor did we ask for one.

I stopped walking and rubbed my face against O. Henry's fuzzy nose. I had learned how to draw water and to make hobbles, how to find pasturage and to follow the tracks of animals, everything necessary to survive in a barren land. The desert had become part of me, hands varnished brown with sand, muscles hardened from loading and unloading the camels, calluses thickened into permanent features of my skin. I was thoroughly permeated with sand, wind, and sky, and I had no need for other, trivial things. As we came closer to Arlit, I wanted to turn away, back into the tranquil emptiness. I could hardly control my emotions, a feeling of impending loss, like death.

For the first time tire tracks scarred the sand. Then a dust cloud appeared on the horizon following a speeding truck. I tried to retain the peace of the desert, but latent images of concrete buildings, highways, and ringing telephones began to stir in my memory.

Flagg reined his camel away from Bilal and dropped back beside me.

"You had better prepare yourself," he said in a voice that seemed far away, muffled. "I have some really bad news, the worst!" Flagg continued, his face serious. "I don't know if I should tell you."

It was late morning, and the sun was hot above us. I tried not to listen.

"Give me the worst," I replied in a flat, uninterested tone.

"He is blackmailing us!" Flagg choked out, face flushing as he looked down at me. "When we reach Arlit, he is going to the police and have us arrested."

"How will he do that?" I replied, plodding along as if I heard only the crunching of my boots on the windswept crust of sand.

"He is going to say we traveled through restricted areas taking many photographs, secretly, without permits. And we hid to avoid the authorities. He will tell them that he did not know why we were doing this, and that he has been afraid."

I stopped and stared north across the empty desert in the direction of the strategic uranium mine that fueled Arlit's economy. O. Henry halted behind me, eyes searching the horizon as if he understood the ways of humans.

The end of the journey at Arlit.

"If the police think we were taking photographs of the uranium mine, we would be in real trouble," I muttered, disturbed by the thought.

Flagg continued, "Bilal says if we give him a camel, all this can be avoided."

A bomb burst in my head. I rapidly mounted O. Henry and trotted straight toward Bilal.

"You! You! You are finished!" I yelled as I reined O. Henry up beside him. I jabbed my outstretched finger at him, screaming, "You are no good! I am through with you. Get off your camel!"

We dismounted simultaneously, and I moved toward him to take his camel's lead rope. Before I could get to him, he handed the rope to Flagg.

"Get your bags off!" I shouted. "You are finished as our guide."

Bilal grabbed the lead rope again but was not strong enough to wrestle it away from Flagg. In a furious rage, Bilal jumped away from us and in one quick motion drew his sword from the red scabbard hanging at his waist.

"This is my country!" he screamed violently. His cold, muddy eyes were piercing mine. "I'm finished with you, you . . . dog!"

He swept the sword above his head, clasping it tightly with both hands. "You will die, even if I must die!"

Flagg and I were stunned. The madman was screaming loudly in Tamasheq, enraged and completely out of control. We stood there unmoved, within striking range.

I turned toward Flagg. "Give him the camel, Flagg." I said in as calm a voice as possible.

Flagg seemed frozen. Bilal was coiled, sword above his head, ready to strike. "Give him the camel, Flagg—now!" I repeated forcefully.

Flagg held the lead rope out toward Bilal. Bilal hesitated, then seized the rein. Sheathing his sword, he mounted in one smooth motion without couching his camel and trotted away in the direction of Arlit.

"He called you a dog!" Flagg said, wrinkling his forehead. "That's the worst insult a Muslim can give. He really hates you!"

We were shaken, but after the initial terror I was glad to be free of Bilal and relieved to know at last that he had been a conniving thief with a hidden agenda all along. Flagg was also convinced that Bilal was evil and could not be excused by cultural differences. While Bilal slowly shrank away we took stock of our situation. We were on an unmarked plain and Arlit was not within sight. It was somewhere to the east, so we rode on with the sun guiding us.

Bilal stopped at the horizon, where he remained a dark specter watching us, a fata morgana that grew tall, then shrank. Each time we moved, he moved; when we stopped, he stopped. My euphoria evaporated.

An hour later a dark band appeared on the horizon: the walls of Arlit. Finally, a vehicle came by on its way to the village, and we signaled it to stop. Flagg caught a ride, trying to get to the police before Bilal, while I continued on with the camels, Bilal watching my every move. When I stopped to eat an MRE, Bilal dismounted and waited. Flagg returned an hour later accompanied by the chief of police and a soldier armed with a rifle.

"Are you a doctor?" the fat Hausa policeman asked. He explained that he had a stomach problem, a gastric ulcer. I gave him my last Alka-Seltzer, explaining that I had the same problem from drinking too much Tuareg tea. He nodded and said he would sort out our problem in Arlit.

Bilal dogged us, watching us from the horizon all the way in. Piles of filth, plastic bags, and garbage littered the wall of the village. The walls were built to keep the desert out, but I was thankful that it kept the villagers and their trash inside, away from the clean desert.

We rode through an opening in the adobe wall and down narrow lanes of soft sand lined by brown, mud-plastered houses with tiny courtyards. Teenage children ran alongside yelling, "Où est le chameau?" Street urchins fought to grab the reins and take control, backing away only when I lashed out at them viciously with my riding stick. They tricked us into a dead-end alley where their friends surrounded us and tried to steal from the baggage camel.

We found the police office with Bilal's camel tied outside and Bilal already inside arguing aggressively with the officer. The uniformed officer listened to our case against Bilal. Then to my surprise Bilal ignored all of it, and in a passive effeminate voice said we had tried to leave him in the desert and cheat him out of his guide fee. The officer found it impossible to believe that after forty days together in the desert, Bilal would threaten to kill us. Neither did he believe Bilal's story. He decided to turn us over to the district administrator. Our "trial" would be tomorrow. Flagg and I were not sure who exactly was on trial.

The street crowd followed us like a plague of hungry locusts. We found a small hotel for overland travelers and led the camels inside its walled courtyard. After unloading, we entrusted them to an elderly Tuareg guardian to corral them safely at the market. Then we checked into a room, took a bath, and drank a Coca-Cola. Having shed the desert in the space of an hour, I felt totally miserable. I held my face and cried.

The district administrator was a thin African with razor-thin tolerance. He was a Djerma, which was not a desert tribe, and had been posted where he had no friends. He seemed irritated at our presence.

We engaged a short, rotund Hausa woman to speak for us, our "lawyer." Before we could explain our case, she jumped out of her chair, leaned her volup-tuous breasts over the administrator's desk and began shouting. Bilal was sitting innocently with his hands folded in his lap, but he quickly lost composure, became angry, and began shouting also, but he was no match for our fat lady.

The noise was deafening as our lady and Bilal turned on each other. The administrator quickly lost control and threatened to throw us all out. Everyone sat back down, and Bilal resumed his innocent hands-folded posture.

The administrator completely ignored our complaint that Bilal had threatened to kill us. For all the trouble Bilal had given us, I was determined to see him arrested or punished in some way. I requested to pay a reduced guide fee; however, the "judge" told me to pay fully and get out.

Flagg was visibly upset. He had never been exposed to a dishonest, plotting person before, and he wanted to end it and get away as quickly as possible. He offered to pay Bilal himself.

As a last resort I convinced the administrator to let me phone Rhissa from his office. He said that Bilal was dangerous and that I must pay him and leave Arlit immediately. Bilal had taken the job, he said, because he wanted the camels. We paid.

During the next two days, Bilal and his Tuareg friend followed our every step. We spotted them hiding behind a telephone pole, loitering outside our window, and watching us from the other side of a mud wall. Finally, I had had enough of the cat-and-mouse game and took his veiled spy friend's hand and led him around town with us.

The camels were sold at the market far above the discounted price we had promised to Bilal. When I asked what would become of them, I was told they would be eaten. There was no longer enough pasturage for camels to survive, so the males were being slaughtered for meat.

That last day in Arlit I went to the market to say good-bye to O. Henry. I untied the black cord around his neck with the leather pouch containing the gris-gris, a magical charm that had been blessed by a marabout. Then a stranger, a large Tuareg, came into the corral and started leading O. Henry away. At the gate O. Henry hesitated, his thin body shuddering as if he knew the fate awaiting him. The impatient Tuareg hauled heavily on the nose rope, causing O. Henry to cry out in pain. In anger I snatched the rope from the Tuareg's hand. O. Henry lowered his head to mine, long eyelashes flickering over deep brown eyes. I rubbed my face for the last time against his fuzzy nose and held his bony head between my hands. Then I handed the rope back to the Tuareg and watched helplessly as he led O. Henry away. ◉

PART
TWO

◈

RIFT VALLEY
BY
HORSEBACK

◈

CHAPTER FOURTEEN

Paradise Waiting

R iding horses as a child in the lowland farm country of South Carolina, I often wondered what it was like for the early explorers of the American West, such as Kit Carson and Buffalo Bill, setting out into wild, uncharted territory. I imagined them galloping across open plains among herds of buffalo, encountering tribal people armed with bows and arrows, and viewing unspoiled landscapes touched only by native camps with smoldering cooking fires. The thrill of such a long, adventurous journey appealed to me, but those days were gone forever, I thought.

Years later, however, I discovered that such an adventure might still be possible in east Africa. Despite a booming tourist industry, travels there in my Land Rover during the 1980s had led me to believe that no other place on earth had such unspoiled magnificence. I had witnessed immense herds of wildebeests and zebras, native Maasai living a nomadic pastoral lifestyle unchanged for centuries, and a landscape that had no equal anywhere.

As I began to research the subject, corresponding with horse lovers, veterinarians, Kenya residents—even retired white hunters—I began to realize the problems I would face. Everyone said that such a jouney could not be made. Lack of water, lions, or tsetse flies would kill the horses, and without vehicle support the whole thing would end in disaster. That made me want to do it even more.

My plan was to travel by horseback straight down the Great Rift Valley in Kenya, which contained some of east Africa's more untouched and uninhabitable wilderness. The Great Rift was a fault in the earth's crust extending six thousand miles from the Dead Sea to Mozambique. Seldom more than thirty miles wide, the valley was created as tectonic plates pulled apart over the last twenty million years, leaving one of the few topological features seen from the moon.

Kenya's rift, also known as the Gregory Rift for the explorer J. W. Gregory who in 1893 gave it the name Rift Valley, was the youngest of the rift system and known for its earthquakes, active volcanoes, and sulfurous steam vents. Fossil remains suggested that human life began in the Rift Valley some three million years ago, migrating out of Africa to populate the rest of the world.

An exhilarating sensation rippled through me as I traced my intended journey on a multicolored topographical map spread out on the floor of my home in California. Starting fifty miles from the equator at Lake Naivasha, the highest of the rift lakes, I would head straight down the valley through an archetypical east African landscape of grasslands and umbrella acacias made famous by Karen Blixen under the pseudonym of Isak Dinesen in *Out of Africa*.

At the lowest and most desolate part of the valley I would reach Lake Natron, a shallow expanse of water sandwiched between the walls of the rift in Tanzania. Unable to proceed farther on horseback, I would then ascend the steep Nguruman escarpment to enter the forest of Naimina Enkiyo, Forest of the Lost Child, a place sacred to and feared by the Maasai.

From there the way would be across the rolling, flower-strewn meadows of the Loita Hills, Africa's version of *The Sound of Music* countryside. Remote thornbush and thorn acacia country would lead to the Sand River, then finally the open plains of Maasai Mara, a northern extension of the Serengeti with its giant migratory herds of more than a million wildebeests and hundreds of thousands of zebras, one of the greatest wildlife spectacles on earth.

By map it was a straight-line distance of 250 miles, but I estimated it to be almost twice that far wandering on horseback. The journey would take nearly two months. I turned away, pale from contemplating the reality of such a plan.

It would be a journey back in time, through the tribal land of the Maasai, who still carried spears to protect themselves from dangerous Cape buffalo and lions that attacked their cattle. I hoped to experience what it was like for early humans walking among giant predators with only a spear and their wits to protect them.

Also I wanted get a sense of what it was like for the explorer Joseph Thomson, who in 1883 was the first European to cross Maasai land. Like Thomson, I would travel accompanied by natives and unsupported except for what could be carried on donkeys. Unlike Thomson, I would have no gun to protect my animals or myself from wild creatures.

It would also be a spiritual pilgrimage for me to live as close as possible to nature, and for the Maasai accompanying me, a journey to their sacred mountain, Ol Doinyo Lengai, the Mountain of God.

I would travel as far as possible from roads and towns with no vehicle support, no food drops, no villages to purchase food should we exhaust our supply, and no means of contacting the outside world in case of an emergency. We would have no radio to follow world news and no watch to check time. Movement of the sun across the sky, cycles of day and night, phases of the moon, and entries in a diary would be the only monitors of our passage.

To thoroughly immerse myself in what I thought would be a more spiritually and physically satisfying way of life—one closer to wilderness, primal forces, and predators—I intended to leave everything behind that reminded me of my own civilization.

Without map, compass, or a global positioning system, I would be completely dependent upon the Maasai to guide me, just as the first explorers through the American wilderness were dependent on Native Americans. Maasai would also be the sole source of human companionship I would have for the entire journey.

Donkeys, faithful but unwilling beasts of burden since the dawn of history, would carry everything I needed. Their survival would depend upon finding wild grasses so they could graze along the way. Each midday rest stop and each night's camp would have to be located near adequate pasturage. Their requirements, and those of the horses, would be given a higher priority than our own, for if they should sicken or die, the journey would end in disaster.

I planned the safari to begin in June just as the rainy season ended, leaving the plains of the Rift Valley flowing tall with red oat and green Kikuyu grasses.

What concerned me most was the extremely arid lower region of the Rift Valley between lakes Magadi and Natron, a region known as Dongilani to the early explorers who had avoided it. It was feared as a hot, dry place without fresh water. One writer called it "the most awful region of the Rift." Other than the Maasai, few had attempted to cross that parched land on foot.

In 1977 the author John Heminway ran out of water there and almost perished. No one I knew had ever been there, and there was no source of drinkable water evident. The water of lakes Magadi and Natron were too caustic to drink, contaminated by carbonate boiled up by volcanic action.

The lower Rift Valley, with its heat and thorn acacias, was also tsetse fly country. African sleeping sickness, carried by the tsetse fly, was endemic there and fatal to horses and donkeys.

Early explorers had given up using horses and donkeys for safari as they inevitably died soon after entering an area infested with the nasty, biting flies. By rendering vast areas of east Africa uninhabitable to cattle and other domesticated livestock, the tsetse fly had been a major factor allowing the wild herds of the region to survive the population pressures of the twentieth century.

Nineteenth-century South African books, such as *Wild Sports of Southern Africa* by Cornwall Harris written in 1852 when hunting was on horseback, made clear to me that traveling with horses was tantamount to trolling for lions. Over the last ten years I had spent many nights camped in Africa, listening half awake to the roaring of lions in the distance; however, the thought of one killing and eating my horse just outside my tent was frightening. So I bought a bullwhip and began having nightmares about trying to drive off a hungry lion with it.

The only horses readily available to buy in Kenya were thoroughbred rejects from the Nairobi racetrack. Their hooves were too frail for the volcanic rock of the Rift Valley and legs too delicate for the steep escarpments we would climb. Somali ponies were tougher and could survive better in the wild, but they were highly valued and impossible to find for sale. My greatest concern, however, was the difficulty purebred European horses would have surviving on lean African grasses.

The risks of embarking on such a journey were therefore similar to those taken by the first explorers. They were, I thought, unavoidable, and an integral part of the experience.

I arrived in Kenya in early June 1987 and drove out to the edge of the escarpment overlooking the Rift Valley, two thousand feet below. The long rains had ended, and the Kikuyu grass stood tall and lush on the Kedong plains, an emerald carpet studded with patchy stands of fever trees and umbrella acacias in patterns of light yellow and mint green.

Longonot, and other more conical-shaped volcanoes, rose sharply from the valley floor while overhead puffy white cumulus clouds drifted lazily in a blue sky. To the north Lake Naivasha was faintly visible, its waters shimmering gold in the setting sun. The valley below seemed a garden of Eden, a paradise waiting. My timing for the journey had been perfect.

I located Sekerot Ole Mpetti, a twenty-six-year-old Maasai of the Ilpurko clan from near the Maasai Mara game reserve. Sekerot was fluent in English as well as in Maa, Kikuyu, and Swahili. We had met the year before, introduced by a Kenyan acquaintance, and hit it off immediately. The Maasai pastoral, nomadic way of life had fascinated me, and Sekerot, whose mother, Elizabeth, was from the line of prophets and spiritual leaders, was eager to open up Maasai land and the culture for me. In addition Sekerot had a great sense of humor and we both loved to laugh, a characteristic that quickly bound us.

That year we traveled together for a month in my Land Rover camping across Maasai land and attending a week-long Olngesherr ceremony in which hundreds of Ilpurko ex-warriors were retired as elders. Excited about the prospect of a new adventure, Sekerot was eager to join up again as my companion and interpreter.

Sekerot was a perfect example of the Maasai warrior age set—six feet tall and 150 pounds of hard muscle rippling beneath flawless brown skin. We were the same height and weight, but I was almost twice his age and not nearly as strong, or brave.

Sekerot lived the traditional life of a layoni herdboy.

As was the custom among the Maasai, and for reasons lost in tribal history, his two lower front teeth had been knocked out when he was a child, leaving an empty space. Circular scars on his thighs were from hot embers self-applied in preparation for undergoing the pain of circumcision without moving, a test of bravery and courage that is the most important event in a Maasai's life.

There was no fat on his body anywhere, and his reflexes were as quick as those of an angry dog. His mind was creative and sharp, solving in ingenious ways the problems of our previous safari. Most important, Sekerot was completely unfamiliar with the *wazungu*'s, or white person's, concept of "It cannot be done." Not only could I rely on Sekerot should things go wrong, but he was a trusted friend without whom I might not have attempted the seemingly insurmountable tasks before us.

As a young boy Sekerot had lived the traditional life of a *layoni,* an uncircumcised herdboy, protecting his father's cattle from lions on the plains east of Maasai Mara. But when it was time for his circumcision when he was about fifteen years old, his father sent him to school in Narok, which prevented him from becoming a warrior, the dream of all Maasai boys, and especially for Sekerot.

Warriorhood was the most highly romanticized and idolized stage in a Maasai's life, and Sekerot was determined to be a warrior. He secretly arranged for his own circumcision, but his father punished him and forced him to stay in school. Sekerot never got over it and still dreamed of being a warrior.

After a ten-day search, I located two thoroughbred mares for sale at Sanctuary Farm, one of only thirty colonial estates that remained in Kenya since the British left in 1963. Owned by a man named Francis Erskin, the farm was located on dry and dusty land bordering the receding shoreline of Lake Naivasha.

Sanctuary Farm, however, was an oasis of green, irrigated from the lake. In the center of the farm stood three colonial-style stone houses surrounded by lawns manicured by Kikuyu laborers wielding *pangas,* or African bush knives. Overhanging pepper trees and giant candelabra euphorbias gave a touch of elegance while marigolds, red-blossomed aloes, and poinsettias added splashes of bright color. Sand lanes led to lush green pastures where thoroughbred racehorses grazed alongside long-legged giraffes that stepped effortlessly over the whitewashed wood fences. Spreading canopies of yellow-bark acacias, often called fever trees for their association with malarial swamps, were scattered throughout the pastures, providing shade for the livestock.

Down by the lakeshore, waterbuck—fuzzy brown antelopes with lyre-shaped horns—grazed on natural grasses that thrived in the black-cotton soil. At night hippopotamuses, more often heard than seen, came out to munch on the verdant landscape, while vervet and black-and-white colobus monkeys slept in the trees.

The lake was on one of the busiest migratory bird routes on the planet. Its fresh water, floating gardens of purple lotus flowers, and immense stands of green, feathery-headed papyrus created a magnet for over four hundred bird species: fish eagles, Goliath herons, saddle-billed storks, marabous, spoonbills, Fisher's lovebirds, Egyptian geese, rollers, kingfishers, bee-eaters, hornbills, and yellow weavers whose inverted nests hung in profusion from the thorn-covered limbs of acacia trees. The weaver nests were protected by the sharp thorns, whose four-inch spikes could flatten a Land Rover tire.

At sixty-two hundred feet in elevation, Naivasha was the highest of a chain of lakes running down the Rift Valley and one of only two that contained fresh water uncontaminated by volcanic-produced soda. Bounded east and west by the rift escarpment walls and by volcanoes Embu to the north and Longonot to the south, the lake was a catchment basin thought to stay fresh by draining through underground channels to Lake Magadi, eighty miles to the south.

Sanctuary's polo field, with its view over the lake, was said to be the most picturesque in the country. During the season, horsemen and other farm owners landed Cessnas and Beechcrafts on the grass next to the field and set up camp under the fever trees to play polo and party.

The thatched-roof stables of Beryl Markham, author and famous aviatrix, were still in use at Erskin's farm. The house of Joy Adamson, author of *Born Free*, was farther around the lakeshore, along with the Djinn Palace, a Moroccan-style mansion that during colonial times hosted wild parties detailed in the film *White Mischief*.

A Kikuyu groom accompanied us to the paddocks where he pointed out two three-year-old mares, one black and the other chestnut, grazing peacefully under the fever trees. He said they were the firstborn of unproven broodmares and too small for the racetrack. Left alone together since birth, they had become inseparable—and that, he said, was the problem.

> *Thirty years had passed since I won first prize riding a bull in a rodeo, and I no longer had the talent or bones to survive a bucking horse.*

Judy Corr, the trainer at Sanctuary, revealed that neither horse had been fully trained. As we walked to the tack house for bridles, Judy explained that they were extremely nervous and unsuitable for riding. She admitted that she had given up and refused to work further with them. Erskin had sent them to a stable in Nairobi for training, but the black one kicked the side off the barn and they had run away. Back at Sanctuary they were for sale, and at a reasonable price.

The chestnut mare had a small white blaze on her forehead, and most unusual, her ears flopped over when undisturbed. She seemed harmless grazing in the pasture, but when I saddled her and put one leg over her back, she jumped forward and began bucking. I held her back, stroking her neck and talking calmly to her until she settled down to a rough but controllable ride. I decided to call her Katy.

I turned Katy over to Sekerot, who, although lacking previous experience with horses, was eager to try his hand. The chestnut mare bucked once, and Sekerot hit the ground, landing on his back with an audible thud. Unperturbed and seemingly unhurt, he remounted with even more enthusiasm. After a few close calls, Katy calmed down, and they rode blissfully across the pasture beneath the yellow fever trees. Sekerot was a quick learner, unafraid, and had a natural way with animals.

The other mare was coal black and as high strung as thoroughbreds come. The whites of her eyes glared at us from the dark interior of the windowless stall we had driven her into in order to catch her. With fits and starts, we finally got a halter over her head while carefully avoiding her back end.

Once outside, she spun around nervously until I blindfolded her with my shirt. As I eased the saddle over her back, her muscles tensed, and she began to quiver. Once mounted, her back arched beneath me like a cat, and her ears pressed back firmly against her head—she was ready to explode.

Thirty years had passed since I won first prize riding a bull in a rodeo, and I no longer had the talent or bones to survive a bucking horse. Nervous beads of sweat formed on my face as the blindfold was removed. All my strength and attention was focused on controlling the trembling mare. She lunged forward, startled by a bird. With every blade of grass that moved in the wind she tried to bolt and run away. After twenty minutes I was exhausted trying to anticipate her moves and hold her back, so we put her back in the stall. I named her Houdini because riding her was going to be tricky.

Near sunset, Sekerot and I saddled the horses again. They were more manageable, so we rode down by the lake. On horseback we did not seem to disturb the waterbuck, wildebeests, and impalas grazing there, and the excitement of riding close among them was thrilling. Houdini almost stepped on a newborn waterbuck calf left hidden in a clump of tall grass by its mother. Curled up in a ball, it looked at us with trusting saucer-shaped eyes, unafraid.

We broke into a canter at the polo field, but Katy bucked Sekerot off again, breaking a stirrup leather. Instead of running away, she stood by quietly, watching Sekerot dust himself off. We put the horses away and turned to the next project—finding pack animals. ◉

WANAICHI TAILORING
& SHOP .
P.O. BOX
SUSWA

OKUU
PLOT no 6

Houdini and I at Suswa.

CHAPTER FIFTEEN

Cowboys in Africa

We needed four donkeys to carry our three hundred pounds of food and gear. After a day and a half searching the countryside and nearby Kikuyu village on foot, Sekerot had located only two donkeys for sale, a pregnant female and its three-year-old offspring. We called them Mamma Donkey and Baby Donkey. Baby had never been trained in any way, or even caught, but I intended to set off in two days so there was no time for training. We would have to use cowboy methods.

At daybreak on June 11, we rounded up the donkeys and horses and tied them to poles. Until more donkeys could be found, we would have to pack both donkeys and horses.

Sekerot and I divided our supplies into equal piles on the ground. Four plastic milk crates were filled with military MREs, pasta, canned butter, coffee, and flour to make bread. Two marine duffel bags were stuffed full with sleeping bags and clothes. Miscellaneous items included a small tent, Coleman stove, fuel, folding stools, cooking pots, jerricans for water, ropes, buckets, an African panga, canteens, a tripod, two English riding saddles, and a bullwhip.

We had few medical supplies and no weapon. For emergencies I was relying heavily on a small, white, leather-bound Bible my grandmother had given to my youngest daughter, Emily. The explorers also usually carried a Bible.

With the sun rising steadily over Lake Naivasha, we bent to the task. Without packsaddles, everything had to be tied down over locally cured sheepskins with ropes of hemp, handmade by Kikuyu laborers. There were no bellybands, girths, or chest straps. Everything was makeshift. It was my first attempt at packing animals, making it even more of a challenge.

"I can't catch that Baby Donkey," Sekerot said as he ran up out of breath dragging a rope behind him. "Every time I get close she just runs away."

Baby squeezed in next to Mamma and Sekerot tried to get his arms around her neck, but she ran off again. I laughed and picked up one of the ropes coiled on the grass. "Watch this!" I said with a smile.

I had not used a lasso since my horse days in high school. The loop landed around Baby's neck, but she was stronger than I thought and ran off, dragging me along with her. Sekerot grabbed the rope and together we dug in our heels and finally stopped her. With one end wrapped around a pole, we began winching her in, bit by bit, like docking a ship.

Baby Donkey stretched out, pulling back as hard as she could with all four legs, trying to break the rope.

"Watch the back feet!" I shouted to Sekerot as he ran in to grab her. Too late. "Crack!" A flying hoof landed squarely on Sekerot's knee, knocking him down. As he fell, Baby landed a second glancing blow to his elbow.

Moaning and rolling on the ground in pain, Sekerot was still within reach of the fighting donkey's rear hooves. I lassoed the belligerent beast around the back legs and pulled her down on the ground, out of commission.

Sekerot got up holding his knee and spitting mad. "I'm getting that donkey!" he yelled as he rushed in and began kicking the struggling donkey until it finally gave up and lay quiet.

We caught our breath, then loosened the ropes on Baby. The fight began all over again, with Baby knocking Sekerot down and stepping on him twice. Finally I got hobbles tied on Baby's front legs, then we began rubbing her neck, gently stroking her ears, and trying to calm her down. This had a soothing effect, but every time Sekerot came near she lashed out at him with sharp hooves.

It was still early morning, but we were already dripping with sweat and had removed our shirts. I used mine to blindfold Baby, then placed sheepskin padding over her back. Working together, Sekerot and I succeeded in gently placing two heavy milk crates filled with food supplies on her and cinching them securely in place. Then I tied her to a pole and turned to Mamma.

Just as the sheepskins and baggage were placed over her back, Mamma began kicking and bucking until baggage and donkey fell down in a tangled heap on the ground. We started over.

"This donkeywork is killing me," Sekerot glared at me. "Why are we doing it?"

It was noon before both donkeys and the chestnut mare were finally packed and stood tied quietly to trees. A crowd of curious Kikuyu from the village had formed around us, laughing and watching our every move, making things worse. They meant no harm, but we had to be constantly on guard or our vital supplies would disappear.

The struggle, the anxiety, and the constant vigilance under the intense equatorial sun had sapped our strength. The precarious state of our packed animals made it impossible to stop and rest or get a drink of water. We were

Fourth day. Mamma and Baby Donkey peacefully being packed..

sweating like crazy, exhausted, and near defeat. The black mare, last to be packed, was eyeing us nervously. We had no strength left for another disaster.

Using the last of my cowboy tricks, I blindfolded Houdini and hobbled her front legs. A loop of rope was placed around her upper lip and tightened with a stick, a method of temporarily paralyzing horses. Her black coat was trembling, but she didn't move as I strapped the remaining items over her saddle. The blindfold and hobbles were removed, and I gripped her halter with both hands as tightly as possible.

I gave the signal, released the rope around Houdini's lip, and we started forward. Sekerot was using switches to drive the donkeys from behind, as it was impossible to lead them. Houdini was terrified by the clanking metal bucket and other miscellaneous items strapped on her back. She leaped forward with such force that I was dragged off my feet. The donkeys scattered and Sekerot was left holding Katy. I could not help him; keeping Houdini restrained was all I could do.

Sekerot quickly employed two Kikuyu boys from the crowd of natives to assist us. They rounded up the donkeys, and we started again. Fifty feet into our journey, Mamma Donkey lay down and rolled over on her back, flattening our supplies. She stood up, with broken crates hanging beneath her belly, back legs tangled in a mass of ropes. The black mare was shaking, on the verge of a nervous breakdown. Baby took the opportunity to lie down and refused to get up. Everything had to be untied, taken off the two donkeys, and repacked.

"These Kikuyu donkeys are smarter than Maasai," Sekerot sighed, sadistically shaking a limber switch at them.

We started for the third time, Houdini trembling not only from the noise and confusion, but because she had not been around donkeys and they frightened her. Each time one of them got close she freaked out, dragging me away with her. All my attention and energy was used up in preventing her from bolting and running back to Lake Naivasha. Our caravan lurched forward, struggling every step of the way.

Two hours down the trail, Mamma collapsed and refused to get up. The weight on her back was just too much for her. We pushed, pulled,

Fourth day, sleeping peacefully on the Kedong plain.

and prodded, but nothing would get her going. We let her rest, then started again. Unless we could purchase more donkeys our journey was doomed.

We ascended the Longonot plateau, a massive outpouring of lava that during Pleistocene times had blocked the drainage of Lake Naivasha. Eventually the lake overflowed, carving an outlet through the volcanic plateau called Hell's Gate, a narrow gorge just to the west of us.

The sun was setting behind us, and Lake Naivasha lay like a silver mirror on the valley floor, a shimmering reminder of what we were leaving behind.

I looked away to avoid the haunting call of "civilization."

Since sunrise Sekerot and I had put in twelve hours of hard labor, but our safari had advanced only three miles down the hot, dusty trail from Lake Naivasha. Sekerot found an open space in the thick *leleshwa,* an aromatic bush with silver-green leaves, that covered the plateau, and we unloaded to camp. I staked out the horses to graze, realizing that they had had nothing to drink all day. Mamma Donkey showed no interest in eating, and she lay down, listless and appearing sick. There was no water source nearby.

There were no thorn trees in the area to make a proper protective corral, so we cut limbs and bushes and piled them into a thick wall that we hoped would slow hyenas or leopards attempting to attack our horses until we could do something. I had no idea what that might be.

When we finally released the horses in the corral, I was exhausted, dirty, and disillusioned. Lying in my tent that night, too worn out to peel off the grimy shirt stuck to my back, I decided that if the horses broke out and ran away, I would quit the safari.

Morning came only seconds after my eyes closed. I shuffled about stiffly in the cold, damp air, body aching all over from the day before. Mamma had recovered and was eagerly munching the wet grass. Katy and Houdini were pacing in their corral, snorting breaths of condensed fog like dragons.

Sekerot and I decided to carry as much baggage as possible on our backs. We distributed the remaining weight on the animals until everything seemed perfectly balanced.

Five minutes from camp, Baby brushed against Katy, and she bolted, bucking off all the baggage. This pattern repeated itself in various permutations and combinations all morning and into the afternoon, until the two donkeys just fell down and gave up completely. We set up camp at the base of Longonot volcano in a dense thicket of tall leleshwa whose leaves the Maasai crush and use under their arms as a deodorant.

The next morning the two Kikuyu boys headed back to Lake Naivasha. It felt like being lost at sea, then losing your life preserver. We had been overwhelmed trying to control the animals and would not have made it that far without them. Now they were gone.

Sekerot and I were so exhausted we decided to rest that day and consider what to do, go back or go forward. We passed the day watching the horses graze and staring up the tortuous ridges of Longonot's eroded slope. It towered thirty-six hundred feet above us and was the youngest and best-preserved volcano in Kenya. I wanted to climb to the rim and look down into the mile-wide yawning crater that had emitted steam for the last hundred years. I was just too weary.

When we set out again the next day, Sekerot and I were refreshed. The loads were better balanced and not such a persistent problem. The horses were calm, free of any stressful anticipation that plagued us humans; even the donkeys seemed more cooperative. Sekerot managed to lead Katy and drive the donkeys. We continued south, around the base of Longonot.

At midday we came to the end of the leleshwa, and the end of the Longonot plateau. Sweeping down the valley before us was an endless sea of brown waist-high grass where shadows of cottony cumulus clouds floating in a brilliant blue sky played on the surface. Antelopes and gazelles were grazing in the distance. I took a deep breath—Africa!

A mile into the waving oat grass we found an island meadow of short-cropped green turf and halted for lunch. A hundred yards away twenty zebras were taking a dust bath in a dry water hole, stirring up clouds of chalky dust as they thrashed about on their backs. Thomson gazelles, tan deer-sized antelopes with a horizontal black stripe above their downy white belly, grazed contentedly in the sunburned grass that surrounded us. They blended into the landscape perfectly, betrayed only by twittering tails that ceaselessly fanned insects. Scattered among them were larger Grant's gazelles and groups of long-faced kongoni with fawn-colored coats and comically bent bracket-shaped horns.

We were in the narrowest part of the Rift Valley, the escarpment walls sharply defined on both sides of us as dark cliffs only fifteen miles apart. All around rose perfectly cone-shaped volcanoes, inactive or extinct. Behind us was the jagged rim of Longonot. Ahead of us to the south was the immense mound of Suswa, the red volcano, which at seventy-seven hundred feet dominated the valley floor.

We unloaded the donkeys, hobbled them, and set them free to graze while we had lunch, a beef MRE with bread. Then I fell immediately asleep on the soft grass, basking in the warm sun.

Houdini had been left to graze on a thirty-foot rope tied to her halter and secured around one of the heavy marine duffel bags. When she reached the end of her rope, she jerked her head, and the duffel bag jumped forward in the grass behind her, an imaginary predator. An explosion of hoofbeats awakened me, and I watched, helpless, as she galloped flat out thoroughbred-style across the grassland back toward Lake Naivasha, the duffel bag bouncing along after her. Nearly out of sight, she passed a solitary tree that the duffel got caught on and held fast. Houdini did a flip in the air, landing hard on her back. When we caught up to her, she was uninjured and waiting submissively to be led back.

Five days after leaving Lake Naivasha, we reached the only road that crossed the Rift Valley. As we approached, a zebra-striped minibus full of tourists sped past at breakneck speed, spooking the horses. The Kikuyu driver was careening recklessly around large potholes in a hell-bent attempt to reach the Maasai Mara game reserve before sunset. Inside, the clean-washed faces of khaki-clad tourists were too frightened to look at anything except the road ahead.

I had driven that road in my Land Rover and each time watched the countryside fly by while wishing I was outside on foot in Africa. Once inside the Mara game reserve, I, like the tourists in the minibus, had to stay inside the Land Rover like a caged animal, unable to touch the earth, smell the grasses, or experience the primitive state of heightened awareness

Archetypal East African sunset with umbrella acacia.

when on foot around lions, buffalo, or elephants. The Land Rover had given me a safe view of Africa, but it was an illusion.

Sekerot stopped at the edge of the road. "We can't go farther. We need more donkeys," he said, face clenched. "This donkey work is killing me. Why are we doing it?"

The creative determination that had keep Sekerot pushing forward had weakened. To him the road was a powerful temptation to quit the safari and hitchhike back to Nairobi before things got worse. He was looking up and down for the next car, all sense of humor gone. Without Sekerot I could not go on. It was serious and tense. "Let's just camp here," I pleaded, "until we find more donkeys. There is plenty of green grass for our horses, and we are in Maasai territory now, so there must be donkeys for sale." Sekerot did not respond.

I hurried the donkeys along, trying to get as far from the road as possible before dark. Sekerot had no choice but to follow. Barely a mile away we tried to cross a swampy area of black mud, but the donkeys got stuck, bogged down to the belly, and could go no farther. The day was over. We unloaded and lugged the heavy baggage fifty yards to higher ground.

While setting up camp, I noticed a Maasai *enkang* on a hill nearby, a family settlement of traditional dwellings called *enkaji*, constructed of cow dung plastered over an oval frame of saplings and sticks. The compound was surrounded by a circular wall of cut thornbush the cattle were driven into at night to protect them from predators. I convinced Sekerot to go there and ask about a donkey.

After hobbling and setting the animals free to graze, I caught up with Sekerot talking to a withered old Maasai at his cattle corral. He lived there with his six wives, one cow dung house for each wife all arranged in a semicircle.

As is typical of elders, the old Maasai was leaning on his walking stick while inhaling a pinch of snuff. A blue and red striped blanket was thrown over his shoulder.

"This elder has a donkey for sale!" Sekerot said, smiling, surprised to have found one so easily. He was back in the game.

The old Maasai gave me a broken-toothed grin, then aimed his walking stick at a huge male donkey bogged ankle deep in the sloshing mud of his thorn corral. A sharp stick had been pushed through its nose and held in place by a loop of rusty wire, a brutal method used to control unmanageable bulls. Deep scars in the raw flesh around its ankles were from prolonged use of tight hobbles. The miserable jack eyed us with hatred.

"That donkey will kill us!" I groaned.

"No, no! This is a strong donkey!" Sekerot urged. "Look at those muscles. He can carry all our baggage, *hacuna matatta*, no problem!"

I was surprised at Sekerot's enthusiasm especially after his painful experience with Baby. "This thing will kick us to the moon!" I replied exasperated. "A wild jack from Mexico was the worst thing I ever tried to ride. It bloodied my schoolmate's nose and threw a farmhand to the top of the barn with the twitch still on! There is no way I'm touching this monster!"

Sekerot pleaded, extolling the donkey's virtues and pressuring me that it was the only one around. I sensed he was giving up again. We returned to camp with my insisting that with all the Maasai living near Suswa we would find others.

The next morning Sekerot searched again for a donkey, but returned empty-handed. We decided to move to a new area and try again.

We camped that afternoon several miles west at the base of Suswa volcano, under two acacia trees. Fresh green grass grew all around, and our horses, which had eaten only tough wild grass for the last six days, began grazing eagerly on the tender shoots.

Near sunset, Sekerot and I climbed a small volcanic mound next to our camp, an eroded satellite of Suswa some three hundred feet above the valley floor. From there we had a view over the emerald grassland that surrounded us, a green tapestry of Africa spotted with tan and white gazelles, flattop umbrella acacia trees, and a variety of cone-shaped volcanoes.

Red bare-earth circles marked old Maasai enkangs, while dark green patches were abandoned nitrogen-rich cattle corrals. Long lines of cattle moved slowly over the rich grazing land forming kaleidoscopic patterns in white, red, and black, while zebras striped black on white grazed, indifferent to the Maasai livestock. Barking stallions reared, kicked, and lashed out with open jaws, competing for the peaceful herds of mares. An orange speckled

Our camp near the Suswa volcano.

giraffe stood with its head down next to a dark acacia forest, a sign that the day was over.

At dusk musical sounds drifted over the plains, clanking cowbells and the birdlike whistling calls of Maasai layoni shepherding their fathers' herds back toward the safety of the enkang before nightfall released the predators.

It was as close to paradise as one could find on earth, one whose intimacies were known best to wild creatures, or to the Maasai who had given meaningful names to each mountain, hill, and stream. It was essential Africa, through and through.

We awoke the next morning to find two curious giraffes staring at our horses. Neither the wild animals nor the Maasai had seen horses before, and they often gathered for hours at camp to watch our every move.

A Maasai elder squatting at our breakfast fire asked Sekerot if Katy and Houdini were a type of zebra. Sekerot laughed, then led him to where

Maasai layoni at sunset.

Katy was grazing, but the old man would not get close, and every time Katy moved, he stumbled backward, afraid.

I spent the morning climbing Suswa, known to the Maasai as Ol Doinyo Onyoke, the Red Volcano. Long ago volcanic outpourings eroded to form the red earth of the Rift Valley, a fine siltlike material that during the dry season blows up into great dust devils that spin across the parched plains coloring everything in sight a rusty red.

We followed a ridge up the steep slope to a plateau on the rim at about seventy-seven hundred feet. The gaping caldera was five miles across, and one side of it had blown out long ago leaving a long, ramping entry into the interior of the volcano. A monolithic lava island, known as the Lost Land, rose from the center of the crater where the Maasai had constructed an enkang. Many caves and lava tubes coursed through the walls of Suswa. I was told that long ago there was a *liabon*, a Maasai prophet, at Suswa who had used them for ceremonial purposes.

That afternoon, Houdini slipped loose of her hobbles and galloped off back in the direction of Lake Naivasha. When she disappeared from sight across the open grassland without showing any signs of slowing down, I panicked.

I quickly saddled Katy and took off in Houdini's direction at a fast gallop but eventually lost her tracks in a thicket of thornbush. A depressing sensation of defeat came over me as I realized that I might have to go back to Naivasha to catch Houdini. That could take four or five days, and without my presence and determination the whole safari would probably fall apart.

Katy was whinnying frantically for her companion, so I let the reins go and trusted her instinct. She took off at a gallop but to my surprise not in the direction of Naivasha.

We galloped for several miles until we reached the village of Empash, Katy whinnying loudly all the way. A large crowd of Maasai was gathered in a tightly packed circle in front of one of the *dukas*, a small Indian-run supply store found all over Kenya. They had surrounded Houdini but were afraid to touch her. They didn't see us coming, and when Houdini suddenly answered Katie's call, they all jumped back. The Maasai were terrified of her every move.

Houdini calmed down when she saw Katy and allowed me to tie a lead rope to the halter. With Houdini in tow, I rode back to camp, relieved to have once again escaped disaster.

Sekerot returned to camp later that day without finding any donkeys to buy; however, accompanying him were two Maasai junior elders willing to join our safari.

Ole Samyo was a thin, shy, and unusually short Maasai, an unlikely candidate for the arduous trip we planned. He did, however, carry the heavy iron spear of a warrior, a three-foot-long blade joined by a short wood grip to an iron butt of similar length. Weighing five pounds, it was a lethal weapon that could easily penetrate the tough hide of a Cape buffalo or elephant.

Young Maasai warriors proved their bravery by killing a lion with their spear, impaling it on the blade as it leaped onto them. The bravest of them cut off the tail beforehand with a sword, which gave them a high status in the ranks of warriors.

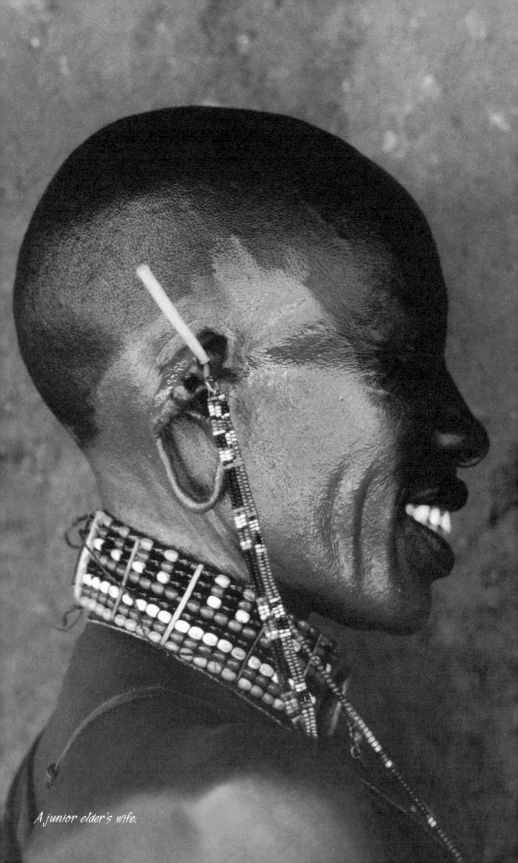

A junior elder's wife.

When Ole Samyo admitted he had never seen a lion, much less killed one, Sekerot laughed so hard that Samyo was embarrassed and threatened to go home. He confessed shamefully that he had never seen an elephant either, since they had disappeared from Suswa years ago.

Samyo's earlobes had been pierced and stretched by wooden disks to the size of an orange, typical of Maasai. He had them looped over his ears for safekeeping. He wore a faded blue and white checkered *shuka*, a rectangular piece of cloth tied in a knot over one shoulder, and a second red and white shuka tied over the other. Beneath that he was bare. A rawhide belt helped keep the shukas from flying open, but Maasai men were proud of their bodies and had no shame about nakedness.

His belt also held a *semi*, a short, broad-bladed, double-edged Roman-style sword, and a *rungu*, a wooden club with a baseball-sized knob on one end. A slender orange gourd containing milk and a red cotton blanket over his shoulder completed all that a Maasai needed for a safari. He would be able to refill his gourd with cow's milk along the way.

I liked Samyo but felt that he would be useless if we encountered dangerous wild animals.

Julius was an aggressive, strongly opinionated Maasai, loud and hard to control. He bragged readily of his bravery as a *moran,* a warrior, saying he had killed five lions; however, it was not clear to me if he was brave enough to run off the lion that might come at night to investigate our horses. He, too, had never seen an elephant, but he enjoyed frightening Samyo by describing how really big and ferocious they must be.

His hair was coal black and curly, cut to one inch with a standard double-edged razor blade. Unlike most Maasai, who have almost no face or body hair, Julius sported a mustache of just a few curly dark hairs. A pencil-sized red plastic rod pierced the top of his left ear and a heavy copper earring hung in the lower lobe. He wore a red and white checkered shuka and carried an elder's walking stick. With only a rungu and a blanket, he seemed ill prepared.

Samyo and Julius both had the typical Maasai tribal markings: missing lower incisors, dilated earlobes that could be worn looped over the top of their ears, and circular burn scars on their legs. Hard calluses on their toes and feet were from wearing rough sandals made of automobile tires. Blue, red, and white beaded bracelets finished them out as typical Maasai junior elders.

Although the normal Maasai diet consisted almost exclusively of cow's milk with an occasional feast on meat and blood when there was a ceremony, we had brought along a supply of cornmeal for them to make the mush called *ugali*. On a pound or two of hot porridge each per day they would be happy and feel they were eating like kings. Sekerot and I were surviving on MREs of only two choices, chicken or beef.

After searching Suswa for six days, Sekerot finally located two untrained and irascible male donkeys. Stronger and larger than Mamma and Baby, they were owned by a clever Maasai who extracted twice the price we paid at Naivasha. Fat, tough, and with ears split down the middle, or notched, in the Maasai method of branding, they had powerful muscles and indomitable bull-like personalities. We named them Tank and Jaws. Two weeks after leaving Naivasha, our journey into Africa was finally beginning. ◉

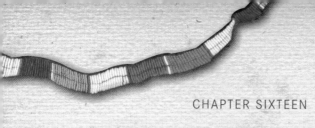

CHAPTER SIXTEEN

Set Free

At sunrise we broke camp at Suswa. Sekerot and I loaded the four donkeys, packing the heaviest loads on the big males before turning them over to Julius and Samyo. Waving spear and rungu, they began driving them forward. Sekerot and I saddled Katy and Houdini and set off at a gallop across the grassland studded with flowers. With the crisp morning air stinging our faces, we began laughing hysterically from the exhilarating sensation of finally being set free in Africa.

By early afternoon we rounded the western side of Suswa, then turned our caravan south toward our ultimate goal, Lake Natron in Tanzania. We had no idea how long it would take us to get there. We never thought in those terms, only that the country ahead was unknown to any of us, and every step forward was a new adventure.

Katy and Houdini stopped suddenly, ears forward as if they had picked up an unknown scent. Their gaze shifted to a zebra stallion that was barking to alert his harem of our strange animals.

The floor of the rift was beginning to slope off in a slow three-thousand-foot descent to Lake Magadi, thirty miles away. The delicate emerald grassland with its quintessential giraffe-trimmed umbrella acacias slowly gave way to a dry, rugged terrain. Sekerot said the thornbush farther south was dense and impenetrable, and even Maasai cattle did not go there. So we turned west toward the edge of the Rift Valley before Loita Hills.

The country grew wilder, and when we approached dense bush I began popping the bullwhip to warn Cape buffalo and lions that we were coming.

Our camp under the yellow-bark acacias.

The worst possibility would be to surprise them; then they would be more likely to attack.

That night we camped next to a small stream under the broad canopies of yellow-bark acacia trees. A Maasai enkang was on a hill nearby and a crowd of around forty women, naked children, and elder men in red, white. and blue striped blankets soon formed a semicircle around us. We needed to be careful, they said, a large pack of hyenas had been threatening their livestock.

Sekerot tied the donkeys to the trees behind our tent for safety, but when he turned around, Baby took her long-awaited revenge by kicking him solidly with both hooves on the buttocks. He crawled moaning to the tent, where he lay without speaking for the next half hour. Later that night I heard the cracking of tree limbs as Sekerot gave Baby a lesson on manners. Afterward, whenever he came near Baby, she held her back foot up for him to inspect.

Sekerot and I bedded down in my small tent, while Julius and Samyo rolled up in their blankets by a fire next to the horses. For the first time, we heard a lion roar far away. Then the fire crackled as Samyo and Julius threw on extra wood. A strange, Tarzan-like yodeling call came from the hill, a signal, Sekerot said,

Katy and Houdini safely corralled at Engare Siapel enkang.

of Maasai warriors approaching an enkang at night. I snuggled down in my sleeping bag, said a prayer of thanksgiving, and fell soundly asleep.

In the morning we rode through Noolpopong, a rolling hill country named by the Maasai for the many tree-size candelabra euphorbias that grew there. Then we marched across Ongado Nado, the Long Plain, to camp at a remote enkang on the edge of a rock cliff overlooking the Engare Siapel River, the Unknown River.

The elders came out to greet us but were so afraid of our horses that when Katy snorted, one of them fell backward on the ground. They were quite accustomed, however, to the forty elephants and the many lions that they said lived in the area. Hyenas had eaten their donkeys, so they offered our animals the safety of their heavily constructed pole-walled corral for the night.

A Maasai boy from the Engare Siapel enkang.

The next day we followed an old trail littered with footprints of baboons, monkeys, buffalo, and giraffes. Once, we lost the path completely and wandered about until we heard the shrill whistling of layoni shepherding cattle; but when the two boys saw our horses coming toward them, they ran screaming with fright into the forest.

Sekerot galloped after them on Katy shouting in Maasai that we were friends, but when he finally caught up, they froze speechless, shaking with fear. About twelve years old, they wore ivory earlobe plugs and ocher-stained cowskins. Both carried lightweight iron spears and were expected to kill any lion that threatened their father's cattle.

Late in the afternoon we forded the Engare Siapel, a fifty-foot-wide, slow-flowing body of milk chocolate. The donkeys refused to enter the water no matter how much we threatened them, and limber switches hissing over their ears or the pop of the bullwhip did nothing. Sekerot, always creative, finally found a technique that gave them courage—poking the male in the testicles with Julius's walking stick.

We set up camp on short grass at the top of the riverbank, then constructed a strong thornbush enclosure for the horses and a second one for the four donkeys. Having been told by Maasai at the enkang that lions were in the area, Samyo and Julius gathered a huge pile of dead hardwood. By nightfall an unusually large wazungu-style fire was blazing. The night was cold, and we gathered around it to keep warm.

Layoni stretching earlobe with wooden plug.

"If a lion comes, I will kill it!" Julius bragged, laughing with a nervous energy. He grabbed Samyo's spear and held it over his head in a throwing position, his sinuous body arching forward, tense as a drawn bowstring. With a thud that shook the earth, he stabbed the iron butt into the ground near the fire.

Julius was good with a spear—I had seen him practicing at Suswa—but Sekerot and I were suspicious of his bragging. He was loud and at times obnoxious.

Samyo, on the other hand, was clearly afraid and admitted it. Julius, who enjoyed scaring him with stories of wild animals, made it worse.

Sekerot insisted that he himself was completely fearless. He told Samyo and Julius of the many times he had run off lions as a layoni while guarding his father's cattle, and how he had spent many long nights awake in the cold rain huddled beneath a single cowskin should a predator come.

I could not stand the thought of a lion killing and eating one of our horses just outside our tent. So I had brought the bullwhip and trained Sekerot how to use it. Sekerot said he was not afraid of lions and would do it, hacuna matatta. However, both Sekerot and I had run like scared rabbits once when we thought a leopard was chasing us. One thing for sure, I was not going out of the tent at night armed with a bullwhip to face a lion. I thought we were all afraid.

"Once I was almost killed by a lion" I confessed, pausing to throw another piece of wood into the fire. "It was my first time in Africa, and I had never seen a lion in the wild. It was hot and I had to empty my bladder, so I got out of the car and started walking toward a bush, unzipping my fly. Suddenly the bush exploded, and I saw two big, yellow eyes flying toward me in a cloud of dust. It was so quick I froze."

Sekerot laughed. Samyo and Julius were standing motionless in the orange glow of the fire, staring at me in disbelief.

"The lioness landed on the ground in front of me," I continued, "skidding to a stop with paws out, sand stinging my face. I just stood there, holding my zipper and staring into those big yellow eyes. She was so close I could have touched her nose."

The Maasai layoni who was frightened by our horses.

I stood up closer to the fire. "At first she seemed as surprised as I was. Then she straightened up on all four legs and began madly lashing her tail and roaring loudly, a powerful deep-throated sound that seemed to vibrate everything and was deafening. For both of us the moment of shock and indecision was passing quickly, and she was not backing off. Still holding my fly, I tiptoed backward around the car and got in."

After pausing to stir the fire and check Samyo's frightened face, I continued. "The window was open, and she put her head up to it and continued to roar. I began laughing uncontrollably and so hard I could not roll up the window. So I just sat there with the lioness's face in the window staring at me and roaring while I laughed. Finally, she got bored and went away, but my adrenaline level did not go down for several hours. I had never felt so acutely alive."

Samyo and Julius were standing by the fire, quiet.

"Samyo, what will you do if a lion comes?" Sekerot taunted him with a grin.

"He will run away!" Julius laughed before Samyo could say anything.

Samyo took his spear from Julius and impaled it on his side of the fire. "I will not run," he said, looking down so we could not see his face.

It started drizzling rain, so Sekerot and I retired to our tent. Julius and Samyo built the fire higher and hunkered down under the shelter of an overhanging tree limb. Rain clouds shut out the stars, and a long night set in, wet and cold.

Then lions started to roar, three males Sekerot said, down by the river fewer than one hundred yards away. Sekerot was unconcerned, saying they were on the other side of the water, but I had no idea how he would know that.

The Maasai seemed to have an incredible instinct about animals, as if their senses were tuned to a higher sensitivity. I had once stood by two Maasai who were discussing a buffalo on a faraway hill. With binoculars I could see only a small black form. I had learned to trust the Maasai about wild animals and nature in general.

The chatter at Samyo and Julius's camp ceased, and I heard wood splintering as they built up the fire. Sekerot giggled as he imitated Samyo's high-pitched almost effeminate voice and imitated them shaking with fear as they struggled to drag impossibly huge logs to the fire. Then Sekerot rolled over in his sleeping bag and was sound asleep.

The lions continued, louder and more persistent, deep throaty echoes that vibrated the very walls of the riverbank. It wasn't the nostalgic, mournful call of a faraway lion, but a terrifying sound, enraged and powerful, so close that it caused me to shrink deep inside my sleeping bag. I lay awake wondering if they had crossed the river, our only real protection, and worrying if Samyo and Julius would be OK.

The drizzle became a downpour, drowning out the lions; then it receded, and the roaring started again, sounding more irritated than before. I could not sleep and took a Valium carried for emergencies. I did not want the trip to end in the bloodbath that three male lions could cause, not on this black, miserable, rainy night in a remote camp. And worse, what if they attacked Julius and Samyo? I tossed and turned, unable to sleep, and for the first time no longer felt safe in a tent.

The lions continued roaring until just before sunrise. When I unzipped the tent door, Julius and Samyo were standing there shivering from cold and fright.

"I am going home," Samyo said, his jaw clenched.

Julius had a firm grip on Samyo's spear. He was shaking and laughing nervously at the same time. "They were just down there!" he said excitedly, jabbing the spear point in highly animated motions toward the riverbank.

"It was not the nostalgic call of a faraway lion, but a terrifying noise, enraged and powerful."

Sekerot sat up in his sleeping bag. "Those lions were hungry!" he said laughing with a big pearly white grin. He had slept well, having heard lions roaring almost every night of his life. However, like Samyo and Julius, I was shaken from the long night's events.

Samyo threw his blanket over his shoulder, gathered his spear, and prepared to start back to Suswa.

"You can't quit now!" I pleaded while struggling half dressed to get out of the tent door. "We're just getting started. You've got to go with us."

"He doesn't want to see an elephant!" Julius laughed nervously. "Yesterday we saw an elephant footprint down by the river. Samyo didn't believe it was an elephant, he said no animal could be that big. He is afraid to see how big they are."

Julius went on, shifting from leg to leg, excited and waving his arms dramatically as if trying to encircle a huge object. "It's bigger than a tree, or even a mountain!"

Sekerot and I pleaded with Samyo, saying he could turn back at the Nguruman escarpment, the place he feared most because of the many elephants in the forest there. We hoped that by then we could find another Maasai to replace him.

Shamed by his lack of courage, Samyo finally put down his spear. "When we get to that forest, I am going back to Suswa," he promised. ◎

CHAPTER SEVENTEEN

The End of the Trail

We had been traveling only ten miles or fewer per day, held back by donkey problems. The old African foot safaris, like that of Henry M. Stanley searching for Dr. David Livingstone in 1871, averaged around eight miles per day.

Stanley had been burdened with twenty-seven donkeys and 153 native porters necessary to carry six tons of supplies and equipment, most of which was cloth, beads, and copper wire needed to trade for food. In his book, *How I Found Livingstone,* he described how his donkeys had caused problems by running off the wrong way, dumping their packs, and falling on the ground. He wrote that this was "natural to the first 'little journey in Africa.'" He also had two horses and was warned that they would die from tsetse flies.

We rode into a country of desert dates, wild olive, and wait-a-bit bushes with reverse-curved thorns that grabbed and held anything brushing against them, thereby making you "wait a bit" before you could come undone. The horses avoided the painful hooks, but the donkeys took great pleasure in racing into them, daring us to come in and try to extract them.

The largest male donkey, Jaws, purposely veered off the trail into a thornbush, becoming hopelessly entangled. Our caravan ground to a halt. Sekerot tried to pull him out by the back leg, but the baggage slid off and fell beneath his belly.

Ticks plagued us by sucking blood inside our horse's ears, and dropping into our baggage from bushes. They often kept Sekerot and me awake at night, pulling them off of our bodies and throwing them out of the tent.

We forded the Engare Narok, the Black River, then Julius drove the donkeys the wrong way and we were lost for two hours. The loads fell off, and while we were repacking, the donkeys succeeded in kicking both Julius and Sekerot. Just another day on our "little journey in Africa."

Two days later we wandered onto an open grassland, the Loita plain, burned crisp in the sun and grazed down to golf-course levels by herds of white-bearded wildebeests. We trekked across the dusty plain scattering herds of zebras and Thomson's and Grant's gazelles. Gray-feathered female ostriches and black-and-white plumed males with red necks that resembled raw flesh, stood by watching our caravan struggle under the harsh midday sun.

Only a year before, there had been a *manyatta* built there, a temporary ceremonial village of two hundred enkajis.

After three more days trekking and camping on the open plain, we came to the beginning of the Loita Hills, a rock escarpment known to the Maasai as Naeni-Nkujit. When making a pilgrimage to the chief liabon, the spiritual leader and prophet of the Maasai, they leave a bundle of tied grass on top of the escarpment to signify that all things evil were left behind.

We ascended Naeni-Nkujit over a narrow trail of hard rock and through chalky dust sprinkled with flecks of mica that left our footprints sparkling gold in the afternoon sun. Then we entered a highlands strewn with wildflowers, pink and white morning glories, black-eyed susans, and fragile violet hibiscus on delicate stems.

Near the end of the day the trail finally ended, and our caravan came to a halt. On one side was Ol Doinyo Loolacho, Mountain of the Calves. At nine thousand feet, it was the highest mountain of Loita Hills. On the other was the rugged escarpment of the Rift Valley dropping precipitously three thousand feet to the valley floor, too steep to descend. Straight ahead was the beginning of a forest that was virgin and undisturbed, and there was no known trail through it.

I had first heard of the forest two years before from the son of a liabon of Loita Hills. He said the forest was dangerous and the Maasai do not go there, afraid of an animal he described as a unicorn. Long ago, however, the Maasai had fled there to hide during a tribal war. A young girl was lost and never found, so they called it Naimina Enkiyo, Forest of the Lost Child.

In the forest, he said, were sacred trees of immense size, strangler figs and podocarpus, where the Loita laibons communed with Enkai, the Maasai God. There they healed the sick, cured the barren, and gave sacrifices to Enkai to make the warriors brave.

Simon Ole Makallah, a senior game warden of Maasai Mara, had told me that forest was like the tropical forests of Congo, something seemingly impossible for Kenya. It was unexplored, and he had once gone there to look for the strange animal the Loita Maasai talked about.

Last enkang before Forest of the Lost Child.

A retired white hunter I had met called it "magical." He and the warden had said it was dangerous because of the aggressive buffalo that lived in its shadows and marshes. To reach Lake Natron, we would have to find our way through the forest.

We found the last Maasai enkang before entering the Forest of the Lost Child. Occupying the top of a small hill, it resembled more a walled fortress than the usual thornbush enclosure. A clear spring bubbled up at the base of

Katy and Houdini frighten the villager's of Pesi's enkang.

the hill in a forest of yellow-bark acacias, and as we started to unload there, a large, heavily muscled Maasai came down from the enkang.

"Sopa," he greeted us. Parsimei Ole Pesi was a junior elder of the Loita clan, married with three children. The enkang belonged to his father who had settled there three years before after migrating with his cattle from higher up in the Loita Hills. Unlike most graceful, storklike Maasai, Ole Pesi was bulky in the chest and thighs. He was also not the typical chocolate or brown but black; however, his skin was smooth and hairless, like that of all Maasai.

Sekerot asked Pesi if he knew a trail through the forest ahead of us.

"There is no trail," he warned. "Maasai do not go to that forest." He spit and hit the ground with his walking stick. "Enkuku Naibor is there!"

Enkuku Naibor, the white beast, was allegedly a zebra-striped creature that attacked and killed people. It was the dangerous animal I had been told of previously.

"Have you seen Enkuku Naibor?" I asked.

"Yes, when I was a moran. It was standing in a clearing at the edge of the forest. It disappeared quickly."

No respectable Maasai would admit fear; however, I had listened to their campfire stories and knew that many were truly afraid of the forest and of the white beast. I felt immediately comfortable with Pesi, more so than with Julius or Samyo. When I asked if he would go with us into the forest, he responded, "I will follow you into hell as long as my stomach is full!" then jammed his spear forcefully into the ground.

Sekerot laughed and glanced at me with a smile, "Hell is not a Maasai concept!"

Sekerot and I were happy with Pesi's immediate decision. He said he would be ready to leave in the morning and would bring one of his own donkeys to ease the work of ours.

Daybreak came cold and wet, grass dripping with dew and a thick gray fog hanging in the trees. Snuggled in my tent beneath the yellow-bark acacias, I awoke to the peaceful sounds of clanging bells and lowing cattle being driven by the layoni down the hill from the enkang corrals.

Ropes, saddles, sheepskins, crates of food, and supplies lay scattered across the wet grass. Several moran armed with spears and rungus were warming themselves by our fire, smoldering with wet wood. The donkeys were grazing nearby, but as the sun rose and the fog began to lift, they moved deeper into the bush.

While I raked coals from the fire to prepare a pot of coffee, Sekerot led the two mares from our makeshift thorn corral, fastened the hobbles around their ankles, and released them near the stream to graze.

"Beel . . . Beel . . . ," Julius called out for me as he left the enkang and wobbled down the hillside toward our camp. He stumbled then slipped on a section of wet grass and fell hard. He stood back up with difficulty, but his blanket slid from his shoulders, exposing his naked body to the cold air. The young warriors around the fire laughed. Julius attempted to cover himself but had trouble coordinating his blanket, rungu, and his state of intoxication. He changed direction, and with an unsteady gait arrived at the campfire.

"Julius," I said in an impatient tone, "we've been waiting on you to help us pack the donkeys. Now they have wandered off somewhere. You and Samyo go find them and bring them back. We've got to get going."

Julius ignored me and started stumbling back up the hill, mumbling "I left something at the enkang."

Sekerot was sipping coffee, sitting quietly with two moran on the gnarled trunk of a fallen yellow-bark acacia tree. They were all staring at me, watching to see what I would do.

"Sekerot," I said exasperated "I've had it with Julius. Every time we camp near an enkang he disappears and drinks honey beer all night, then delays us in the morning. Only two days ago we wasted time looking for him, then he was too drunk to help us pack the donkeys. We warned him. Let's just get going without him."

I began lining up the ropes and crates. Sekerot and Samyo disappeared into the bush to search for the donkeys. Thirty minutes later they returned with our split-eared beasts of burden. The empty stares and passive resistance of the donkeys added to my frustration.

Samyo held Mamma by the head while Sekerot adjusted the sheepskins and began loading crates of food onto her back. I caught Jaws, fastened the hobbles around his ankles, then padded the sheepskins over his withers. With effort I lifted and settled our two fifty-pound marine duffel bags filled with camping equipment over his back, but before I could cinch down the ropes, the unruly beast reared and lunged forward, then hopped away with his front feet still bound together. Baggage, ropes, and sheepskins lay tangled in a mess on the ground.

I noticed Julius had returned and had joined the crowd of Maasai that had come to watch us. They were joking around and laughing at our struggles.

"Julius!" I shouted. "I need some help. Come hold this donkey."

He turned his back and continued talking. I gave up trying to tow Jaws back to the fallen baggage and began counting out the money I owed Julius.

"Sekerot, give this to Julius and tell him he is finished." I handed the stack of Kenya shillings to Sekerot and felt a sadistic rush of pleasure. We were fed up with Julius's honey-beer binges and had discussed getting rid of him, but now that I was actually doing it, Sekerot appeared shocked. Julius drew a blank stare when Sekerot gave him the money, then grinned broadly at the large wad of paper Kenya shillings in his hand.

He rejoined his Maasai friends triumphant and I thought everything was all right, but then as he and others examined and reexamined the money he began to frown and started shouting, demanding more. I gave him another two days' pay, enough to cover the twenty-mile walk back to Narosura where he could hitchhike a ride home to Suswa. Julius stared at the extra shillings, then wanted more. He came toward me waving the money and shouting angrily.

I firmly refused to give Julius any more money and turned to continue packing the donkeys. It was tense, no one moving, everyone quiet waiting to see what Julius would do. Sekerot's face stiffened.

Sekerot was a fighter, and his friends said he was good at it. He had recently slugged a seasoned policeman unconscious in Nairobi. I did not want to see him tangle with Julius, not because Julius was bigger than Sekerot, but because Julius would fight dirty, using his semi or his club. And Sekerot would fight to the end.

Finally Julius quieted down and rejoined his warrior friends. They kept passing the shillings around, examining and reexamining them with puzzled expressions.

Sekerot laughed. "None of them can count!"

When Julius realized that he had to trust me to give him the correct amount, he came running furiously toward me again, shouting that I had cheated him. I almost felt sorry for him. He wasn't going to fight, the moment had passed, and he had embarrassed himself in front of the warriors. I gave him another two day's pay, then Sekerot and I just ignored him.

We finished packing the donkeys, released the hobbles, and turned them over to Pesi and Samyo. Although the elephants that Samyo so dreaded were now immediately ahead of us, he made no move to join Julius and return home. The sound of green switches hissing over the donkeys' ears said that we were moving off.

Sekerot and I mounted the horses, forded the small stream, and rode up the hill to Pesi's enkang. The enkang was set on a green meadow at the summit, enclosed by a stockade wall of cut poles eight feet high. The cattle were brought inside at night for protection, the entrance plugged with thornbush to keep out predators.

We found Pesi's father wrapped in a blanket sitting on his wooden stool near the gate, warming himself in the morning sun. At sunrise he always stood at the gate watching the cattle depart, giving instructions to the layoni and singing praises to Enkai for another day in paradise.

"The old men, even the moran, sing praises to Enkai," Sekerot said. "When the morning sun begins to warm the earth, Maasai feel joy to be alive."

That was a beautiful way to live, I thought, one that I envied. But their pastoral lifestyle made it a lot easier to see the beauty in nature and feel the presence of God than living a Western existence where time was money.

"All Maasai believe in God," Sekerot continued. "Enkai created everything, and is a good God. And when you die, there is no hell."

Sekerot dismounted to greet the old man. "Sopa, Ole Pesi . . . Sopa."

The old man smiled without rising from his stool. His withered skin and drawn face resembled that of an Egyptian mummy. Sekerot paid the

An unmarried Maasai girl.

Young Maasai bride.

respect due a Maasai elder by bending forward so Ole Pesi could place the palm of his hand over his head and receive his blessing. Then Sekerot asked of his cattle's health and of his many children and several wives.

Customary greetings over, we remounted and bent low over our horses' necks to pass through the tunnel-like entry into the stockade. The ground inside was bare of vegetation, cow dung compacted by hooves and human feet to a soft, brown carpet, several feet deep. The air smelled of earth and livestock.

The enkang was typical of a Maasai settlement. A protective stockade pole wall 8 feet high enclosed a circular space 150 feet across. After the cattle were brought inside at sunset, thornbush was used to seal the two entries to keep out predators. Many enkangs' outer walls were constructed entirely of thornbush instead of poles.

Inside were eight traditional enkajis, oval houses each the size of a large pickup truck with a slightly curved roof that made it not quite high enough to stand up when inside. The whole thing was constructed of bent saplings plastered over with cow dung and had to be constantly repaired during a rain.

Situated side by side along the inner wall of the stockade, the enkajis' oval doors faced the interior and were always open. Six of the houses were occupied by the wives of Ole Pesi's father, the other two by Ole Pesi and his wife. Inside the dung houses were typically one room with a fire hearth, a sleeping platform, and a small enclosure for baby goats. There were a few oval holes in the wall to let in light and to let out the smoke of the fire.

After several years, when the pastures become overgrazed or the enkang becomes too deep in dung, they migrated to another area as Ole Pesi had done.

In the middle of the compound a group of married women dressed in ocher-stained cowskins with round leather neck collars of red, white, and black beadwork were clustered together in a circle singing. One of them had worked herself into a frenzied fit and was rolling across the ground with others trying to restrain her. Sekerot said they were preparing to trek to the Loita Hills with cows for Mokombo, the head liabon and spiritual leader of the Maasai, in exchange for his blessings to make them fertile.

An unmarried teenage girl with long beaded earrings that hung down over her chest was staring at the horses from the shadows of an enkaji doorway. She seemed friendly, but when I started toward the oval entry, she quickly disappeared inside. Tying Katy to a pole, I stooped low and entered the doorway, then groped in the darkness along a curving passage.

On the earthen floor inside was a simple hearth, three blackened stones around glowing embers that bathed the cloistered interior with a warm orange glow. A shaft of white light came through an oval hole in the wall, illuminating specks of swirling dust. My eyes burned from acrid smoke that escaped through cracks in the cowdung roof. A stick-frame sleeping platform covered with a cowskin was on the far side, otherwise the room was bare.

The young girl was busy swirling hot embers around inside a milk calabash to sterilize it. She was unafraid and spoke to me softly in Maasai, but when she discovered I only knew a few Maasai words, she threw her head back laughing.

She had flawless caramel skin, full lips, a thin Nilotic nose, and a broad smile that radiated inner joy. Her dark eyes were widely open as if to take in all the love the world could offer.

I envied the carefree pastoral lifestyle of the Maasai, especially that of the children. During their teenage years the boys became warriors and until around thirty years of age enjoyed an unrestrained lifestyle of heroism and romance envied by Maasai of all ages and sex. But the transition to maturity for girls was abrupt, harsh, and at an early age.

Although it was common for premenstrual Maasai girls to enjoy uninhibited sexual freedom with age-mates and even warriors, after their first period signaled fertility they were brutally circumcised and married off to elders several times their age. Life then took on the monotonous drudgery of hauling firewood and water and the pain of frequent childbirth.

Sekerot said, however, that an unspoken custom allowed the young wives to have lovers, former boyfriends who as warriors freely roamed the countryside. When these men arrived at an enkang, they stuck their iron spear up by the enkaji door of a girlfriend notifying everyone that they were inside.

Although husbands did not like this, Sekerot said they would not challenge a warrior. So the old men retired to the house of one of their older wives and allowed the young couple their tender intimacies for a night. ◉

CHAPTER EIGHTEEN

Day of Horrors

"Ole sere, ole sere . . ." We said good-bye to Pesi's father, then rode through the opening on the far side of the wall. Outside the walls women were beginning their daily work, gathering fresh cow dung to repair leaking cracks, carrying loads of firewood on their backs, and hauling water from the stream. At the sight of the horses they screamed and ran for the safety of the enkang, followed by children crying with fright.

We pushed the horses into a slow gallop across the hilltop, the smell of fresh grasses and morning air perfumed with a thousand fragrances rushing over our faces. I let Katy's reins go, and she began to gain speed, neck stretched out and back flattening beneath the saddle. The sound of rushing wind and pounding hoofbeats drove her faster. Then her ears turned back against her head, and she bolted at full speed, an equine instinct honed by thousands of years of pursuit by predators.

Houdini spooked and took off also, so we let them run out of control, Sekerot and I laughing wildly from the all-out chase in the crisp morning air. At the end of the meadow I slowed Katy to a canter, but Sekerot veered off down the hill, unable to stop Houdini. They returned moments later, Houdini's nostrils dilated and blowing with Sekerot pulling desperately on the reins.

We located the hoofprints of the donkeys and tracked them through bush over our heads to find Samyo driving them alone. Pesi had gone back to the enkang for a final good-bye to his family.

"Sopa, sopa." Pesi joined us at a run carrying his blanket, a rungu topped by a shiny iron transmission gear from a truck, a Maasai sword, and a calabash of fresh milk—everything a Maasai needed. Pesi was someone I could rely on. He also brought one of his own donkeys, a large male, which I had agreed to rent. The extra donkey would allow us to reduce the loads, giving our four a chance to rest. The ropes, although padded by layers of sheepskins, were beginning to cause pressure sores on their backs.

The donkeys moved along at a snail's pace, despite continuous efforts to speed them up. Tank, our lead donkey, purposely veered into a thornbush and stopped. Before I could dismount, Jaws careened into a tree limb, scraping off his cargo. Two milk crates of food, pots, pans, and my folding stool hung upside down beneath his belly, the entire mess tangled in rope around his back legs. Sekerot and I were convinced the donkeys hated us.

In twenty-three days of donkey safari we had not traveled a single morning without having to stop because of a shifting load, falling baggage, or some other problem. We had given up lunch to march nonstop eight to ten hours a day to make time on the trail. Before stopping to camp, we had to locate a place for the horses to graze; otherwise, we continued into the night. In spite

In the Forest of the Lost Child.

of such Herculean efforts, the greatest distance as the crow flies covered in a single day had so far been only ten miles. Donkeywork was killing us.

Nineteenth-century African explorers had similar problems: festering sores, lack of proper packsaddles, tsetse flies, and wild animals wreaking havoc with their beasts of burden. One unfortunate donkey made it all the way to the Ituri rain forest with Henry M. Stanley, only to be eaten by the men who had brought it there. When I told Sekerot about that, he said with a grin, "It must have been a satisfying meal."

At midmorning we rode into a meadow of red oat grass speckled with red and yellow daises and trumpet-shaped white morning glories. Orange butterflies wafted about in the purified air over tall grass that was untouched by Maasai cattle. We were beyond their normal grazing grounds.

Here was a truly wild part of Africa, inhabited by Cape buffalo and elusive elephants that gouged red scars in the earth digging with their ivory for salt. Unlike animals protected inside a game reserve and accustomed to seeing people, they were afraid and would flee unseen. However, many of them had been speared by Maasai or shot by poachers and would attack.

A male impala with three-foot-long spiral horns trotted toward the safety of a thornbush thicket. Stopping short, his expressive wide eyes turned to stare at our horses. He snorted and shook his head as if to clear his nose of an insect, then bounded off, followed by eight doelike females. At the edge of the meadow, his harem suddenly spooked and exploded into spectacular leaps, then vanished into the forest of silver thorns.

Mint-green acacia trees growing in the meadow had had their limbs recently twisted and torn away, leaving long strips of white inner-cambium bark dangling from their mutilated trunks. Leading away from the destruction were two huge wakes plowed through the grass. The grass was still popping up in places, meaning the path was fresh. We followed until it vanished into the forest.

"That elephant is near, just there, inside the forest," Pesi pointed, then shifted his blanket higher on his shoulder. "I can hear him moving," he continued. "Many elephants live here, but they are afraid. They run into the forest."

"Pesi, have you ever seen the elephants?" I asked, shifting sideways in the saddle to face him.

"A month ago, near this place, I threw my spear into a big elephant. It made a loud noise and ran off into the forest, over there." He pointed again, using his rungu. "I ran after the elephant, but it was too fast for me." Pesi stopped and looked down with despair.

Sekerot laughed. "The elephant took your spear! That's why you did not bring one."

Pesi confessed that he had searched all day, but when he found it, the shaft was broken and the steel blade twisted and bent.

Samyo was nervous, holding tightly onto Mamma's rope halter. When Pesi indicated the size of the elephant by tapping high up on a tree trunk with Samyo's spear, he threatened to go back to Suswa.

Pesi did not say why he had speared the elephant. The Massai do not eat wild animals, and I knew it was either for sport, as a warrior might do, or to sell the ivory in the illegal market.

We continued across the meadow, passing oval beds where the grass had been pressed flat against the earth. Pesi stopped.

"A small herd of buffalo rested here last night," he indicated with his transmission gear club. "At sunrise they got up and went there, into the forest."

From a hilltop I saw the meadow ending at the edge of a forest where a profusion of yellow and orange wildflowers grew. As we rode closer it became a wall of tall trees, the tallest I had seen in Kenya, with huge spreading crowns, some in full tropical bloom—red-blossomed flame trees and white-flowered trees that filled the air with a sweet, cloverlike fragrance.

"It's Naimina Enkiyo," Pesi said, pointing ahead to the Forest of the Lost Child.

It was nearly noon with intense sunlight burning clouds of steam off the wet grasses. The air was thick and muggy, my clothes saturated with horse sweat. Our passage into the forest was blocked by a formidable tangle of bush, vines, and creepers grown together in a solid mass. Sekerot and I rode along the edge of the forest searching for an opening but returned, unsuccessful.

Pesi approached the impenetrable barrier cautiously, stopping to look and listen. Drawing his semi, he hacked into it once, then stepped back quickly. Sekerot and I remained mounted a safe distance behind while Samyo attended the donkeys, preventing them from wandering off. No one spoke; we knew the danger.

In dark edges of the forests, solitary Cape buffalo hide, waiting out the heat of the day. They lay up in the thickest bush, ticks plastered to the thin skin between their legs and inside ears, leaches sucking their tender throat membranes. Sick, aged, injured by a Maasai spear, or cast out of the herd by a stronger bull, they wait in an unrelenting state of misery, irritated and defiant.

They attack suddenly when unexpected and in full fury. Unlike any other animal they are intent on nothing less than total destruction. Even after they have killed, they continue to grind the victim's body with their sharp hooves or the hard boss of their horned head, until nothing is left but shreds and a moist spot on the ground.

Sekerot yelled and I cracked the bullwhip, hoping to awaken or run off any creatures ahead of us. I had a growing anxiety I always felt when entering dense bush in Africa, a primitive instinct that flared out of control, pouring adrenaline into my muscles, supercharging them to flee an unseen predator. The same apprehension had come over me in the Loita Hills two years before.

At the time it had seemed like a great adventure, myself and two friends from San Diego exploring Naimina Enkiyo on foot for a week. It was their first trip to Africa. But on the third day, things began to go wrong. One of the Maasai porters came down with malaria, my friend Joe was awake most of the night vomiting, and my other friend Robert had a fever. We were all exhausted from a sixteen-hour trek to the edge of the Nguruman escarpment the day before.

We had decided to end the safari and were on our way back across the Loita Hills, walking in single file. A meadow led us to a narrow corridor between two forests. I was following Ole Supeti, our Maasai guide, Joe and Robert behind me, followed by our four porters. It was a beautiful day to be alive and on foot in Africa.

I heard the sharp crack of a tree limb breaking, then saw muscles tense in Ole Supeti's back as his spear rose above his shoulder. A low bellow came from just inside the forest on my right, and as I turned to run, a huge black form filled my field of vision. Then the buffalo was galloping after me, and I was running full out for my life. In my mad dash across the meadow, the anticipation of sharp horns slamming through my back was for a moment replaced by an uncontrollable urge to laugh, the kind of laughter that one feels when waterskiing over a wake at impossible speeds or galloping flat out across

an open field. Then with one great leap, I landed safely seven feet up in the fork of a tree.

I scanned the meadow below, then heard the bellowing noise again and to my horror saw the buffalo chasing Joe around a clump of saplings too small to climb. Back and forth they went, first one way, then another. Joe was slowing from exhaustion. I screamed for the Maasai to use their spears and distract the buffalo.

Two spears were thrown into the buffalo's hindquarter, but when he spun around to chase after the Maasai, the spears fell out. Joe sprinted desperately across the meadow toward my tree, but the buffalo saw his escape and gave up pursuing the Maasai. He caught up with Joe at full gallop in the middle of the meadow. At the moment he lowered his horns, Joe's legs gave way, and he fell facedown in the grass. The horns missed their mark and a ton of hoofed destruction passed over his body.

The buffalo spun around just as Joe got to his feet. He slammed headfirst into Joe's chest, tumbling him backward and breaking his spine. Wheeling around, the buffalo came at a gallop, horns skimming the grass. He hit Joe violently throwing him fifteen feet in the air to land at the base of my tree.

Again the buffalo hit Joe, lifting him on his horns and tossing him into a bush; then he was on top of him, pounding with the ironlike piles of horn that grew over the front of his head. Over and over the buffalo bashed into Joe,

thrusting his head from side to side, trying to gore him with the curved tips of his horns. Joe stopped screaming. He was covered with blood, silent and still.

Robert got out of our tree and moved cautiously toward the buffalo, pausing each time the featureless brown eye left Joe to stare at him. Then, when Robert was less than ten feet away, the buffalo came after him, bellowing as he chased him around the base of our tree.

At that moment Joe regained consciousness and moved his leg. Immediately the buffalo left Robert and started for Joe again. I took a heavy marine duffel bag from a Maasai higher in the tree and threw it onto the buffalo's head. He attacked it furiously, smashing it into the saplings. During the distraction, Joe crawled toward the base of our tree and Robert lifted him up. I pulled him into the fork of the tree, then Robert climbed up and held Joe's limp body.

> A Maasai had told me that a buffalo would wait you out, for days, until dehydration or exhaustion finished you.

When the buffalo discovered his prey missing, he frantically searched the area below. Then he saw Joe up in the tree with us and furiously rammed his horns into the trunk below our feet, over and over, sending chunks of bark flying.

Joe began to vomit, spewing yellow liquid over the buffalo's face and horns only inches below our feet. Then Joe turned pale and lost consciousness. I cut tree limbs with a semi and made a platform in the tree to lay Joe down. He regained consciousness but was unable to move. A quick exam showed Joe had not been gored, but was covered in blood from the buffalo's spear wounds.

An hour passed, or two; it was impossible to have any true sense of time. A grass fire swept up the hill, tall yellow flames passing beneath our tree, licking the trunk and causing us to move higher. The previously green meadow was transformed into a blackened battlefield seething with clouds of acrid smoke. And when it had burned its way through and the smoke cleared, below our tree among the smoldering clumps of tussock grass stood the buffalo, unmoved, staring up at us and waiting.

A Maasai had told me that a buffalo would wait you out, for days, until dehydration or exhaustion finished you. Despite yelling for our Maasai to spear the buffalo, they refused to help us. Ole Supeti shouted to the others not to risk their lives for us wazungu.

Finally Ole Supeti's son came down from a tree some distance away. He broke into a short trot across the meadow and launched a spear into a perfect Olympic javelin trajectory, arcing seventy-five feet through the air. With a hissing thud the heavy iron spear sank three feet into the buffalo's chest. After twenty minutes the animal weakened and lay down. A second spear was thrown into its chest, then with a solid "crack" of steel hitting bone, one of the Maasai hamstrung the monster with his semi.

I ran through the forest and across miles of tall grass until finally reaching the enkang where we had left the Land Rover. Then I drove recklessly back to the tree, zigzagging around termite mounds and praying not to hit a warthog hole that would take off the axle.

After sixteen hours of anxiety and stress, careening over potholed dirt roads with a dangling shock absorber and a broken spring, we arrived in Nairobi in the middle of the night. Joe was alive but in severe pain. A broken spine without paralysis seemed a blessing. For a time after that day of horrors, I hated Africa and thought I would never return. ◉

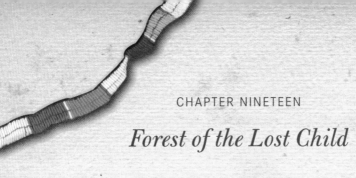

CHAPTER NINETEEN

Forest of the Lost Child

Pesi emerged from the dark tunnel he had chopped into the forest, sweat dripping from his forehead. We drove the donkeys forward, disappearing one by one into the black hole. The air inside was cool and moist with the smell of fresh earth, a welcome relief from the bright sunlight and suffocating heat outside. The dense canopy, nearly 150 feet overhead, created a twilit, tomblike silence. Deep shade stunted the growth of underbrush, and instead of claustrophobia, there was an unexpected open, airy feeling.

Sekerot and I mounted the horses and rode behind the donkeys, moving silently beneath columnar giants with plank buttresses and immense strangler figs that embraced tropical hardwood trees in a choke hold. Walking ahead of us, Pesi hacked away the long vines that hung down to entangle the donkey's baggage.

We discover the elephants' trail, a broad avenue that led to a stream lined by head-high bundles of papyrus. Potholes left in the mud by the elephant's huge feet were slowly filling with water, indicating their recent passage. Fresh mounds of warm dung the size of soccer balls lay in piles.

The horses waded in to drink, then we moved on. Broken tree branches hung across the trail blocking our way, left there by the elephant that was feeding somewhere just ahead of us. Periodically we heard the sharp snap of a limb breaking or a tree splintering.

Pesi halted. "A small herd of elephants just passed this way," he said, studying several platter-sized leathery imprints. "They are keeping a distance ahead of us."

We followed the elephant path out of the forest into rolling grasslands, hills spotted with tender mint-yellow acacia trees—perfect browse for an elephant. To my surprise, they were nowhere to be seen.

"The elephants are hiding, watching us," Pesi said. "They are so big, but they disappear easily."

From the crest of a hill we had a faraway view of what lay ahead, miles and miles of forest in variegated shades of green, broken by brilliant splashes of the red and white of tropical trees in bloom. We continued south, crossing deep valleys with cathedral-like forests whose rushing streams cut narrow clefts in the escarpment wall.

Just as the sun disappeared, a lion roared far away, a descending set of hoarse utterances echoing throughout the hills. We watered our horses at a shallow stream that rushed over rocks and smoothly worn stones, filling the forest with a tinkling musical sound. As we hurried to set up camp on some nearby grass, the air turned cold, clouds formed overhead, and drops of rain began to fall.

Sekerot and I joined Pesi and Samyo squatting around a fire near the horses' picket line. It was too dark to build a thorn enclosure, so our animals were tied up, unprotected. Again the lion roared, a hollow groan that seemed neither far nor near.

"Are you afraid of the lion?" Sekerot asked Samyo. He looked away, avoiding Sekerot. Although I knew he had never seen a lion or an elephant, I was shocked when Samyo pointed to a herd of wildebeests on the Loita plain and asked what kind of animals they were.

"Pesi, tell me about the white zebralike beast, Enkuku Naibor," I asked.

Pesi seized his rungu lying on the ground beside him and stood up. "I saw it with my own eyes!" he said emphatically.

Samyo shifted nervously around the fire.

Pesi's voice grew tense, his body animated as he dramatized the start of his story by spitting on the ground and bashing it with his rungu.

"We moran were at an *olpul* [a secret camp for warriors] in that forest and saw many strange animals. Three of us were hunting with spears and saw an old man, white like a wazungu, very old and with long white hair and big ears. He was taller than we moran and completely naked."

Pesi shifted his red checkered blanket farther back over his shoulder.

"His body was covered with hair. One leg was a sharp stump that left holes in the ground when he walked. At first we thought he was some kind of an animal, but he began making ropes from tree bark and setting traps. He caught a bushbuck and ate it without cooking the meat, ripping off big pieces of flesh with his hands."

Pesi reached for Samyo's spear, stuck upright by the fire, and began to crouch and move around the fire imitating the wild creature.

"He moved slowly, like a madman, walking straight through bushes, pulling them up and throwing them aside. One *morani* wanted to kill him

Wildebeests on the plain at sunset.

with his spear, but we held him back. We were afraid to follow him because he walked so close to the elephants, like they were nothing."

With an emphatic thud, Pesi sank the steel shaft of the spear into the wet ground and sat down again by the campfire. Resting his elbows on his knees he stared into the flames. Samyo shrank away, frightened.

"Let's go into Naimina Enkiyo and search for Enkuku Naibor and the hairy wazungu," I suggested, expecting a response out of Samyo.

"It was not a wazungu," Pesi insisted looking at me with big eyes, "he was some kind of a creature! Maasai call him Nenauner."

Samyo pulled his blanket tightly around him. "I am not going any farther."

"Ole Samyo are you, a Maasai, afraid of Enkuku Naibor and the old white man?" Sekerot challenged him.

Ole Samyo sharpening his spear.

Samyo looked away, to the darkness. "I am leaving in the morning."

Pesi turned toward Samyo with a grin. "You will have to go back through the forest. Will you walk through Naimina Enkiyo alone?"

Sekerot and I held our faces, almost laughing out loud. Pesi went to check the horses, and Sekerot and I retired to our tent, leaving Samyo sitting by the fire, lonely and miserable.

The African night took over, a wax-and-wane trill chorus of cicadas and tree frogs, the resonant "rurr, rurr, rurr" of colobus monkeys settling themselves in the trees behind our tent, and the hypnotic gurgle of water rushing over stones in the forest.

"Samyo is really afraid," Sekerot whispered. "He believes Enkuku Naibor will get him."

We pulled our sleeping bags over our heads, trying to muffle the laughter. Every time we thought of Samyo sitting alone by the fire, we giggled until our stomachs ached.

Far away the lion roared, wet and forlorn. We laughed at him too. Finally Sekerot was asleep, and the lion's roar faded away into the night. I felt badly that we had teased Samyo so much, as he was really afraid and felt alone.

"Coo coo . . . coo coo . . . coo coo." We awoke to the sound of a red-eyed dove, a soothing mother's lullaby sound that I identified with Africa. The colobus monkeys were creating confusion in the tree behind our tent with their clacking chorus, then they descended to water at the stream and moved off in search of food. As we packed the donkeys, zebras barked on a nearby hillside.

We saddled the horses and, with Pesi and Samyo driving the donkeys, started out following the ambling road of an elephant. The path led us to cross and recross heavily eroded streambeds, one of which had been deeply gouged out by tusks in search of salt. Loaf-sized piles of brown dung, dry and scattered on the white mineral-laden earth, were evidence that the elephant had not been this way in several days. Then we left the convenient trail and made our way cross-country over hills so rocky and steep that we had to dismount and clamber over them on foot to avoid damaging our horses' hooves.

Our camp at the Entosopia River.

At sunset we came to the edge of the escarpment and found a narrow, tree-filled canyon to set up camp. A clear-water stream flowed through the canyon, which Pesi called Entosopia, a Maasai word for clean, pure water. Ferns, lacy euphorbias, and other exotic plants hung from the precipitous canyon walls, thriving in water that dripped constantly down the rock faces and mists that blew off the falls. The roar of a waterfall echoed throughout the canyon, bouncing off rock walls and creating a constant din.

We set our tent on a bank of yellow quartz sand at the edge of the twenty-foot-wide stream, between a stand of head-high papyrus and the trunk of a giant podocarpus being encapsulated by a strangler fig. Sekerot led the horses into the waist-deep water, and we gave them a bath. The cold water seemed to soothe the tick and insect bites that I thought were causing white spots on their coats. We set them loose to graze, then followed the stream down to the roaring falls.

The Entosopia waterfall.

Black boulders held back the stream, but a broad sheet of swift water flowed over the top to fall thirty feet into a deep, olive-green pool where frothy white spray was spiraling upward. Sekerot and I stopped to swim in the pool and explore a small cave behind the waterfall, then continued downstream until the canyon walls narrowed enough for only one person. The stream was compressed between the walls and shot out through a slot with great force over the edge of the escarpment, where it fell cascading in a thunderous roar to the Rift Valley floor several thousand feet below.

Carefully I threaded my way into the narrow slot, and holding on to the rock wall, I made my way to the edge of the escarpment. Far below was an arid plain, shimmering in rising thermal currents and shrouded in a brown haze of dust. Twenty miles to the east I could see a white expanse of solid soda, the undrinkable caustic water of Lake Magadi.

Between Magadi and Natron lay the hottest terrain in the Gregory Rift, one of the most inhospitable places in Africa. It was one of the few places on earth so hot and dry that rain evaporated before it could reach the ground. The surface of Lake Natron had been measured at 150 degrees Fahrenheit. It was the rift's furnace, a place I both dreaded and found irresistible.

The Nguruman escarpment continued another twenty-five miles south to end in Tanzania, but the pounding of the horse's hooves on the rocks and boulders and the strain of traversing the steep riverine valleys had caused Katy to go lame. We decided to descend to the Rift Valley floor where the flat plain would be easier on the horses' fragile legs. But the intense heat, lack of water, and tsetse flies would test all of us to the limit.

Once off the escarpment we would be irreversibly committed to the dreaded valley, for until we reached Lake Natron, the escarpment was an unbroken steep rock wall two thousand to three thousand feet high and impossible for our animals to climb. I estimated that it would take us three days to reach the lake, but I knew of no source of drinkable water along the way. The horses would not survive the heat unless we found water. ◉

CHAPTER TWENTY

Cauldrons of the Earth

We rested two days at Entosopia, allowing the horses to graze and Katy's lame leg to heal. Sekerot and I enjoyed swimming in the pool at the bottom of the waterfall, but Pesi and Samyo did not like the cool, damp air of the canyon and were anxious to move on. Samyo was relieved that we were leaving the Forest of the Lost Child and Enkuku Naibor, but now he planned to quit and go home as soon as we reached Loita Hills.

We broke camp early and started leading the horses and donkeys down the rock cliff. Katy was limping badly on her left front leg and slowing our progress. She stopped in pain several times, and it was difficult to get her going again.

The scorching heat rose up from the Rift Valley and hit us like an open oven. Sekerot and I were dripping sweat, and the horses were lathering between their legs. Halfway down the escarpment, tsetse flies attacked the horses, leaving welts on their necks and bellies. With each sharp sting Katy swung her head around, yanking hard on the lead rope. For the first time I felt overwhelmed, confronted by the reality that our journey might end in disaster. I quickened the pace, hoping to move rapidly down the parched valley to Lake Natron and ascend the escarpment before things got worse.

At the base of the escarpment we found a spring. The heat was overwhelming, even lying in the springwater did not relieve the hammering of the sun's anvil in my head. We decided to camp by the water and start again in the early morning.

That night was sweltering hot, the ground burning beneath my tent. Malaria-carrying mosquitoes prevented me from sleeping outside, so I baked. Sleep evaded me, the anxiety of impending disaster almost unbearable. I no longer worried about water or my own survival. Tsetse flies would kill the horses, and the donkeys would soon follow. I had made a mistake bringing innocent animals here. My only thought was to quickly get to the end of the valley and reascend the escarpment.

At the first light of dawn I crawled out of the tent, head throbbing and exhausted from the unrelenting heat during the night. The sun had not yet risen, but the ground was still hot from the day before. The horses were standing motionless, covered in gray dust that pervaded everything—heads down, ribs showing, listless. There was no grazing anywhere, only dust and dry earth. It was a valley of death.

We started at sunrise, fiery rays already scorching the ground. We were leading both horses to make it easy for them. Katy limped forward in pain, throwing her head up with each short step. After four hours she gave up and would go no farther. Sekerot and I debated leaving her behind, a certain death. Time was our enemy, the risk of sleeping sickness from the tsetse fly was increasing with each stinging bite. West of us was the Ewaso Ngi'ro river, a source of water but two hours out of our way. We decided to risk all and try to get Katy there, rest for a day, and hope she might improve.

We camped on a steeply eroded bank overlooking the river, red with mud and silt. The grass was sparse, dry, and brittle, worthless nutrition for the horses. The next morning both horses were limping badly, ankles swollen above the hooves. They were also weak from weight loss. Our situation had worsened. We had no choice but to press on.

We started out again on foot, leading the horses and driving the donkeys before us. We were committed to a forced march, covering the remaining twenty-two miles to the border of Tanzania in one day. If Katy could not keep up, Sekerot and I had decided to leave her behind.

Sekerot and Pesi set a rapid pace. The horses suffered badly the first mile, but somehow Katy managed to stay with us. Nervously eyeing our caravan, a small herd of zebras raced across the dry plain, stirring up yellow clouds of dust that layered out suspended over the valley floor. The cloud drifted, sluggish as if paralyzed in the heat. Two miles to the west rose the three-thousand-foot wall of the Nguruman escarpment, blanketed along its summit by the tempting lush green forest of Naimina Enkiyo. We struggled down the hot valley, a madman and his accomplices walking into hell.

By late afternoon the valley had narrowed, and I realized we were near the unmarked border of Kenya and Tanzania. On the flat, empty plain ahead of us was a small patch of dust-covered acacia trees. We followed the trees to the base of the escarpment where Sekerot discovered a tiny stream of clear water flowing from higher up. Our immediate problem—water—was solved.

We set the animals free to graze on a thin ribbon of green grass that grew along the edge of the stream. It was no longer necessary to hobble them, they were too weak to run away. I lay in the water to cool off, ignoring the risk of *Bilharzia*, a potentially fatal disease carried by snails that thrive in warm African water.

We had reached the end of the Rift Valley, and my goal, Lake Natron, was only a few miles farther on. I decided to go there on foot alone before dark, for early the next morning we would ascend the escarpment to escape the tsetse flies. The horses and donkeys had almost certainly been infected with sleeping sickness from the tsetse flies; we would know in five days, the period of incubation.

Sekerot and I sat on the stream bank under a tree, watching the horses and donkeys graze. We wondered if they would make it. They ate with renewed energy, sensing the end of the ordeal. The sun dropped over the escarpment behind us, casting a shadow that slowly advanced across the scorched earth.

Although weary from the long day, I started south on foot alone. About three miles away, a broad, mirrorlike expanse of steel-gray water shimmered in the rising heat waves. The only thing between Lake Natron and me was raw earth, red and cracked open as if it had bled.

The desolation, glaring heat, and solitude combined to make Natron unlike any place I had ever experienced in Africa. It seemed as if I were walking straight into the cauldrons of the earth. Enclosed by the extinct domes of Shombole and Gelai in the east, and by Ol Doinyo Sambu and the Nguruman escarpment in the west, Lake Natron and its soda mudflats were a formidable challenge to human existence.

Lake Natron with its blood red pools and white soda crusts.

The earth beneath my feet was seething with energy. Steam rolled up from the lake, and on the mudflats it vented through oozing spouts. Fish thrived in hot-water springs of 112 degrees Fahrenheit with alkalinity at the end of the scale. Extreme evaporation left sodium carbonate precipitates that formed giant white spirals on the lake's surface. So silky and smooth was the water that it mirrored exactly the blue sky overhead, complete with puffy white clouds—a reverse image so perfect that pilots and birds became confused and crashed into the caustic water. In places, algae thriving in the hot alkaline water turned the lake a deep forest green, while other sections were blood red, pools of scarlet carnallite edged with lacy white soda crusts in honeycomb designs. Near the shoreline the shallows were shimmering pink, alive with flamingos.

Each year millions of lesser flamingos congregate at Natron to nest and raise their fuzzy gray chicks. One of the few animals whose legs are so leathery and tough, they can wade in the caustic water without the flesh being eaten away; however, they do lift their legs quickly because of the extreme heat of the water. As a result, their nests are safe from predators.

The more I walked, the more the lake receded. On the far side, the ash-white slopes of a dramatic cone-shaped volcano towered 7,650 feet over the lake—Ol Doinyo Lengai, the sacred Maasai Mountain of God. It had exploded in 1966, covering the area with chalky-white soda dust.

A liabon told me that when the volcano spit fire and rumbled, Maasai came from far away bringing cattle, sheep, and goats to sacrifice to Enkai, their God. Their sacrifices were taken by a liabon deep inside a cave in the mountain. When the Maasai returned the following day, they put their ears to the ground and heard the animal's cries beneath the earth, proof that Enkai had accepted their offerings.

Reflected in the mirror waters of Natron, the volcano appeared like a silver throne at the end of a pillared hall, a fitting place for a god.

I pressed on in failing light across the cracked earth, but the thin crust of dried mud began to crack and my boots sank into a sticky black substance. I gave up and returned to camp at dusk, fulfilled and relieved. The horses had survived, and I had traversed the Rift Valley and made a pilgrimage to the sacred mountain. I had lived on foot in Africa, and the experience would always be with me. ◉

CHAPTER TWENTY-ONE

Prophets and Sacred Trees

"Ke, ke, ke, ke," a yellow-billed hornbill cried as he fluffed his black and white feathers in the acacia tree over the stream at our camp at the foot of the escarpment. Various species of doves alighted at the water's edge for their morning drink.

As we finished packing the donkeys, two natives appeared dressed in shorts, shirts, and car-tire sandals. Sekerot immediately recognized them as Sonjo, a tribe from Tanzania that was a traditional enemy of the Maasai. Both carried a bow and a cowhide quiver full of arrows tipped with black poison, an extract from the morigio tree, which was fatal.

After the usual introductions, Sekerot asked in Swahili, the cross-cultural trading language, what they were doing in Kenya outside their tribal land without legal permission to cross the border.

"We are *askaris* [native guards]," one of them answered. "A wazungu hired us to patrol the forest at the top of the escarpment. We are here to see that you do not go there."

I recoiled with fear. The man who had hired them was Herman Stein, a suspicious character with government connections whom I had been told was run out of Tanzania for illegal traffic in gemstones. A Maasai said that he had gained control, through trickery, of some two hundred thousand acres of Naimina Enkiyo along the Nguruman escarpment. What he was doing there no one seemed to know, although a pilot had told me he had seen mining tailings from the air.

I had been previously warned about Mr. Stein, so before leaving Nairobi, I invited him to the Trattoria Restaurant for lunch. He proved to be an interesting and very intelligent German from South Africa, with a PhD in structural physics. His mother died when he was born, and he had survived by being breastfed and raised by a female bushman. He could speak several click dialects and other African languages.

When I told him of my plan to go by horseback down the Rift Valley, he was intrigued, but when I mentioned Naimina Enkiyo he suddenly cut me off.

"That is my land, that forest!" he said in an unfriendly, threatening tone. "If you go there, I will arrest you and put you in my jail out there. And you will not come back unless I say so."

With that the conversation ended. He stood up and left.

The askaris revealed that over three hundred Sonjo were employed to prevent anyone from entering the forest, including the local Maasai. They had seen our campfire during the night and came down the escarpment to investigate. When they discovered us preparing to ascend, they first offered to show us the trail, then when we refused they insisted on going with us to make sure that we did not enter the forest. At the top of the escarpment they left us.

From the summit of the escarpment we skirted the base of Ol Doinyo Sambu and rode north into the Loita Hills, a highland at six thousand feet. Green trees dotted the yellow-grass landscape like leopard spots, while dark riverine forests filled the valleys between hills. The countryside rolled gently beneath our feet, sprinkled with yellow daisies, black-eyed susans, orange lion tails, red pincushions, white mallows, purple bachelor's buttons, and myriad other wildflowers in lavender, lilac, blue, and red.

In the forests, flame trees dropped red and orange blossoms, and the air was filled with sweet fragrances that permeated every living cell. Songbirds flew from tree to tree, chattering vervet monkeys shook branches above our heads, and baboons fled into the bush, barking warnings that constantly reminded us of the hidden life all around. Herds of zebras raced away with the sound of pounding hooves rumbling across the grasslands. At such an altitude the days were sunny and warm, but the nights were cold and mornings wet with fallen dew.

Five days after leaving Lake Natron we reached the settlement of Entasekera, the spiritual center of the Maasai world and home of the liabon prophets. We camped on a close-cropped green meadow at the edge of a forest of yellow-bark acacias. A small clear-water stream ran next to our tent, convenient for drinking and bathing. On the opposite side of the meadow was a dense forest containing a spring-fed swamp hidden behind tall reeds.

Pesi and Samyo began constructing a protective enclosure of cut thorn limbs for the horses, while Sekerot and I unloaded the donkeys and began setting up camp. I was dragging up some dead firewood when a group of five Maasai elders approached, two of which I had met before.

"Sopa, Ole Nyambwale, Sopa," I held my hand out to the old man who was struggling to cover his thin frame with a dark blue blanket. Born near the turn of the century, he was the oldest living liabon and the son of Senteu, who had been custodian of the sacred *enkedong*. Passed down from father to son, the enkedong was a set of stones that came from heaven fifteen generations ago and were used by the liabon to predict the future.

Raphael, a tall, thin Maasai who was once the bodyguard for Kenya's president Jomo Kenyatta, accompanied him. They settled down on the grass in front of our tent.

"Where are you coming from with those horses?" Raphael asked in an educated British accent, a sign of his higher education and past association with Kenya's elite. If I had not met him previously, I would have been fooled by his traditional dress and mode of living.

"Lake Natron," Sekerot replied, smiling with a broad grin.

"Ayeee . . . that is far away!" Raphael exclaimed, waving his walking stick east in the direction of Natron. Sekerot and I noticed the sky there was rapidly taking on an ominous dark brown color.

"A big sandstorm is at Natron," Raphael explained. "It is good you have left that place. There is much wind there."

"Raphael," I asked, "what do you know of Sonjo askaris from Tanzania?"

"Yes," he frowned, "they are trying to prevent us Maasai from going to Naimina Enkiyo. You know, that forest is our reserve grazing ground, where we Maasai take our cattle during a drought. Two years ago I myself had 250 cows, but lost 100 of them when the rains stopped. We cannot survive without that forest."

He spit and hit the ground with his walking stick, angry. "That wazungu Stein cheated us. One day we will run him off with our spears!"

Raphael had once been a formidable soldier in the Kenya Army, but now seemed far too fragile for warfare. After his retirement from Kenyatta's service, he had turned to alcohol—Maasai honey beer. He had been in a coma for a week, almost dying, before giving it up.

"Ole Nyambwale," I asked impatiently, "tell me about the sacred trees of Naimina Enkiyo." The old man could not speak English so Sekerot translated.

"What you speak of is at Olasuru," he said, "the waterfall on the Nguruman escarpment." He pointed his walking stick toward the Forest of the Lost Child and continued. "There are two *oreteti* trees, strangler figs, one in a pool of water. Maasai leave sacrifices under one tree, milk or goat intestines, then the liabon blesses them under the other one, tying a piece of oreteti bark around their wrist.

"My father, the great liabon Senteu, went there," Ole Nyambwale continued. "Now the sacred enkedong, the one that was brought down from heaven nine generations ago, has passed to my father's grandson Mokombo." He banged his stick against the ground with frustration. "Everyone is waiting to see what will happen."

Mokombo, I learned, had only recently inherited the sacred stones after his father, Simel, had died. He had not yet assumed the power that would make him the chief of all liabon and the spiritual leader of the Maasai. Unfortunately, Ole Nyambwale admitted, Mokombo stayed drunk on honey beer most of the time. The old liabon expressed fear that the end of Maasai customs was near.

I recorded in my diary as Ole Nyambwale traced from memory the liabon family lineage back nine generations to Kidongoi, the first liabon. He had descended from heaven bringing the sacred enkedong that had since been passed down from father to son. Concealed in a hide-sealed cow horn, the stones empowered the liabon to see into the future. Using the stones, Mabatian, chief liabon at the end of the nineteenth century, foretold the coming of the white man long before the first wazungu set foot on Maasai grazing land.

That night Sekerot and I ate like gluttons, feasting liberally on our two-month supply of pasta and rice carried by the donkeys. Samyo and Pesi had stuffed themselves with ugali, while Katy and Houdini's bellies were filled with the tender grass of the green meadow.

We were sitting around the campfire with Samyo, telling stories of Enkuku Naibor and laughing, when the loud bellow of a buffalo came from the swamp. Pesi, who had left to visit relatives at a nearby enkang, ran out of the dark forest short of breath.

"A buffalo almost got me!" he shouted waving his rungu. "There are many buffalo, just there in the swamp!" he pointed behind him. "I heard them and hid behind a tree, but one of them came after me. It chased me around the tree, but I got away in the dark."

In true Maasai fashion, Sekerot and Pesi laughed, as if being on foot among wild animals was all a game, a continuous but comical sequence of narrow escapes—Maasai versus lion, Maasai versus elephant, Maasai versus buffalo. Even the stories with tragic endings were told with humor. And naturally in tune with Maasai humor, I laughed as hard as anyone.

> We bedded down that night feeling safe and secure. As we nodded off, the clattering of colobus monkeys vibrated the trees behind us, then a lion's roar rolled across the hills.

"Lepish, my uncle," Sekerot chuckled, "was guarding my father's cattle at Maasai Mara. He found a baby buffalo alone in the bush, but it started crying . . . waaahhhhh! The mother heard it and came after Lepish." Sekerot imitated the bellow of a charging buffalo while throwing up his arms and rushing forward. "Lepish climbed a thin sapling, but it bent over. The buffalo saw him and began pressing the sapling down by straddling it and walking it down. When the buffalo got to Lepish, the top of the sapling hit the baby, making it cry so loud that the mother left and ran to comfort it. Lepish sprang back up into the air. This went on over and over until Lepish just ran away." Sekerot and I laughed so hard our bellies hurt.

We bedded down that night feeling safe and secure. As we nodded off, the clattering of colobus monkeys vibrated the trees behind us, then a lion's roar rolled across the hills. The night sounds quieted down, and an owl began to hoot, a sound that Sekerot said in a serious tone was an omen of death.

We awoke to the many songbirds whose melodic voices fill an African morning with tranquility. Then a Hadada ibis flew from one of the trees in the swamp and began a rakish cawing, a haunting sound more sonorous and drawn out than that of a common crow. Sekerot looked up from the breakfast fire. "That ibis is a bad sign!"

As we finished our oatmeal, I noticed Katy was not grazing but standing listlessly with her head down. An hour later she lay down and rolled over on her side. Together, Sekerot and I tried to get her to stand, but she was just too weak. Her breathing slowed, mucus clouded over her eyes, and she began to die. It had been six days since we left the Rift Valley, the time it takes tsetse flies to do their dirty work.

African equine sleeping sickness carried by the tsetse fly was an incurable disease; however, I had obtained a new drug, Berinyl, intended only for cattle. The problem was that in severe infections, sudden death could occur immediately after injection of the medicine. I plunged the needle into her neck and injected the full dose. Then we sat, waiting and worrying. An hour later her breathing improved, then at midafternoon she rolled over onto her chest. Slowly she put her front legs forward and stood up. By the end of the day she was grazing again.

The next day, Matampash Ole Suki, a young liabon, came to our camp bringing his enkedong, an oblong orange gourd with a rawhide leather cap and stones inside. He said he could look into my future, for a fee. Using a chalky powder kept in a second small gourd, he painted white stripes on his face. Then he showed us a third gourd containing a plant extract that he said produced a trancelike state that allowed him to see into the future better. That, he said, was dangerous and would cost more money. I decided to forego the extra expense.

Ole Suki removed the cap on the enkedong and poured fifty or so smooth black, white, and gray stones onto a red and white cowskin brought

200

Liabon Ole Suki tells my future with enkedong stones at Loita Hills.

for the purpose. After rolling them around for a moment with the palm of his hand, he formed them into eight small piles. He stared for a minute, transfixed, at the stones, then mixed them up again and formed new piles. After the third time he seemed satisfied, smiled, and pronounced my prophesy—"A long and happy life."

That afternoon we set off on foot with Ole Suki into the Loita Hills to visit Mokombo, the chief liabon and keeper of the sacred enkedong. At the entrance to Mokombo's enkang we met a group of Maasai elders who had walked three days to consult with the chief liabon. They were plying him with honey beer in hopes that he would solve their problems.

Ole Suki showed me inside one of the enkajis where Mokombo was sitting on a wooden stool. He was a moderately plump Maasai of middle age. Next to him was a big gourd of honey beer propped against the interior wall. He was so drunk I almost had to shake him to get a response.

With Sekerot translating I asked him to tell me about the sacred trees, but his breath reeked of honey beer and his speech was slurred and unintelligible. He was just too drunk to answer any questions. However, he did manage to bring out the sacred enkedong and display it on a black and white cowskin. The magical stones were contained inside a large polished cow horn with a rawhide handle and cap. To predict my future with the stones, he said, would cost forty cattle, which was the price he was demanding from the elders.

I was getting nowhere with Mokombo, so we decided to see if Ole Suki would take us to a sacred tree he had told us about. But before we could leave, another exasperating problem arose.

Ole Supeti, the Maasai guide who had been with me during the buffalo attack two years ago, had joined us for the day. While I had been inside with Mokombo, he had been helping himself to the honey beer and now had disappeared with one of Mokombo's wives into one of the dung houses.

Frustrated, I went from dung house to dung house shouting his name while Sekerot and the elders laughed. Finally he emerged sheepishly, retrieved his spear and rejoined us.

Ole Suki led us to a giant strangler fig some thirty feet or more in circumference, located just inside the forest a few miles from Mokombo's enkang. Years ago, he said, the massive strangulating roots and buttresses of the fig had formed an arch that those being blessed by the liabon could pass through. Now it had fused into one big mass. That tree, he said, was the most important of all the sacred trees of Loita Hills.

Liabon Ole Suki shows us a sacred fig tree at Loita Hills.

When Mokombo finally assumed the full power as spiritual leader and prophet of the Maasai, all the people of Loita Hills would go to the sacred tree and slaughter a cow. Mokombo would take official possession of the enkedong and be blessed and accepted as leader by all the Maasai people.

The tree was also used by the liabon to foretell the future of a new generation of warriors, select their chiefs, and bless them. All the sacred trees were places where the liabon went to commune with God.

That night Sekerot and I were awakened by a loud rasping in-and-out "urrrrrrr–rrrrrr . . . urrrrrrr–rrrrrr" near our tent. It was a leopard, and its terrifying growl was loud and bloodcurdling. We lay awake thinking it was just moving through the camp, but after a time it didn't go away, and the growling persisted with growing irritation.

"Sekerot, that leopard is not going away!" I said, groping in the dark over the floor of the tent to find the bullwhip. My hand found the wood handle. "Here, take the whip and go run him off!"

"He's going away," Sekerot responded sleepily, brushing it off as if it were a natural occurrence of no importance.

"No he's not!" I insisted. "He's been hanging around too long. He smells the horses and is getting ready to go after them. Here's the whip. Do it, you said you would!" I thrust the whip under his shoulder.

"He's going now," Sekerot said, turning over and ignoring me.

Pesi and Samyo had not made a sound. They were rolled up in their blankets next to the horse corral without a fire and with only the one spear. If the leopard started after the horses, they would not be able to prevent a bloodbath, or even protect themselves.

Every leopard story I had heard of went through my mind, how they were creatures of stealth, killing silently without warning, sometimes for no reason at all. Once in the Serengeti I had discovered a leopard stalking me, sneaking up behind on its belly. In Maasai Mara I had driven a leopard off a fresh kill by running at it. Still, I did not have the courage to go out in the night with a bullwhip and chase the angry leopard away.

"Sekerot, you've got to do something!" I begged.

"That leopard is not hungry," he insisted. "It ate two goats last night at the enkang."

Sekerot pulled his sleeping bag over his head and ignored my pleas. Finally the growls began to weaken, trailing off into the forest behind our tent.

Despite the sleepless incident during the night, I was up before daybreak, stoking the fire and preparing coffee. We finished the oatmeal in a hurry, trying to get to a nearby enkang before sunrise, when a circumcision was to be performed.

For the Maasai, circumcision of boys was the most important of all ceremonies, for that was when they became warriors, the most respected, revered, and romanticized of all Maasai. Young boys prepared themselves years in advance to tolerate the pain of the procedure, as there was no anesthesia and any flinch or movement discredited them and their families for life.

For girls, circumcision was a brutal, less-celebrated procedure signaling only that the girl had had her first menstrual period and would be ready for marriage.

As Sekerot and I ran breathlessly through the dark across the Loita grassland, boots soaked with dew, the western sky began to light up with a dusky gray glow, outlining the enkang stockade at the top of a hill. Wisps of smoke indicated that people were already awake, preparing for the ceremony.

We arrived at the main cow entry, an oval passage of bent saplings and crooked tree trunks, where a boy about fifteen years old was standing completely naked. Although I was wearing a down jacket, his lean, pencil-thin body seemed indifferent to the cold.

"Sopa," I said, greeting the elders who were wrapped tightly in blankets against the crisp highland air and were gathered just inside the gate of the enkang.

An elder turned to receive a black earthen pot carried by the boy, as well as the circumciser's knife, which the boy had keep safe since sharpening it the day before.

Sekerot explained, "The boy filled the pot with cold water from the stream during the night. A hand-forged ax head was put in the water to make it colder."

After circumcision, Maasai bird boys travel the country together.

The elder held the pot above the boy's head and poured the icy water over his thin body, drenching him. He did not shiver or react in any way, despite the bone-chilling air. The boy was then taken quickly by the elders to the center of the cattle corral and seated, legs spread, on a cow skin ringed with olive branches stuck upright in the ground. Immediately his body went limp, falling into the arms of his uncle, who had positioned himself behind him. A calabash of fresh milk was poured over his penis.

"One cut!" the circumciser announced, then the knife blade sliced around the head of his penis cutting into the foreskin. The boy did not move or flinch a single muscle; there was no sign of pain. Some age-mates and warriors taunted him, trying to make him react and discredit himself; others, including relatives, shouted courage and sang praises to the boy.

His face remained blank, expressionless, eyes open without blinking as if in a trance. His entire past and future, and that of his family, depended on the moment. Each probing eye searched for a sign, or some slight motion that would dishonor him for life.

For five minutes the knife did its work, pausing only to rinse off the coagulating blood with milk. The crowd continued to scream words of encouragement, while others accused him of acts of cowardice.

When the final cut was completed and the customary tag of foreskin was witnessed hanging below the penis, the crowd erupted in screams of joy.

A Maasai layoni endures without flinching the rite of passage that will make him a warrior.

Shaken but still unmoved, the boy was carried away by his uncle into the dark seclusion of his mother's dung house.

Two age-mates in black cowskins rubbed with charcoal and sheep oil stood near the enkaji doorway shouting words of encouragement. Their faces were painted in white polka-dot designs, and a crescent rack of red, green, and yellow stuffed birds adorned their heads, signs of their recent circumcision. When healed, the newly circumcised boy would join these "bird boys" and travel the countryside shooting birds, flirting with uncircumcised girls, and attending circumcision ceremonies all across Maasai land.

Finally, when the entire age set had been circumcised, they would demand that the elders transfer the power to them and create a new generation of warriors.

Three junior elders started a ceremonial fire, symbolic of passage into manhood and life as a warrior. Rapidly twirling the *olprion*, or male fire stick, between their palms, they produced a smoking ember on the *entoole*, or female part. Puffs of breath caused the ember to glow red and ignite a ball of dry moss. A kindling fire was built up around it, then the ceremonial olive branches were pulled down and thrown into the flames.

In the middle of the enkang, two Maasai junior elders restrained a cow while another shot an arrow into its jugular vein. A gallon of blood was drained into a calabash and sent to the circumcised boy to drink for strength. Cow blood was a rare delicacy, and they were honoring the boy by doing this.

I followed the calabash into the dung house, squeezing my way through the tightly packed flesh of excited Maasai. The fire inside gave off a soft glow, but the thick smoke and jostling bodies excited and stimulated by honey beer quickly drove me out.

A warrior arrived at the enkang carrying a buffalo-hide shield and wearing a tall yellow headdress made from the mane of a male lion he had killed. His bravery and high ranking among the moran was shown by the red and white design painted on the shield. Long ocher-stained braids hung down the middle of his back, a sign that his warrior days were growing old and that the new generation would soon take over. Then he would cut his braids and retire as a junior elder. Everyone, Maasai and wazungu alike, wondered how much longer this traditional way of life could survive in a modern world.

The government had forbidden cattle raiding, an essential part of warrior life since the Maasai believed that God had given them all the cattle in the world to care for and protect. The government had also forbidden killing lions, which to the Maasai was a necessity to protect their cattle as well as another essential part of warrior life. Even the possession of a shield was forbidden. And yet, the Maasai refused to give up their cherished lifestyle. So all of these things continued to a lesser degree, hidden from government eyes.

I felt I had slipped through a time warp. The ancient practices and ceremonies, so fulfilling to the human spirit, so missed when the romance of them was all that remained, were still available for an unknown time for those few people who wished to be part of it.

We returned to camp accompanied by Ole Supeti. I was making bread and had placed a pot of risen dough on the hot coals when I noticed a long tree limb lying across the grass. It had not been there before, and there were no overhanging trees it could have fallen from.

"Pesi, did you bring that piece of firewood into camp? "I asked, staring at the suspicious limb.

"No," he replied as he bit off a chunk of goat meat skewered on his spear.

I went to drag the deadwood over to the fire, but recoiled quickly when I realized it was a huge snake. Its head was hidden inside a bush at the edge of the meadow, but the body was stretched out about fifteen feet across the grass and was as thick as my arm. When I tried to locate its head to identify the snake, it slithered off unhurriedly into the forest. Its skin had no pattern, so I thought it was a mamba or a cobra.

"Oeee!" Pesi yelled as he came running, "That snake was big like a python!"

"It came out of the swamp," Supeti said, shaking his head. "A big python once lived there. It swallowed my cousin. He went to get water just before dark, but did not return. The next morning we saw the python lying on the grass with a big bulge in his middle. We killed it with my semi and cut it open. My cousin was inside." ◉

CHAPTER TWENTY-TWO

River of Sand

We left Entasekera the next day. Although we had traveled for thirty-five days across some of the most difficult terrain in Africa, we felt rested and well fed.

The flowered hills rolled effortlessly beneath us, and we felt a renewed sense of adventure and excitement. Even Samyo was enthusiastic, having given up the idea of returning home. He spoke excitedly about a civet cat he had seen the night before nosing around our fire. A herd of wildebeest thundered off in front of us, then we passed Mokombo's enkang, laughing as we shouted farewell to the "liabon of honey beer," as we had dubbed him.

Pesi's belly was full of goat meat, and the donkeys trotted well ahead of his threatening rungu. Katy had completely recovered from her near death from sleeping sickness, and even her old shoulder injury was finally well. Sekerot and I were riding the mares again.

We passed a forest of acacia trees where a cluster of giraffe heads suddenly popped up through the branches, flicking their ears as they questioned our little caravan. Loita Hills and its lush tender grasses faded slowly behind as the countryside ahead flattened and turned dry. The grass took on the yellow stain of parchment, and brittle, whistling thornbush stretched as far as we could see, hardened black in the scorching sun.

"These," Sekerot said, pointing to brown, nutlike balls attached to a limb of thorns, "are the houses of ants. When an animal disturbs the bush, the ants swarm out angry, biting so it does not eat the leaves. The ant hole in the ball whistles when the wind blows. That's why these bushes are called whistling thorn."

Our donkey Jaws rammed into the thorns, and the air reeked of formic acid, a warning secreted by the vicious ants.

As the afternoon wore on, the blue sky faded behind dark clouds. Bolts of lightning thrust jagged electric spines into the distant mountain ranges, lighting the horizon with brilliant pyrotechnic displays. The wind began to blow, then the long-awaited rains came, soaking us to the bone. A bitter cold brought our miserable caravan to a halt, and we just stood there wet and shivering like the wild animals around us. Finally the soggy clouds drifted away, and the sun and heat returned. A herd of impalas raced in front of us, leaping over the thornbush.

We had filled only our canteens at Entasekera, planning to reach the Sand River before nightfall. After marching nonstop all day our canteens were now empty. A dark line of trees wandering across the plain indicated a river several miles ahead of us, but as the afternoon dragged on, it seemed to be coming no closer. Finally, nearing sunset, we reached the forest and came to the river's edge. There was not a drop of water, only soft white sand, churned up by animal hooves. We explored the dry riverbed in both directions but found nothing, not even an undercut bank to dig beneath. Sand River was appropriately named.

Sand River.

For the first time, I felt defeated. We had pushed hard all day, intensifying our effort as the afternoon wore on. My throat was parched. Every ounce of energy gained by our three-day rest at Entasekera had been used up. I was exhausted, all the enthusiasm and excitement gone. I stood in the middle of the dry riverbed with my head down, too tired to even sit on the sand. I had given up.

"We'll find water farther on," Sekerot said, seeing the despair on my face.

I looked at him, trying to focus. "Where?" I said, my voice cracking from dryness. "This is the only river before Maasai Mara, days away."

"We'll find it," he replied, stone-faced.

Sekerot was different from me, a Maasai melded to an incomprehensible endurance that all Africans seemed to have. Submission, acceptance of fate—whatever it was, a wazungu could not possibly understand. Africans persisted against impossible odds, overwhelming forces that nature constantly threw at them—drought, pestilence, sandstorms, famine, disease—without the aid of Western technology or the slightest hope of an antibiotic or a simple medical procedure that could cure them of such things as an infected appendix.

Sekerot was braver than I. I admitted it. His life had been a never-ending struggle: to protect his family's cattle with a stick or rock against lions, to survive on a monotonous diet of milk and cow blood, to endure the forced confinement and discipline of a schoolroom in Narok, and severe beatings from his father and teachers. And yet, despite all these hardships, Sekerot always laughed, a trait I had come to love about him and Africans in general. I had also learned to trust Africans in times of despair.

Reluctantly, I remounted Katy and followed Sekerot into the empty plain beyond. It seemed an absolutely worthless effort.

In the last dusky light we entered an area of granite boulders the size of houses. At the base of a huge rock, Sekerot discovered a stagnant pool of water. I dismounted and waded through the sopping mud and piles of wet cow dung to fill my canteen. The stench of urine was repulsive, but the sight of water gave me a giddy sensation.

"Not here," Sekerot stopped me. "We will dig, over there." He pointed to a sandy wash where water had previously flowed.

A Topi antelope.

We dug like thirsty dogs with our hands until hitting moist sand, then waited until the hole filled with a yellow-tinted liquid. It was clearer than the pool, but still reeked of urine. We had no choice but to drink it.

That night the moon was nearly full, outlining the shapes of hills around us and casting long shadows across the grassland we were camped on. We no longer hobbled the horses but set them free. They always came back at sunset, seemingly aware that nightfall brought predators. Now they were lying down beside my tent, exhausted from the long day.

We were heading west toward Maasai Mara, the Spotted Plain, the grazing land of the Ilpurko clan, Sekerot's people. His mother, stepmother, three brothers, and two sisters lived there in an enkang, two days away near the border of the famous game reserve of the same name. Wild animals would increase dramatically in number the closer we got.

The following day we encountered large numbers of plains animals: zebras, Thomson's gazelles, topi with rust-colored coats and burned-purple shoulders, and a herd of agile elands, the largest and most majestic of the antelope. I once saw one jump over a moving Land Rover.

A Maasai boy who was hunting with a bow told us he had shot a wildebeest with a poison arrow. It had run a hundred yards before dropping. He showed us one of the arrows covered with a black, gummy substance prepared from the morigio tree. He said it would kill an elephant in five minutes.

That night we camped on an open plain. As I began preparing supper, a pack of spotted hyenas were whooping themselves into a frenzy, issuing high-pitched, shrieking screams as they fought among themselves over a kill. With so many predators around, Sekerot took the horses and donkeys to an enkang a half mile away and put them inside their stockade.

Venus appeared in the west accompanied by early-appearing stars, then the moon rose full, bathing the enkang in a golden glow. Singing and waves of laughter drifted over the plain, mixing with the hyenas' whoops.

A plains zebra mother and foal.

"The women are celebrating," Sekerot said, staring at the moon, a yellow disk now hovering just over the enkang walls.

The contaminated water we drank had given me diarrhea, and I felt sick. "You go, I'll guard the camp," I said. "Take Pesi and Samyo with you." I sat down by the fire and placed a pot of pasta on the hot coals.

Pesi grabbed his blanket and rungu, and they disappeared into the night. We had been on safari for forty days, and our time together was running short. I knew they needed to be among their own people. They would stay all night at the enkang. Pesi would get drunk on honey beer and tomorrow would be a drag. I didn't care. They had been more in every way of companions and friends than I could ever have imagined.

The star-filled sky clouded over, and it started to drizzle rain. I finished cooking and went inside the tent to eat. A lion began to roar far away, and I pitied him out on the open plain, alone and soaking wet. I swallowed an antibiotic pill without water for the diarrhea and lay down.

Flickering shadows moved over the tent wall as the fire died out. The slow pelt of rain on the fly, the lilting voices of the Maasai, and the faraway roar of the lion had a soporific, hypnotic effect. Soon I was asleep.

I awoke suddenly with a severe pain in my chest, like an elephant was standing on it. The pain was so unbearable I was sure I was having a heart attack. I sat up groaning, clenching my ribs and searching for the nitroglycerine I had packed for an emergency. The tiny white tablet caused an immediate pounding headache relieved only by lying down, but that made the chest pain worse. So I propped myself up against the tent wall, writhing, moaning, and unable either to lie down or sit up.

The lion's roar was moving closer, so I tried to muffle my groans to prevent attracting him. After some hours, Sekerot returned and the lion went away, but I spent the night sitting up in pain and unable to sleep.

By morning I began to think it was not a heart attack but an esophageal ulcer caused by the highly alkaline antibiotic.

Each time I swallowed, it felt as if a sharp stick were being jammed in and out of my chest. Oatmeal was impossible, and I almost passed out from pain trying to sip water. Sekerot packed the donkeys while I lay curled up on the ground. It was the first time we had not packed together. I mounted Katy and slumped forward over her neck. She followed the others.

We started up a rock-strewn mountainside with Pesi hacking a tunnel-like path through the thick brush. Each time we stopped, I dismounted and fell asleep on the ground holding Katy's reins.

From the summit we had a view over the Mara plains swarming with huge herds of wildebeests and zebras. It was part of the vast migration of more than a million animals that arrived earlier in the summer from the

Serengeti. I had not eaten or drank anything all day, but when we descended, I could not resist galloping Katy headlong after a herd of Thomson's gazelles, despite being dehydrated and weak.

We camped at the foot of the Megwarra Hills, next to Sekerot's mother's enkang. A blood-red African sunset formed over the Oloololo escarpment thirty miles to the west, while the blue eastern sky became streaked with fading brushstrokes of rust and gold. Then the moon rose full in the fever trees behind us—a swollen orange globe accompanied by the whooping of hyenas out on the open plain. The singing voices of Maasai women trailed like a mist over the yellow grass, celebrating their blessing by an elder to make them fertile. Then the lion began to roar, continuing through until early morning when the women took up the strain with a song of joy.

I was still unable to eat or swallow. Weak and in constant pain, I was slowly beginning to starve. After forty-three days on foot in Africa, our safari had come to an end.

Samyo returned at last to his home in the Kedong Valley, eager to tell of his wild experiences and the many unfamiliar animals he had seen. He had no intention of ever leaving Suswa again.

Pesi set out with his donkey back to his enkang on the Nguruman escarpment, his stomach full and a bundle of Kenya shillings tied up in his shuka. As he left, he turned to say, "I am ready to join you, if you should ever go again to the Forest of the Lost Child."

The horses I gave to Sekerot, who planned to start a safari business. Tourists at nearby Sekenani Lodge were already inquiring to ride them. He built a protective high-walled pole stockade for Katy and Houdini on lush green grass next to a flowing stream, and his two uncles, LePish and Tarounkie, guarded them with spears. The two Maasai loved the mares, watching over them as they grazed by day and sleeping with them in their pole-walled enclosure at night; however, it wasn't long before Houdini was killed by a lion, her neck broken.

The donkeys I gave to Sekerot's mother, and they grazed peacefully for a time with their cattle on the acacia-spotted plain at the eastern border of the Maasai Mara game reserve; then one by one, hyenas ate them all.

In forty-two days on horseback we had traveled more than three hundred miles across Africa. Although the land was still wild in places, it was clear that the wilderness and the Maasai culture were changing. When I had asked Ole Nyambwale, the ninety-year-old liabon, what changes he had seen, he replied, "The government of Kenya did not recognize the value of traditional ways, and when the Maasai had lost knowledge of the old customs, they would become dependent upon the government and no longer be able to take care of themselves."

The same prospect, I thought, awaited the wild animals we had encountered. When lions were found only in game reserves, and the Maasai no longer needed their spears, then the spiritual fulfillment of traveling on foot in such wild places would be lost forever.

I often thought back to our camps in Africa—the musical sound of a forest stream, the fresh smell of distant rain on parched earth, the forlorn call of a lion on an empty plain, the soft touch of green grass, a new moon shining through a canopy of yellow-bark acacias. I had often lain awake at night listening to the horses just outside my tent, the sounds of their grazing, and the clocklike cycles of sleep and wakefulness that stirred them. And when I could no longer hear Katy's movements, I would look outside to find her standing motionless with ears forward, scarcely breathing, brown eyes straining to pierce the African night, and wondering what strange creature had passed in the dark.

After the lion killed Houdini, Sekerot transported Katy to a riding school in Nairobi where she remains today, carrying children on her back.

Painfully swallowing only sips of water, I returned to California for medical treatment. But in the years that followed, Sekerot and I often met to laugh again about the donkeywork that almost finished us and to relive the safari that forever bound us. ◎

Part
THREE

◆

ITURI RAIN
FOREST
ON FOOT

◆

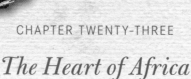

CHAPTER TWENTY-THREE

The Heart of Africa

When I first saw the African rain forest in 1984, I had driven myself there in an old Land Rover purchased in England for the purpose of satisfying my childhood dreams of Tarzan and the primeval rain forest. Six weeks after leaving London, and after another two months crossing the Sahara desert and west Africa, I finally had a view from a hilltop in Cameroon of an immense wall of dark trees rising just across the border in the Central African Republic. The rainy season had been long overdue, and as I watched, an evil black cloud rapidly formed over the menacing vegetation and descended in dark spiny fingers, throwing out jagged bolts of lightning. A diluvial rain poured down, and in contrast to the drought-stricken country I was leaving, the road ahead was suddenly transformed into a slippery ribbon of red clay.

From there the equatorial rain forest spread unbroken for some twelve hundred miles to the Mountains of the Moon and the western branch of the Rift Valley, features formed by tectonics that separated the Congo River basin from the Serengeti plains of east Africa. Two weeks later I reached the Oubangui River and ferried my Land Rover across on a rusting barge into the even taller and darker rain forest of Zaire, formerly the Belgian Congo, and currently the Democratic Republic of the Congo. Here the single-lane clay road had become a deep-rutted nightmare, a dark tunnel that snaked its way through massive bamboo beneath towering trees that often fell in the lightning storms and torrential rains and blocked all passage. And after another two weeks of agonizingly slow travel on jungle pathways whose potholes swallowed Mercedes-Benz trucks, and crossing swollen rivers by

An Efe leaf home in the Ituri rain forest.

driving across slippery logs or by straddling abandoned train trestles whose timbers had rotted, and after turning the Land Rover over on its side in sloshing mud, I finally arrived, after a journey of four and a half months, at the very heart of Africa—the Ituri rain forest.

Here was the place Joseph Conrad had written about in *Heart of Darkness,* and the scene of the greatest expedition disaster in history when the rain forest took the lives of three hundred of Henry M. Stanley's men during the ill-fated rescue of Emin Pasha in 1887–1889. It was a place Stanley hated and loved.

The natives of the Ituri, tall Bantu and Sudanic tribes, were afraid of the rain forest, and they lived along the road subsisting on small garden plots. They seldom ventured far into the dark forest. However, I was naturally adapted to the claustrophobic darkness and damp air in the forest, having grown up exploring a cypress swamp that I loved behind my family's cabin on the Edisto River in South Carolina. Any experience I might have with these natives would be strained, unnatural, and not satisfying.

Ituri rain forest canopy.

Then for the first time, I discovered pygmies, and I followed them into the forest and watched them paint their bodies and dance. They preferred the forest to the open sunshine, and their camps were in deep shade beneath the tall trees. They called the forest home, and they had lived there as long as anyone could remember, long before the other tall tribes migrated there.

As hunter-gatherers the forest provided them with what they needed: materials to make their oval leaf houses, clear streams to drink from and bathe in, and a variety of things to eat—antelopes, monkeys, honey, termites, mushrooms, and forest fruits. They knew the names and habits of all the animals, as well as the plants and what they could be used for. In addition, the forest was to them a spiritual provider, and it was good. Friendly, happy, and humble, the pygmies were the perfect companions, and if I ever wanted to connect spiritually with the forest and learn its secrets, it would be by going there with them.

The Land Rover, however, was an albatross around my neck and could not be left alone by the side of the road. It would be stolen, or the locals would take it apart for the metal. So I continued to east Africa, unable to fulfill my dream. I pledged to return.

Six years later I returned, hitchhiking through the forest. But to my eye the pygmies I had met before, net hunters known as Mbuti, seemed to have been too influenced by the overland tourists and the trade that came along the road and by the growing Bantu village of Epulu with its beer and corruption. So after a week of camping and trekking through the forest with the Mbuti, and locating the place where Stanley's men starved to death at the junction of the Epulu and Ituri rivers, I decided to walk north through the forest to a remote area far from the trans-Africa road. There, I was told, lived the Efe pygmies, who of all the pygmies were the remotest and least disturbed by the outside world. They were also the shortest of all pygmies. In fact, at four and a half feet, they were the shortest people on earth.

Unfortunately my destination was forty miles into virgin rain forest, and no Mbuti at Epulu knew how to take me there. It was simply beyond the end of their hunting grounds and the end of their trail. After nearly two weeks hanging around Epulu, three Efe pygmies arrived for unknown reasons. Although the Mbuti and Efe speak completely unrelated languages, I found out that they were willing to take me back with them.

Carrying enough food for one month, alone and with no interpreter and no possible way of communicating with them, I followed them back into the forest. For six days I traveled with them through the rain forest without seeing the sun and unable to speak even a word to my companions. Sometimes there was an animal trail, but most of the time there was no trail at all. I had no way to know where we were or which way we were going.

All around us the presence of buffalo, elephants, and forest leopards was evident, sometimes heard but not seen. We crossed a crocodile-infested river where a man prospecting for gold had recently been eaten, and once, my Efe pathfinder leaped over a twelve-foot-long black mamba, Africa's most vicious snake.

The Efe moved silently through the forest, blending in so perfectly with their surroundings that when they stood still they were hard to see. Once I paused by a stream where there were fresh tracks of a leopard hunting a baboon. When I looked up, my companions were gone.

I followed their bare footprints up the bank, then lost them in the leaves that covered the forest floor. There was no trail, and I had no idea which way they had gone. My calls, "ooo…ooo…oooo," went unanswered. Then I saw Imbi standing right beside me, smiling with big expressive Bambi eyes. He had been there all along, waiting for me.

On the fifth day of no communication, I began to wonder if we were getting closer to their camp. At one point, I placed a green leaf on one end of a fallen log saying, "Epulu." Then I put another green leaf on the other end of the log saying, "Cambi," the word they had used for their camp. Then I positioned a third leaf up and down the log while asking emphatically, "Here?" and pointing to the ground where we were standing. Suddenly Imbi's face lit up! He stuck his finger into a rotten knothole on the other side of the log and grinned from ear to ear. After that I just followed.

On the seventh day we came to a clearing in the forest, several acres of clean-swept red clay occupied by mud-dabbed, stick-frame dwellings with thatched roofs. Fully exposed to the blazing tropical sun, it was not an Efe camp but a village of Lese, a tall tribe that had migrated there from the grasslands of the Sudan to the north. I was immediately stopped from going any farther by the Lese chief, a large, powerful man who informed me in French that if I wanted to travel in his hereditary kingdom I would have to pay *hongo,* just as the early explorers had.

He also told me that his great-grandfather remembered Stanley coming to his village and how one of his men had chopped the head off of a Lese man to get an example of the exotic hairdo they wore at that time.

With the hongo fee quickly settled, the chief became friendly and told me that the Lese had migrated there from the Nile two centuries earlier, at which time the Efe were living in hollow trees or holes in the ground and eating their meat raw for lack of fire. The Lese survived by planting gardens of manioc, rice, and yams, and by trading with the Efe for meat and honey.

There was only one trail into the immense and virtually unexplored region beyond the village, an area occupying twenty-eight hundred square miles of virgin rain forest. Around the turn of the century the trail had been a main trading route, but now even the chief seemed unsure of where it went.

He refused to let me go with the pygmies, or even alone, and insisted that I go with his men. That, I knew, would ruin the experience.

The next day, accompanied by two of the chief's Lese henchmen, one of whom was an alcoholic with breath that reeked of rotgut palm wine, I hastily set off following the trail that led away into the jungle to the east. Near the end of the day we left the main trail and discovered a small Efe camp, six fragile leaf dwellings hidden in the deep forest beneath tall trees. Each head-high dome-shaped dwelling was constructed of bent saplings thatched with forearm-length, paddle-shaped leaves of the *kilipi* plant. It was dark in the camp, no sunlight reached the ground, and the small clean-swept common area between the dwellings was damp and smelled of fresh earth. It seemed more a part of the forest itself than something created by humans.

Seeing immediately that the Efe were intimidated by the Lese men, I stayed back until I could pay them off and send them away. From the shadows of the forest just outside the camp, an adolescent Efe mother stared at me, her infant slung in a cloth beneath breasts heavy with milk. She was clad in a black-and-white painted bark cloth, rectangular flaps hanging in the front and in the back from a string around her waist. Stems of bright red berries dangling from pierced earlobes adorned her body.

In front of one of the leaf dwellings, a young man wearing a plain loincloth of beaten tree bark squatted at a smoldering hearth, while several completely naked children with round, protuberant bellies and red-tinged fuzzy hair stared wide-eyed from behind trees as if ready to bolt and run. I moved slowly knowing that many Efe, especially children, believe that white people eat pygmies.

As I came closer, the women and children ran inside their leaf dwellings while a young man came to meet me at the edge of the camp clearing and kneeled down. Averting his eyes, he extended one arm toward me while supporting it with the other, as if trying to prevent it from trembling. I took his hand and gently urged him to rise, but he turned his face away and remained kneeling on the ground.

At the edge of the camp I put down my backpack, sat next to it and waited. Gradually, curiosity overcame the women, and faces began to appear in the shadowed doorways. Several Efe men and children gathered, standing in front

Dume and the children of Pembo's camp play with a trumpet made from bongo horn.

of me quietly. I offered them a bag of rock salt, an essential nutrient unavailable in the forest. They ate handfuls at a time, quickly devouring the entire two-pound bag. The women took my gift of rice, which disappeared quickly into small, black earthen pots with green leaf lids placed over the open fires.

I moved cautiously into the center of the camp. Gray wisps of smoke spiraled upward from the cooking hearth, formed of three hardwood logs with their burning ends placed together in a three-point star. Near the entrance to one of the leaf dwellings, a teenage girl lay with her head in the lap of an age-mate who was attentively grooming her hair.

Peeking inside the leaf dwellings I discovered two frightened children clinging tightly to an older woman, but in the next one a young girl seemed unafraid. Sitting on the bare earth, her attention was focused on a small bundle cradled preciously close to her chest. As she lifted one edge of the stained cloth, a warm smile, a glow, came over her. Swaddled in the bundle a tiny pink face stirred, lids momentarily flickering open as the unsure eyes of a newborn baby met those of its mother. Only a day old, the infant had a wrinkled face, and its nose and lips were not yet perfectly formed. For a moment, its delicate fingers extended toward its mother's breast, then the baby's eyelids closed, and it slipped back into blissful sleep.

With the Efe watching my every move, I began setting up my tent just outside the camp circle. Two men voluntarily joined me with forked sticks to clear a space of leaves and rotting debris. One of the men took some embers from a hearth and started a fire in front of my tent while a group of children sat on a nearby fallen tree trunk watching, laughing, and jostling each other. I had no idea what the pygmies felt about my uninvited arrival in their midst, but I felt safe and comfortable among such humble people.

A monkey stirred in the treetops nearby, and a young archer seized his bow from the side of a leaf dwelling and silently disappeared into the forest.

With the coming darkness the camp began to fill with Efe drifting in from the forest, women carrying baskets of mushrooms and nuts on their back, and men with bundles of fresh antelope meat wrapped in green leaves and slung over their shoulders. After dispensing with their loads, the fruits of a day's hunting and gathering, the women began preparing food while the men and youths gathered around the log, a sort of seating area conveniently located in front of my tent near the fire. The jesting among the youths increased until one boy fell backward off the log and the entire camp came alive laughing, a relaxed mood that I thought indicated my acceptance.

A young boy dragged over a drum, a hollowed section of a tree trunk with its ends covered with a red fur antelope skin stretched tight with rawhide strips. He heated the skin near the fire to increase the pitch, then began pounding on the taut skin and along the wooden edge of the drum with two hardwood sticks. He was quickly joined by a second boy banging on the small end of the drum. After a few fits and starts a throbbing and repetitive rhythm was established.

Pembo's daughter and wife of Bezangu.

Everyone in the camp gathered and began to dance, a rambunctious crowd of fifteen pygmies pushing, shoving, and laughing while moving in a circle around the fire. It was chaotic fun, twisting and cavorting, and occasionally someone fell over laughing. An eerie singing added to the odd scene. The song was not formed of words, but of a peculiar cascading blend of haunting forest sounds: "eee, eee, ooo . . . eee, eee, ooo . . . eee, eee, ooo . . . ," spiraling downward in repeated sequences with each note of the triplet taken up by one or more individuals in the style of a children's round. Round and round it went, with the musical quality of a rusty wheel turning in some long-abandoned workshop. After some time, I noticed countermelodies evolving, and after several hours, just when I thought I was bored of it, other intricate vocal patterns emerged that seemed to intertwine and blend in complex sequences, subtle harmonic forms that were always repeating but never quite the same. It went on late into the night, seemingly powered by some reciprocating madness, and periodically accompanied by loud bursts of laughter, which often brought the entire process to an abrupt halt with pygmies yelling, screaming, and laughing uncontrollably as they rolled on the ground. Then the throb of the drum would start up and the whole thing begin all over again.

As the night progressed, the fire grew higher, the singing and drumming became louder, and the outbursts of laughter more often ended in shouting arguments. I retired to my tent and lay there, sleepless until around midnight when the raucous party began to fade. The drumming fitfully trailed off, and I fell soundly asleep.

Some hours later I awoke to the sound of wind rustling the dead leaves outside my tent. Strange, I thought, as wind, no matter how strong, does not penetrate the dense canopy to the floor of the rain forest. Then, faintly,

A dance at Zaiku's camp.

I heard a finger tapping on the drum skin, and the subtle crack of a fire being rekindled.

With no further warning the drumming began at full intensity and the rustle of wind became the pattern of many bare feet moving quickly across the leaves. All at once voices came in complete harmonic unison, "eee, eee, ooo . . . eee, eee, ooo . . . eee, eee, ooo." For hours I lay without moving, caught up in evolving patterns and the unstoppable throbbing of the skin drum. There was none of the laughter or the jostling that had been so much a part of it before.

The night wore on, and I sensed that this was no longer just a good time but something serious and meaningful. The dance continued without pause, unwavering in its stride until the first dim light of day penetrated the canopy and spread a gray shroud across the forest floor. Then the voices trailed off and the drumbeat stopped. I looked outside but saw only the faint form of a lone hunter with his bow disappearing into the mists that drifted among the giant trees.

When I arose, the camp was empty, and except for the aged and the newborn, I was alone. I did not know the meaning of the dance, or even if there had been one, but I felt that something spiritual had occurred that tied the pygmies to their forest world. ◉

CHAPTER TWENTY-FOUR

Efe Hunting Camp

During the years that followed I spent another four months camping with a different group of Efe, Pembo's clan, consisting of his wife and sons and their wives and children. Pembo was a respected Efe elder, and often his camp merged with those of his childhood age-mates and their families. It was a typical pygmy camp, ten to twenty igloo-shaped leaf houses constructed in a clean-swept circular space. The open entries faced inward, toward each other, and each house had a fire hearth in front.

The Efe moved their camp every month or so, depending on the hunting-gathering season, or if the fragile leaf structures needed to be rebuilt. So each year I found the camp in a new location, sometimes settled between huge growths of overhanging bamboo, or among granite boulders grown over with green moss, but always in an idyllic setting in the forest beneath the tall trees.

Early on I befriended two young Efe hunters, Bezangu and Kaluli, who became my constant companions, guides, and finally close friends. We developed basic communication using sign language, miscellaneous words of French and Swahili, and words we seemed to invent, as I had no idea what language they belonged to, if any. We could get around together, but I understood little of what was said among them.

The last time I was there was in July, the honey-gathering season, a time when the rain stopped briefly. This was the happiest of all seasons for the Efe, as honey was their favorite food and normally plentiful after the white-blossomed *Brachystegia* trees perfumed the forest with their sweet fragrance.

Pembo's camp.

I expected plenty of excitement, dancing, and singing in the camps, relocated deep in the forest where the trees would be in full bloom.

Bezangu and Kaluli were excited to see me, but they explained with long faces that the honey season had failed completely, as well as the Lese gardens, which were their backup source of food through trading. The torrential rains had continued incessantly right through the three-month dry season, preventing the trees from flowering and the Lese from burn-clearing their garden plots. Hunger had plagued the Efe for several months, and all those who were able had gone deep into the forest to hunting camps. Kaluli, with five children to feed, looked especially thin. His ribs were showing and his cheekbones protruded. With the top of his head reaching my midchest, he weighed little more than seventy pounds.

Carrying my supplies, Bezangu and Kaluli led me through a tunnel of giant bamboo, then across a small familiar stream with a bed of yellow quartz sand, to the camp of old Pembo, Bezangu's father-in-law and a respected elder, storyteller, and keeper of all manner of forest lore. "Ahh!" came a staccato note of surprise as Pembo looked up and saw me entering the camp. We had not seen each other in over a year. "Ooo yea, Pembo, maendeleo!" I greeted him.

"Ooo yea!" Pembo called back and came toward me with a broad smile across his elfin face. I clapped a cupped hand three times over my bent elbow, trying to make a popping sound like the Efe do when they are happy. "Eeeeeeeeeeeeaaa!" shrieked three young women laughing with excitement, bodies shaking at my muffled attempt to express joy in the way of an Efe.

The ethereal sound of harp music wafted across the camp, a sound that immediately transported me back again into the world of the Efe—a world of music, laughter, and love. A world that I envied and loved. Lobaki, a young hunter, stopped playing and leaned out of his leaf dwelling, smiling to see me in the camp again. His harp, five strings stretched from a curving neck to a carved wooden box, was the instrument portrayed in Egyptian hieroglyphic paintings. It looked like a pygmy hunting bow attached to a box and was thought to be the origin of stringed musical instruments. I had first heard the lilting music years before as an Efe hunter passed me on a trail deep in the

A kilipi leaf house at Pembo's camp.

forest. He played effortlessly as he sped down the narrow pathway, bow and arrow tucked under his arm, seemingly in rapture. In an instant he was gone, but the music seemed to linger in the trees.

We set off in the morning for the hunting camp, deeper in the forest. We departed after the dew had dried from the foliage, Bezangu with a machete, and Kaluli carrying a chunk of smoldering hardwood from a hearth fire that he periodically blew on to keep the embers alive. Three other hunters—Ouchotoofe, Tomas, and Zaiku—came along bringing their spears, bows, and arrows. We followed a narrow trail beneath mahogany and other hardwoods, passing an abandoned elephant trap, a pit dug ten feet deep tapered in a wedge shape to trap the creature's massive legs together and render him unable to climb out.

The pit was a Lese contraption, but the Efe occasionally hunted elephants with spears, which provided them with a giant feast. I had once helped them haul a big chunk of smoked elephant back to camp.

We skirted the base of a granite mountain covered with cycads, tree ferns, and other primitive vegetation left over from the time of dinosaurs, then waded across a dark stream and through massive strangler figs draped with spiral vines larger than my chest. We made our way deeper into the forest among giant trees with moss-covered plank buttresses that spread like wings on a Gothic cathedral to form cloistered chambers where antelopes hid their young. Somewhere up above the canopy came the sawing sound of a crowned eagle's feathers rasping the air as it searched for primates

Susu, a spear hunter of the Ituri rain forest.

Tomas and the monkey he caught.

down below. Then we heard the booming mating call of a crocodile, a terrifying sound. We scurried beneath the giant trees feeling like moles, a sensation the early humans must have had while fleeing from pterodactyls and other flesh-eating reptiles during the era when reptiles ruled.

Near the end of the day we stopped at an abandoned camp Bezangu called "E-Ma-Boom-Goofy." The more I pronounced it, the more the Efe laughed, and it became a regular joke for the next few days.

Bezangu and I found a small stream to wash off the day's sweat and the rotting debris that constantly dropped from the canopy into our hair. While we lay in the refreshing, cool water, a clap of thunder rolled over the forest. "Mvua [Rain]," Ouchotoofe said and pointed with his bow in the direction of the approaching tropical storm.

We quickly returned to the camp where Kaluli had a fire going with the embers he had carried. Mushrooms and corpulent white grubs, gathered from a rotten log found along the trail, were wrapped in green leaves and already cooking in the hot coals of the fire.

The Efe started fires so quickly with their embers that I had stopped bringing matches or a small camp stove. It was easier just to do it their way and cook over hot coals. However, I always brought my own food because as hunter-gatherers they lived on the edge and I did not want to stress them further. I occasionally tasted their delights, however, monkey and forest products such as their roasted nuts, which were exquisite. Also, I loved wild honeybees—wings, bodies, combs, and all.

I envied the Efe's ability to live in nature, making the things they needed from what was available around them. While I struggled to put up my tent, they watched from a comfortable bed of soft leaves by the fire, and when it rained, they either constructed a primitive shelter or endured without. They never liked my tent, preferring to be outside, even in the rain. And if during a tropical rainstorm one of their shelters was available, I preferred that, as it was much drier than my soggy tent.

After supper we sat staring into the fire and waiting silently for the storm to arrive. I noticed everyone staring while I flossed my teeth. They had never seen dental floss before. Without saying anything I tore off pieces and passed them around. They knew exactly what to do, and the six of us just sat there by the fires flossing away together as if we had done it every night of our life.

With the coming of night the forest erupted in a symphony of cicadas, tree frogs, and myriad other unknown sounds while, beyond our tiny firelit space, fireflies twinkled like stars between the trees. The torrential storm arrived with a vengeance, raking the treetops with a fierce wind that shook the canopy, spewing leaves and branches all around. Then a flood poured down while lightning split trees in the forest nearby, crashing with a loud noise.

An hour later the tropical storm moved off, leaving the sodden trees dripping with water, and the cicadas to begin all over again. Far away a tree hyrax screamed. Although a small, football-sized animal, it is related to the elephant, and its blood-curdling, high-pitched, repetitive screams were characteristic of nights in the rain forest. When I first heard it, I thought a baby was being strangled to death. It sent shivers up and down my spine, and I never got used to it.

In the morning three long-tailed black monkeys were playing in a nearby treetop. Ouchotoofe and Zaiku went after them, firing a barrage of arrows. Standing with them beneath the tall tree, I heard crisp rattling sounds on the dry leaves next to me. Suddenly I realized that those lethal, poisoned shafts were landing all around us. Ouchotoofe laughed and fired another arrow. Perched safely on a limb high up in the canopy, the monkeys looked down at us with indifference. Nearly fifty arrows were fired before our supper took a few flying leaps through the treetops and escaped.

Stopping along the trail to gather mushrooms and dig grubs, we made slow progress. By midafternoon we arrived at another abandoned camp. Although I wanted to press on to the hunting camp, Zaiku insisted on stopping for reasons I could not understand to spend the night.

Zaiku was often volatile and loud, releasing his opinions in uninhibited outbursts of emotion. He was also one of the funniest and most fun loving of all the Efe, occasionally degenerating into absolute silliness. Once, I gave his wife, Ndoleungu, a small perfume sample, which Zaiku quickly seized for himself. Later on, he sped past me on the trail, giggling and reeking of perfume. He had been flirting with a younger girl.

After a half hour of rest I approached Zaiku, who had started a fire and was lounging in the doorway of a leaf dwelling. "Tuende cambi nyama, tuende, Zaiku [Please, let's get going, Zaiku]," I said to him. He turned his head and pointed to the green canopy, "Mvua [Rain]!"

There had been no thunder all day, and the little bit of sky that was visible through the canopy was clear. Nevertheless, the others, led by Zaiku, moved all the bags inside one of the leaf dwellings. Before I could get my tent up, a rainstorm drenched me.

We reached the hunting camp at midmorning the following day. While still some distance away, Bezangu pounded on a plank buttress with a stick to announce our arrival. The laughter and sounds of children playing were undetectable until we were almost upon the cambi, "E-A-Ke-Le," eleven freshly made dwellings of green leaves set in four separate circular spaces, each with a connecting path.

Tall trees overhung the camp, and it was impossible to see the sky overhead through the dense canopy more than 120 feet above the forest floor. An odor of fresh meat hung over the camp, carried on layers of acrid blue smoke that rose from the meat curing racks. Red and blue hides of small antelopes, duikers of various species, were being used as sitting mats in front of the leaf dwellings. Hunting nets were lying in piles on the ground, often occupied by a sleeping child or a dog.

As I walked into the camp a brown and white mongrel basenji dog bared its teeth and growled, a line of hackle hair sticking up along the ridge of its neck and back. Clucking chickens flapped their wings and scattered, along with some of the younger children who were naked except for a fibrous string around their waists. Women looked up from their cooking hearths near the oval opening to their leaf dwellings. Black clay pots rested in the flaming embers, occasionally bubbling over with boiling mushrooms or wild tubers. Young mothers sat peacefully against the outer wall of their dwellings suckling babies while singing softly to them. Spears were propped up beside doorways, bows and arrows rested on top of dwellings. The vibrant melody of a finger piano floated about the camp, punctuated by the shrill overtones of a songbird in the forest nearby. It was a typical idyllic Efe camp scene.

learning to climb.

Two boys were preparing their father's hunting net, stretching coils across the camp to undo tangles and repair any breaks in the mesh. Gathering the long loops of the net over their shoulders, the boys looked more like fishermen preparing to set out from some seashore than hunters deep in a forest. Other nets were tied in coils and left hanging across meat racks to dry out the ever present moisture.

Lobaki, who had arrived the previous day, was sitting in front of his leaf dwelling weaving a new net. Only twelve feet of the web were completed, and it would take months before the nearly two-hundred-foot-long net would be ready to use. The thick cord was made by his wife, who spent many hours rolling plant fibers across her thigh with the palm of her hand. Brown seeds, woven at intervals into the mesh, served as a rattle to signal the hunter when an antelope ran into the net. Because making a net was such a lengthy joint effort between husband and wife, each family owned only one, and a successful hunt required the participation of several families. Lobaki was recently married, and this was to be his first net.

One of the hunters hoisted the heavy brown coils over his shoulder, picked up a broad-headed spear, and quietly disappeared into the forest. One by one others followed in an unhurried manner, carrying nets, bows and arrows, and spears. A sleeping dog awoke suddenly and trotted out of camp, following the scent of his master. The lonely "tok, tok, tok, tok" of a wooden clapper, tied around the dog's neck with a vine, trailed off into the forest. Had I not witnessed this quiet scene before, I would not have noticed their departure.

Bezangu and I raced after them along a tiny trail, knowing that the hunters would move rapidly once outside the camp. After ten minutes of breathless running we found six hunters sitting calmly on their nets piled beneath a tree. A small fire had been started with embers brought from the camp, and puffs of blue smoke belched upward as a young boy held branches of green leaves over the flames. Each hunter took a handful of the charred leaves and painted black lines across his forehead and below his eyes, markings that would magically increase their ability to see animals in the dark forest. Once before I had witnessed the Efe using magic, when a

hunter had tried to make an approaching storm go away by preparing
a similar leaf ash and blowing it in the opposite direction.

We waited until a group of young, unmarried girls joined us, then
the hunt set off in earnest—six men with nets, four boys, five girls, and
three dogs with wooden bells. The hunters moved swiftly, their bodies
shrouded in long folds of the nets that draped from their foreheads across
their shoulders and down their backs, almost touching the ground. Moving
silently, they floated through the dark shadows of the trees like the ghosts of
a funeral procession.

We followed a narrow trail made by forest buffalo, wading across streams
and through a black mud marsh. Then we left the trail and went up and down
forested hills, rapidly weaving our way through tangled vines and thin saplings
straining to reach the sun. The women, accompanied by Lobaki and the dogs,
separated and went to position themselves about a half mile away, ready to
beat the underbrush and drive the animals into the nets. Every few hundred
feet one of the hunters dropped out of our group to string up his net, hooking
the bottom to bent twigs at ground level and the top edge to saplings. Silently
and quickly the quarter-mile-long semicircle of nets was erected, with hunters
stationed at various sites armed with spears or bows.

Bezangu and I sat down behind a tree, quiet, unmoving. Voices trailed
off quickly and the world about us was suddenly still. We waited. The
forest seemed strangely quiet, as if every insect and bird were aware of our
presence. The sound of each falling leaf or rotten branch caught our ears. No
matter how carefully I tried to reposition a foot or shift my position it created
a disturbing noise. The silence became almost unbearable, and whenever
I looked at Bezangu he turned his face away, knowing that one of us would
surely laugh and ruin the hunt.

Light penetrated the thick leaf blanket overhead in tiny rays, yellow disks
that danced across the forest floor in speckled patterns like those cast by
mirrored globes on ballroom walls. The forest seemed to be spinning dizzily
around us, and in my intense concentration I almost fell off the root I was
sitting on. An Efe hunter appeared suddenly nearby, his copper body painted
in a confusing dappled pattern that blended seamlessly into the forest.

Mateso and his friends practicing archery.

A mile away we heard the beat begin, the women shouting and thrashing bushes while Lobaki urged the dogs into an excited state. "U-ya, u-ya, u-ya . . . aii, aii, aii." Slowly the beaters moved closer. The hunters signaled by popping their wrist guard that they had shot an arrow at a fleeing duiker.

"U-ya, u-ya, u-ya," the tension mounted in Lobaki's voice. The "tok, tok, tok, tok" of a wooden clapper signaled that a dog was approaching. Running hooves pounded the forest floor only a few yards away as two okapis (shy, giraffelike large antelopes) easily leaped over the four-foot-high net. "U-ya, u-ya, u-ya," a hunter yelled. Bezangu grabbed my arm, and we ran down the net to find two hunters kneeling on the chest of a red male duiker with its hooves tangled in the web. With two fingers jammed up its nostrils and its mouth held closed, the duiker grunted in a final death struggle.

Three more hunts netted only a small blue duiker and a francolin captured alive. We returned with the antelopes slung over the backs of two of the women. Tankaoso, one of the unmarried girls, had cut off the testicles and was wearing the furry white scrotum on a green vine as a necklace. Two duikers were not much meat for the twenty-five Efe at the camp, so the men planned to hunt a different area in the afternoon.

Zaiku and Ouchotoofe were off monkey hunting. Kaluli sat by our fire roasting a plantain in the hot coals. He removed it with a metal-tipped arrow and began to eat. There was little meat in the camp, and the hunting in general had been bad. We had assumed that there would be plenty of fresh meat available and had brought only palm oil, salt, and a stalk of green plantains. Zaiku and Ouchotoofe returned at dusk empty-handed. Supper was a pot of spiny caterpillars that Kaluli had collected.

By late afternoon the persistent booming of thunder signaled another tropical storm. A massive tree nearly 150 feet tall dominated the camp. About fifty feet up the trunk lightning had splintered it, leaving a jagged fork on one side and the huge, spreading top hanging like a giant flyswatter over the entire camp. I had surveyed the tree for an hour before deciding where to set my tent.

What bothered me most was that, during a heavy tropical rain, this king of the forest, whose branches were covered with spongelike mosses and ferns, would become heavily laden with water. Then, aided by storm winds, it might suddenly collapse. After a century or more of growth, tons of wood and vegetation would fall, dragging down even more vines and limbs broken from other trees nearby. Falling trees are highly feared in forest camps, and the Efe are professed experts in predicting just when and where these big trees will fall.

Each time I suggested another tent site it was flatly rejected by either Bezangu or the others. Bezangu insisted the leaning tree was "Hacuna matatta (no problem)!" He showed me exactly where it would fall, twenty feet to the left of my tent. That put it right into the main camp where there were six leaf dwellings, but no one seemed concerned.

Kaluli jumped up and loudly disagreed, saying it would fall on the other side of the camp, where two leaf dwellings occupied a small hill. The older Efe man living there came out and said he was not at all worried. Soon all the Efe were heated up, taking sides about where the tree would fall. Finally Bezangu yelled louder than everyone else, and they all went back to what they were doing.

"There is the problem!" Bezangu reassured me, pointing to an innocuous-looking tree of another species whose limbs, he said, were easily broken off in strong winds. He waddled around waving his arms and shaking his head, imitating the sound of blowing wind and flailing tree limbs. "*Kabisa!*" Kaluli said with finality, as if the whole thing were stupid. Despite Bezangu's objections, I cleared a new space and moved the tent.

The full force of the tropical storm descended just after dark. Outside it sounded as if hell itself had come loose. For an hour the storm raged, like water from a broken dam, before settling into a hard but continuous rain. Water flooded my tent and deep pools formed all around the camp.

Finally it slowed and I went to sleep. During a black hour of the night I was shot awake by a horrible cracking sound, the splitting open of immense timbers above my head. Nature's largest living landmass was coming down! In the absolute darkness the precious moments allotted for escape slipped by as I failed to find the tent zipper, so I curled up on the floor and prayed. Tree limbs and falling debris crashed all around, then a deafening silence. My hand found the zipper, and I ran blindly into the forest. I didn't know which way to go, so after I cleared the camp I just stood there, naked, in the dripping vegetation, unable to see a thing and afraid to move. Gradually the Efe, who had also run into the forest, came back. The tree had cracked but not fallen, so we gathered in the most precarious position of all, beneath my rain tarp, to wait. The black, rainy night seemed to go on forever while we huddled together listening, ready to run at the slightest noise. In the morning I moved the tent again.

We were desperate for food, so I gave everyone a fishhook and line and we went fishing. Ouchotoofe went monkey hunting while the net hunters and their dogs set off to try a new area. We waded up and down small streams, over mud banks, and across rotting logs, places that were ideal for snakes. I was used to snakes from my river swamp days, but crocodiles worried me plenty. Kaluli assured me there were none around, but twice before in the Ituri I had been told this only to find out after swimming that someone recently had been eaten. Our entire catch was only eight small fish, but Ouchotoofe, who returned with a large white-nosed monkey, saved us.

Late in the afternoon Asena, a young mother, brought me her month-old infant. It was her first baby, born only a year after her *ima* celebration, the puberty rite held after her first menstrual period. The baby's lips were

blue, its nostrils flaring, and it was having a difficult time breathing. Only a faint rasping sound could be heard when I pressed my ear to its tiny chest. Listless and unable to suckle, it was rapidly declining. As a medical doctor, I could see that the baby was in extreme respiratory distress, with cyanosis and a retracting chest. I knew it would die within just a few hours.

With death imminent, there was nothing to lose. I ground up two different antibiotic tablets on the trunk of a fallen tree and mixed an unknown dose of the powder with milk from the mother's breast. When the potion was dumped into the baby's gaping mouth, it neither struggled nor swallowed. I turned away, sure it would aspirate the mixture and die on the spot. Asena went back to her dwelling. Soon darkness came, then a sudden wailing from Asena's hearth. The other women of the camp joined her and for hours the wailing continued, loud and mournful.

I saw Asena by her fire, holding the limp body cradled in her arms, all the youthful beauty of her motherhood now dashed in a flood of despair and tears. The extreme anguish on her face told me all I needed to know, but I decided to see further. The fire had been built up by the crowd of wailing women, and I saw clearly the baby's naked body, motionless, limp, and cold in Asena's arms. Its head had fallen back and mouth hung open; there was

A spear hunter with his body painted.

no longer any flaring of the nostrils or movement of the diaphragm. There
was not a single clinical sign of breathing. I was sure the baby was dead.

The wailing continued for most of the night, then everyone slept,
awakened only by Asena's lingering outbursts.

When I awoke in the morning, Bezangu was staring at Asena's hearth with
a perplexed look on his face. "*Kabisa!*" he exclaimed, shaking his head. "The
baby is alive again!" Asena came over with a concerned but pleased look in her
eyes. Sure enough, the baby was breathing—cyanotic and struggling, but alive.
I mixed up more of my antibiotic potion and over the next two days Asena's
infant improved. If miracles do occur, surely this was one.

Kasongo was the oldest man in camp, perhaps sixty. His wife had died
some years before, leaving him childless. Basically he was alone in the world.
Thin, frail, and seeming as ancient as an Egyptian mummy, he was by far
the best of all the bow hunters, and his reputation as an archer commanded
absolute respect from everyone in the camp.

While the hunters set out with their nets, I followed old Kasongo into
the trail-less forest. Carrying only two heart-shaped, metal-tipped arrows
and a bow, he moved effortlessly and with total stealth, his bare feet caressing
the leaf- and twig-strewn forest floor without creating a single sound.
Broad-leafed kilipi plants seemed to part magically before him, and he slid
effortlessly through tangles of fallen vines and over projecting roots. His
movements were slow and without fault, and he often paused, frozen like
a wild creature, to listen or to sense, and feel the world about him in ways
unknown to me.

Silently he searched the dense overgrowth created by fallen trees, under
fallen logs, and in the hollow spaces where antelopes often hide their young.
Although he moved slowly, he often had to stop and wait for me; so I let him
go on alone and I joined the net hunters. After the hunt had ended, I found
old Kasongo squatting over a red duiker, gently inspecting a gaping arrow
wound in its chest. It was the only *nyama*, fresh meat, taken from the forest
that morning.

Zaiku, Kaluli, and Tomas returned from fishing with only two small fish;
Ouchotoofe had shot no monkeys. There was little laughter in the camp that

night as everyone went hungry. Discussions went around the fire, lamenting the bad hunting and lack of nyama in the forest. Bezangu and Kaluli hotly argued over what to do. Kaluli, of a more practical nature, wanted to give up the hunt and go back and get some plantains from the Lese gardens. Bezangu said that he was Efe and would not go begging to those villagers. Tomorrow he would fill his belly from the forest. Perhaps he would find a honey tree, although everyone laughed knowing the season had failed completely.

The men settled into their sleeping positions around the fires, lying on beds of freshly cut kilipi leaves. Voices grew softer, fires flickered, and the camp gradually darkened and became quiet. The last women finished cooking what little food they had and retired. Orange sparks from fire sticks—Efe "flashlights" used to avoid snakes in the night—lit the darkness like a child's sparkler. The occasional burst of a campfire flame cast an Efe silhouette against the forest wall that encapsulated us.

Bezangu stood in the center of the clearing and began his nightly speech. For an hour he carried on in serious tones, emotions rising in heated crescendos only to crest and fall back again in waves. An occasional communal "ahh" punctuated the lonely monologue when his performance struck a resonant chord. One by one the Efe edged closer to the warmth of the dying embers, then all slept profoundly.

Bezangu continued alone for another hour, addressing the sleeping camp, or perhaps the forest itself. Once his voice trembled and took on a high-pitched tone that merged with the song of a nightjar singing far away in the forest. Then he, too, faded into the night. I lay awake listening to the sounds of the forest and to the blood-curdling screams of a hyrax broadcasting his territorial call. It was like no other sound on earth and on such a dark night struck fear into the heart of anyone not familiar with it. But on that night it seemed to be the voice of the forest itself in pain, giving birth to a new life creation.

I set off with Bezangu and Kaluli in the early morning, at the hour when worker bees fly from the hives. We walked far and fast, until the sweet fragrance of the white *Brachystegia* fell upon our noses. Bezangu stopped to listen, turning his ears from side to side like a bat. He took another step with his head cocked upward, then his eyes widened. "*Asali* [Honey]!" he said pointing into the canopy.

As if by magic he and Kaluli were gone. I found them at the base of a large tree, pulling down slender vines and tying them together. Kaluli had started a smoking fire and was making a basket from the large paddle-shaped leaves of the kilipi plant, conveniently present everywhere in the forest. Bezangu excitedly pointed to the hive, a small opening in a limb some one hundred feet from the ground. The tree trunk was eight feet in diameter and rose like a slick column to its first branch at around sixty feet. Kaluli shinnied effortlessly up a nearby sapling, then rode its swaying top over to a second, taller tree. From there he threw the vine rope around the first branch of the honey tree and secured it. Then, nearly one hundred feet up, he crawled acrobatlike across the vine and quickly ascended to the bees' nest.

A vine rope coiled around Kaluli's chest was lowered to Bezangu, and the basket containing the smoking fire and a small honey ax were hauled back up. Kaluli smoked the hive, then chips flew as he chopped wildly into the opening. Standing untethered on the tree limb with angry bees swarming over on his face stinging him, Kaluli kept up an excited, yelled conversation with Bezangu about his progress and how much honey there might be in the hive.

Soon the chips stopped falling and Kaluli jammed his hand through the enlarged hole. Bezangu screamed with jealous anguish while Kaluli stuffed his mouth full. Then he threw down a few pieces, which Bezangu caught and immediately swallowed without looking at them. I bit into a chunk of comb, which burst not with honey but with a milky white cream that tasted like fresh grass. Live grubs oozed out of the corners of my mouth. The hive was barren of honey, but Bezangu and Kaluli enjoyed a meal of warm bee larvae before returning slothfully to camp.

Ouchotoofe returned with a monkey slung over his shoulder, and Zaiku had six small fish. In the forest behind one of the leaf dwellings the net hunters were butchering four blue duikers on a bed of green leaves, the dogs waiting to finish any scraps left behind. Two women chopped open orange-sized tree fruits to obtain the highly valued central nut. When cut into thin slices and roasted, it tasted like almond-flavored potato chips. In the last gray light of dusk, a lithe-figured girl with budding breasts came from the forest balancing an amber calabash of water on her head.

The night was moonless, and the flickering of the hearth fires in front of each leaf dwelling cast eerie shadows of trees and women tending pots. We ate our monkey in silence, then watched the flames die out with an occasional shower of sparks that spiraled upward with the blue smoke. One of the hunters began a lonely speech, but nobody listened and soon we were all asleep.

An hour or so later the old man in the leaf dwelling next to me awoke, his bones stiff and cold. He talked to himself in an irritated voice as he blew on the smoldering hardwood logs of his hearth. Flames leaped from the embers, and the orange glow that filled the dwelling began to warm the old man's withered flesh. As smoke belched from the oval entry, his paroxysmal fit of coughing shook the camp.

Soon the entire camp was awake, talking as they stoked fires. Then everyone fell asleep again. Some hours before daybreak this sequence repeated itself in a waking and sleeping pattern that is typically Efe.

During one of the quiet spells I needed to empty my bladder. Everyone was soundly asleep so I slowly unzipped my tent door. In the darkness around me resounded the loud "ZEEEEEEP!" of the zipper, then twenty voices in unison mimicked perfectly the strange sound they had heard each night. When I returned to my tent the "ZEEEEEEP" was mimicked again. No one said anything, and no other sounds were heard. I laughed—even in their sleep the Efe are mimes and jokesters.

Several days later, with Mboko (the "Buffalo") speaking nightly about the bad hunting, the group decided to move deeper into the forest to a place near the Nduye River where they had not hunted in years. They expected to find nyama plentiful there and perhaps some honey. Years before, Mboko had killed his first of many buffalo in that area, finding it stuck in a mud wallow and bellowing like a cow. Bezangu, as a boy, had traveled there with his father, and gave a detailed description of a rhinoceros they had seen bathing near the river. In their youthful memories it was a fine hunting ground.

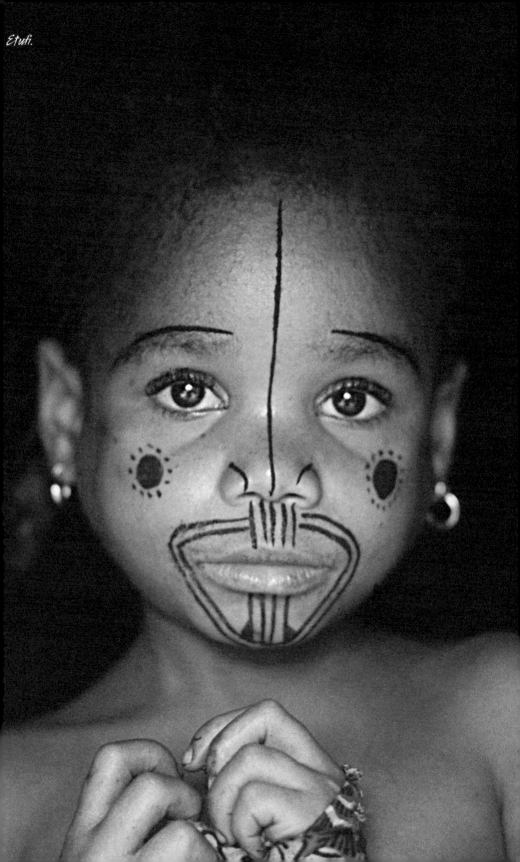
Etufi.

By midmorning the last woman had gathered her household possessions in a basket woven from the *anjiani* palm. Using a forehead trump line of beltlike strips of the *ndulu* plant, she hoisted the basket onto her back. Inside were all her worldly possessions: one blackened clay pot, a crudely hammered iron knife blade, and a gourd for carrying water. Her baby rode on her hip.

Zaiku, Kaluli, Ouchotoofe, and Tomas had departed just after daybreak for the Lese village. Bezangu and I sat on a fallen tree trunk watching the woman leave. At the last minute she spotted a bush knife lying on the ground. Digging her toe beneath the heavy blade, she lifted it balanced on the top of her foot to within arm's reach, then disappeared into the waiting forest.

For a moment the camp was silent, empty . . . dead. Then birds began to sing in the trees nearby, and the drone of cicadas and a thousand insects began to fill the empty space. Purple butterflies wafted about in the light shafts and dead leaves drifted down from the canopy overhead. As I watched, the clean-swept little clearing was quickly recarpeted by falling debris. From the trail at the edge of the clearing I looked back at the hunting camp, just minutes ago filled with laughing voices, music, and the joyful sounds of children playing. Now the leaf dwellings were brown and lifeless, already falling down. How quickly, I thought, the forest reclaims its own.

Then, far away, I heard the music of Lobaki's harp, drifting faintly among the trees. Here, I thought, was all one needed to know of life—all of its joys, all of its sorrows. ◎

Andekufe's wife painting a barkcloth.

❖ EPILOGUE ❖

When I returned home to California from the Sahara, the noise of the freeway was deafening, and the quick pace and confusion of modern life disorienting. I spent long periods sitting quietly alone. Although six feet tall, I weighed only 125 pounds, having lost 20 percent of my body weight. I would eat slowly, for hours. Clear water in a crystal glass was to me more precious than gold, and I regarded the common faucet with sacred respect.

It was years before I could talk openly about the desert experience without breaking down emotionally. The Sahara, in its vast emptiness and untouched beauty, had given me an inner peace, a nirvanalike state unlike anything I had ever experienced. But I had paid a terrible price, and the remembrance of the desert was like grieving the loss of a loved one. The fate of Bilal and O. Henry was tied together by the fragile cord of good and evil. God and the Devil.

After the buffalo attack, I cursed Africa and thought I would never go back. I returned home to marry the girl I had loved for seven years, and I could never bring myself to work again cloistered inside a building, shut away from the beauty of the natural world outside.

But a gloomy sensation persisted until the lure of the Rift Valley brought me back. I could not resist the intense sensation of being free and alive when on foot among its wild creatures. It taught me the true value of nature, that humans are spiritually and genetically wedded to it. For 98 percent of our time on earth, humans have lived close to nature, outdoors among wild animals, and such evolutionary adaptation cannot be undone so rapidly without consequences.

The Efe pygmies were the happiest and humblest people I have ever met. Their love of family, especially children, and their respect for elders is a model for how people should live. And yet they are among the most primitive people left on earth today. They live closest to the way it was for all of us ten thousand years ago when we were all hunter-gatherers. Perhaps that is the reason they are so happy and loving, lacking the necessities we are so miserable without. They made me realize that in the end, love and compassion were all that mattered.

Since these journeys, the places that I traveled in have undergone vast changes. Agadez, the dusty little oasis in the Sahara, became a booming tourist destination with weekly flights from Paris, a four-star hotel, an ice cream parlor, and many excellent European restaurants. I even know a lawyer from San Francisco who built a vacation house there.

Rhissa Boula, the man who introduced me to Bilal, emerged as leader of the Tuareg rebellion. Mano Dayak, respected by everyone, was also a prominent Tuareg rebel leader. He was killed in a plane crash that was thought to be sabotage. The Tuareg continued to revolt such that by 2008 all tourism to Agadez and the desert had vanished, the ice cream shop gone. I never heard of Bilal again.

Flagg, the T. E. Lawrence protégé, returned to graduate from Dartmouth and went on to Oxford as a Rhodes scholar. He did PhD fieldwork among the mountain tribes of Yemen and is now a professor of Arabic studies at the University of Chicago.

I finally located El Bechir at a remote oasis in northeast Mali, and in the winter of 2000 we completed the promised camel journey that for sixteen years had eluded my grasp. At that time the government had given up trying to subdue the Tuareg and the desert was under traditional tribal rule. That was the last of my twenty-six trips to Africa.

The Rift Valley near Suswa where our caravan trekked across emerald grass plains, and herds of zebras grazed peacefully alongside long-necked giraffes that trimmed the umbrella acacias so archetypal of Africa, now is an endless vista of commercial wheat fields. And huge flower farms are sucking Lake Naivasha dry.

A luxurious lodge sits on the once remote Nguruman escarpment overlooking the scorching desolation where we floundered with our horses and donkeys. There is even a tourist camp in Lashi Valley where Sekerot and I once lived for nine months in complete seclusion, alone and on foot among the wild animals.

But the game reserves are a growing tourist destination, which in the end will preserve east Africa's inspiring landscape, save the exotic creatures from total destruction, and keep alive the vision of endless free-ranging wild herds to inspire future generations.

Currently, however, all is not perfect in Paradise. Tribal war and ethnic cleansing has come to the Rift Valley, and as this book is being published people are fleeing Lake Naivasha.

In the Ituri Forest, I helped start a dispensary with missionary Lester Green to provide basic medical care for the Efe. A pygmy committee was formed, and I trained Bezangu to treat wounds and tropical ulcers. For a time everything worked well.

Then in 1997 General Laurent Kabila's rebel army overran the country, ending the corrupt thirty-two-year reign of the hated military dictator Mobutu. Zaire became the Democratic Republic of the Congo and everyone expected conditions to improve. Instead, chaos ensued, unleashing ancient tribal enemies to massacre each other in the grasslands just outside the Ituri Forest. In addition, hundreds of thousands of Hutu and Tutsi fleeing the genocide in nearby Rwanda worsened the situation.

Neighboring countries, desiring Congo's rich gold mines and minerals, began supporting renegade armies of teenagers with AK-47s. Riled up by witch doctors to believe they were invincible, and starving for lack of food, they resorted to cannibalism and mutilating horrors as nightmarish as anything in human history. The Ituri region descended into a living "Heart of Darkness," with soldiers capturing pygmies along the edge of the forest and eating them because they believed that their hunting and survival skills would be assumed.

Since 1997, four million Africans have died from starvation, disease, or violence. Five hundred thousand women and children are wandering about the countryside, displaced and starving.

The Efe pygmies, hidden away in remote forest camps, have remained elusive and distant from it all. However, all communication with the outside world was cut off, making it impossible for me to supply medicines to the dispensary. Without simple and inexpensive medical care, old Pembo, the respected elder of the pygmy clan, as well as my close companion Kaluli have passed away.

But maendeleo (progress) arrives. The recent appearance of e-mail in a distant village has allowed me to obtain news of the dispensary. After years of being unable to get medicines to the Efe, I am now providing monthly medicines and a salary for the nurse.

Finally, at sixty-one years old, I was told I had incurable cancer. With chemotherapy I was given a 40 percent chance of surviving one year. My immediate reaction to this unexpected news was a warmth that spread over my body, the same comforting sensation experienced in my childhood vision. My first thought was how thankful I was to have solidified my relationship with God; my second, how lucky I was to have fulfilled my dreams. Then I remembered the voice saying, "Put him back," and I was grateful for having been given that second chance to live.

❖ GLOSSARY ❖

THE SAHARA

Allahu Akbahr... Allahu Akbahr (Arabic). "God is great." The call to prayer.

As-salaamu alaykum. "Peace be upon you." Arabic greeting.

Azali. The annual camel caravan from Agadez 400 miles across the Ténéré sea of sand to get salt at the oasis of Bilma.

Balek (North African Arabic). "Watch out!" "Out of the way!"

Bismallah (Arabic). "Praise be to God."

Boubou. A pullover gown typical of desert village dwellers.

Chèche (Arabic). A 12-foot long cotton headcloth that desert nomads wear to protect them from sun and wind and to hide their faces. The Tuareg head-cloth is called *tagulmust*, and it is only worn by men.

Chef de marché (French). Chief of the market.

Djerma. A sedentary agricultural tribe.

Erg (Arabic). A vast sea of sand with large sand dunes several hundred feet high. Mostly devoid of vegetation.

Fata Morgana. A mirage.

Fatiha. The six verses that comprise the opening chapter of the Koran.

Gendarmerie (French). Police station.

Gris-gris. Magic charm.

Guelta. A natural basin of rock or sandstone that catches and holds rain water. The water may not be replenished for many years and may dry up.

Guerba (Arabic). A water bag made from a goat- or sheepskin by tying off the legs.

Halal (Arabic). Islamic law regulating allowable food and drink and the method of preparation.

Hamdullah (Arabic). "Praise be to God."

Harmattan. A seasonal arid north wind that blows across the Sahara through Mali, Niger, and as far as the west coast of Africa. It fills the sky with dust, turning it gray and blocking out the sun. It can cause lethargy; cracked lips; parched throat; eye, ear, and respiratory disease.

Hausa. A black African Muslim tribe of farmers and traders. The men wear long white flowing robes and embroidered hats. Houses of adobe.

Imam. The prayer leader at a mosque.

Jinns (Arabic). Spirits of the desert that can bring evil.

Marabout. An Islamic teacher or religious scholar.

Oued (Arabic). A dry sandy riverbed. A seasonal Sahara rainstorm may fill the riverbed with a rushing torrent that quickly sinks into the ground leaving the streambed dry again.

Palmeraie (French). A grove of palm trees that mark a desert oasis. The oasis is created when ancient water trapped deep beneath the desert surfaces in a natural spring or is shallow enough to be tapped by hand-dug wells. The date palms and gardens are irrigated by hand.

Peul. Nomadic cattle herders of the Sahel. French for *Fulani*. *Wodaabe* is a subtribe.

Piste (French). A desert track, not a road. A commonly used direction of travel marked by old tire tracks.

Reg (Arabic). A flat open plain of sand and gravel.

Soudure. An annual period of hardship that occurs during the summer heat when the grasses are depleted and the animals and nomads run out of food and starve while waiting for the rains.

Tagulmust (Tamasheq). The cotton head covering and veil worn by Tuareg men to hide their faces from strangers; also, to prevent *jinn* from entering their nose and mouth. The most highly prized for ceremonies, dressing up, or status are stained with indigo, which rubs off on their skin and has given them the name "blue men."

Tamasheq. The Tuareg language.

Tanezrouft. A Tuareg word translated as "desert of fear," "desert of thirst," and so forth. A vast, waterless, and absolutely lifeless plain of pebbles and sand. A desert within a desert; extreme aridity.

Tifinar. The Tuareg writing system of lines, circles, and dots related to ancient Phoenician and Lybian script.

Tuareg. Nomads of Berber origin who occupy the southern part of the Sahara.

Wa-alaykum as-salaam (Arabic). "And upon you be peace." Response to Arabic greeting.

RIFT VALLEY

Askari (Swahili). An African guard. Usually armed with only a bow and arrow or a club.

Duka (Swahili). A small Indian-run supply store found all over east Africa.

Ekuku Naibor (Maasai). "White beast." A zebra-striped creature that lives in Naimina Enkiyo. It attacks and kills people.

Enkai (Maasai). "God." The Maasai God.

Enkaji (Maasai). An oval Massai house constructed of bent saplings plastered over with cow dung and mud.

Enkang (Maasai). A Maasai family settlement of oval, cow dung dwellings surrounded by a protective wall of thornbush or poles.

Enkedong (Maasai). Stones kept in a cow horn or gourd that are used by a *liabon* to predict the future.

Glossary

Hacuna matatta (Swahili). "No problem!"

Layoni (Maasai). An uncircumcised Maasai boy.

Liabon (Maasai). A spiritual leader and prophet of the Maasai.

Morani (Maasai). A Maasai warrior.

Naimina Enkiyo (Maasai). "Forest of the Lost Child." A forest along the Nguruman escarpment that is both sacred and feared by Maasai.

Nenauner (Maasai). A manlike creature with one leg and a stump that lives in Naimina Enkiyo.

Olprion (Maasai). The ceremonial Maasai fire stick, known as the male part. It is used to start fire by inserting it into the female wood part *(entoole)* and twirling it rapidly between the palms.

Olpul (Maasai). A secret forest camp for new Maasai warriors where they eat meat and learn the ways of a warrior.

Oreteti (Maasai). A strangler fig tree. Sacred trees are often huge strangler figs.

Panga (Swahili). African bush knife. A machete.

Rungu (Swahili). A wooden club with a baseball-size knob on one end. *Orinka* is the Maasai word.

Semi (Maasai). A short broad-bladed Massai sword. Thought to be modeled after the Roman stabbing sword.

Shuka (Maasai). A rectangular piece of cloth worn by Maasai warriors.

Sopa (Maasai). Maasai greeting.

Ugali (Swahili). Cornmeal cooked into a thick paste. Typical food for east Africans.

Wazungu (Swahili). White person.

ITURI RAIN FOREST

Asali. Honey.

Cambi. A pygmy camp.

Hacuna matatta (Swahili). "No problem."

Hongo. Gifts or money given to a tribal chief for permission to travel in his land.

Kabisa. An expression meaning "crazy."

Kilipi. A ubiquitous broad leaf plant that grows from the forest floor and is used for building pygmy houses and to make disposable containers and baskets.

Maendeleo. "Progress."

Mvua. Rain.

Nyama. Meat, bush meat.

❖ ABOUT THE AUTHOR ❖

William F. Wheeler is the author and photographer of *Efe Pygmies: Archers of the African Rain Forest*. After practicing medicine for sixteen years, he bought a Land Rover and began traveling Africa on his own. After 40,000 miles in the Land Rover, he began to explore the most exotic and remote areas on foot. His photos have appeared in *Condé Nast Traveler, Outside, Sierra, Utne Reader*, and other magazines. More than 5,000 of his photos and 300 artifacts from his travels are in the permanent collection of the Smithsonian National Museum of Natural History. He lives in Solana Beach, California.

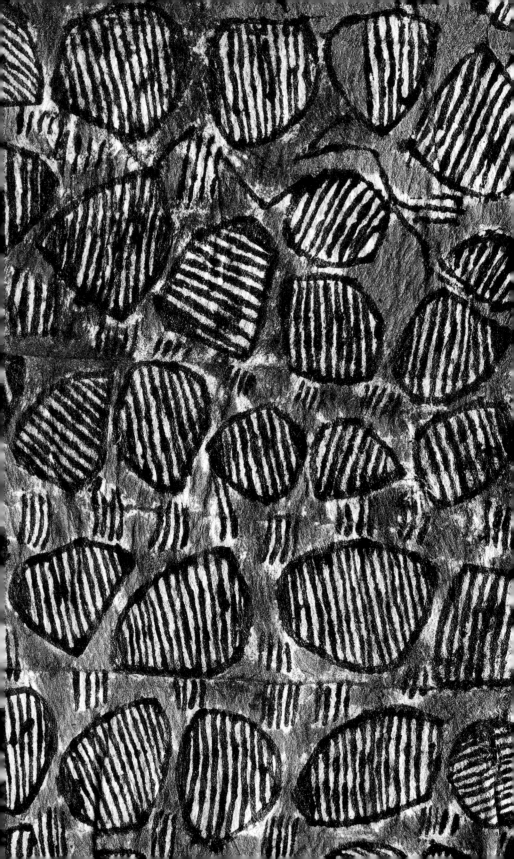

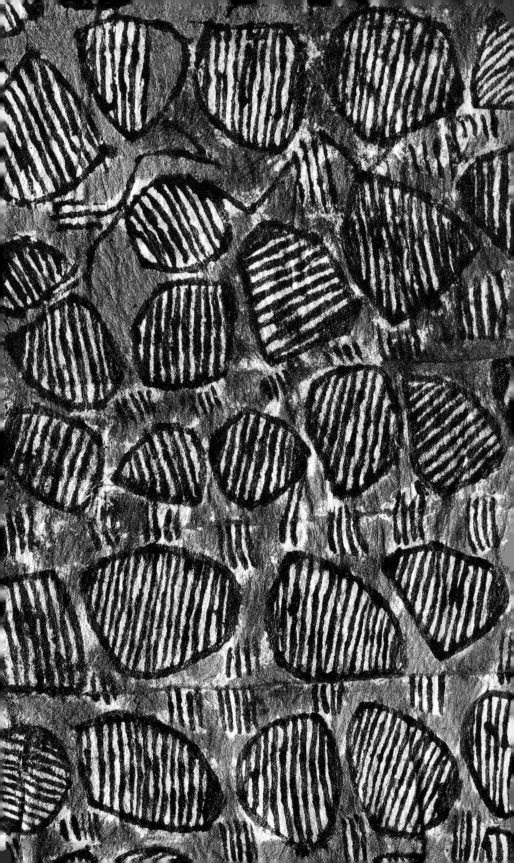